Agricultural Finance and Management

S Subba Reddy
P Raghu Ram

Oxford & IBH Publishing Co. Pvt. Ltd.
New Delhi
(*A Unit of* CBS Publishers & Distributors Pvt Ltd)

CBSPD

CBS Publishers & Distributors Pvt Ltd

New Delhi • Bengaluru • Chennai • Kochi • Kolkata • Lucknow • Mumbai
Hyderabad • Jharkhand • Nagpur • Patna • Pune • Uttarakhand

Agricultural Finance and Management

ISBN-13: 978-81-204-1022-0
ISBN-10: 81-204-1022-X

OXFORD & IBH

New Delhi
(A Unit of CBS Publishers & Distributors Pvt Ltd)

Published by Satish Kumar Jain and produced by Varun Jain for

CBS Publishers & Distributors Pvt Ltd
4819/XI Prahlad Street, 24 Ansari Road, Daryaganj, New Delhi 110 002, India
Ph: 011-23289259, 23266861, 23266867   Website: www.cbspd.com
Fax: 011-23243014   e-mail: delhi@cbspd.com;
                                         cbspubs@airtelmail.in.

Corporate Office: 204 FIE, Industrial Area, Patparganj, Delhi 110 092, India
Ph: 011-4934 4934   Fax: 011-4934 4935   e-mail: publishing@cbspd.com;
                                         publicity@cbspd.com

Branches

- **Bengaluru:** Seema House 2975, 17th Cross, KR Road, Banasankari 2nd Stage, Bengaluru 560 070, Karnataka, India
  Ph: +91-80-26771678/79   Fax: +91-80-26771680   e-mail: bangalore@cbspd.com
- **Chennai:** 7, Subbaraya Street, Shenoy Nagar, Chennai 600 030, Tamil Nadu, India
  Ph: +91-44-26680620, 26681266   Fax: +91-44-42032115   e-mail: chennai@cbspd.com
- **Kochi:** 42/1325, 1326, Power House Road, Opp KSEB, Power House, Ernakulum Kochi 682 018, Kerala, India
  Ph: +91-484-4059061-65,67   Fax: +91-484-4059065   e-mail: kochi@cbspd.com
- **Kolkata:** 147, Hind Ceramics Compound, 1st Floor, Nilgunj Road, Belghoria, Kolkata-700056, West Bengal, India
  Ph: +91-9096713055/7798394118, 9836841399   e-mail: kolkata@cbspd.com
- **Lucknow:** Basement, Khushnuma Complex, 7 Meerabai Marg (Behind Jawahar Bhawan),Lucknow-226001, UP, India
  Ph: +0522-4000032   e-mail: tiwari.lucknow@cbspd.com
- **Mumbai:** PWD Shed, Gala no 25/26, Ramchandra Bhatt Marg, Next to JJ Hospital Gate no. 2, Opp. Union
  Bank of India, Noorbaug, Mumbai-400009, Maharashtra, India
  Ph: 022-66661880/89   e-mail: mumbai@cbspd.com

Representatives

• Hyderabad	0-9885175004	• Jharkhand	0-9811541605	• Nagpur	0-9421945513
• Patna	0-9334159340	• Pune	0-9623451994	• Uttarakhand	0-9716462459

Printed at Mudrak, Noida, UP, India

PREFACE

The period of early nineties in India has witnessed self-sufficiency in food production by nearly achieving four fold increase in foodgrain production, compared to production level of independence period. This was largely owed to adoption of seed-fertilizer technology and impact of nationalisation of major commercial banks in India. Particularly the latter has helped the farm-sector to apply an array of requisite new techniques in crop production and livestock management. The catalytic role of farm finance strengthens the farming business and augments the productivity of scarce resources. Provision of finance is basic and instrumental for narrowing down the imbalances existing in income and wealth levels of different farm-groups in regions, states and the nation. The requisite supply of agricultural finance is imperative to establish, strengthen and develop agribusiness units, farm input and output markets in the country. Indeed, it is the most basic instrument to break the vicious cycle of poverty and place the Indian farmers into the cycle of prosperity and for socio-economic development of the country.

Thus, considering the significant role of agricultural finance in the overall development of the country, many courses/subjects under varying heads of agricultural finance and management are now being offered by many Agricultural Universities to their graduate, and post-graduate students. The same subjects are being taught to the students of economics, commerce and management in the traditional universities at graduate and post graduate level.

Immense literature is available on the subject of finance particularly with reference to sources of finance and use of finance in agriculture and industry. The attempts in this direction by the Economists are noteworthy. However, books which have dealt with management aspects of agricultural finance are very few. No Indian book contains exhaustive information on all aspects of agricultural finance and management. The application part of management tools to agricultural finance with a bent of mathematical and programming models is not found in most of the Indian books related to agricultural finance. Indeed very few Agricultural Economists made an earnest attempt in this direction. Keeping this in view, the authors made sincere attempt to highlight the application part of agricultural financial management along with micro and macro aspects of agricultural finance.

The authors with a deep sense of gratitude and regard acknowledge their indebtedness to authors of various books, journals, periodicals, reports and bulletins from which they have conceived the subject matter of the book. The authors are greatly indebted to various officials working in cooperatives, Farmers Service Societies, Nationalised Banks, Regional Rural Banks, and Agricultural Departments for their valuable suggestions. The authors would like to place on record the help received from the officials of SBI Regional Office, Tirupati particularly in the provision of requisite data on agricultural projects and financial aspects. The authors are highly thankful to their colleagues who helped in bringing out the book.

Any suggestion for the improvement of the book is welcome.

S. SUBBA REDDY
P. RAGHU RAM

CONTENTS

CHAPTER 1

AGRICULTURAL FINANCE— CONCEPTS AND SCOPE

Agricultural finance generally means studying, examining and analysing the financial aspects pertaining to farm business which is the core sector of the country. The financial aspects include money matters relating to production of agricultural products and their disposal. When we speak of the financial aspects in agriculture, issues that figure are capital required for agriculture, the way necessary funds are raised and the pattern of utilization of funds so raised. Murray (1953) has defined agricultural finance in the following words, "It is an economic study of borrowing funds by farmers; of the organisation and operation of farm lending agencies, and of society's interest in credit for agriculture." Tandon and Dhondyal (1962) defined agricultural finance as a branch of agricultural economics which deals with the provision and management of bank services and financial resources related to individual farm units.

The following are implied in the above definitions of agricultural finance:

1) All the farmers should be purveyed requisite finance,
2) Finance should stimulate and enhance the productivity of farm scarce resources, and
3) Farm finance has a vital and catalytic role for agro-economic development of farmers.

Agricultural finance is viewed both at macro level and micro level. Macro finance deals with the different sources of raising funds for agriculture as a whole in the economy and it is also concerned with the lending procedures, rules, regulations, monitoring and controlling procedures of different agricultural credit institutions. Thus, macro finance pertains to financing agriculture at the aggregate level. On the other hand, micro finance refers to financial management of the individual farm business unit and it is concerned with the study as to how the individual farmer considers various sources of credit, quantum of credit to be borrowed from each source and how he allocates the same among the alternative uses within the farm. It is also concerned with future use of funds. In sum, macro finance deals with the aspects relating to total credit needs of the agricultural sector, the terms and conditions under which the credit is avilable and the method of using the total credit for the development of agriculture. On the contrary, micro finance refers to financial management of the individual farm business.

IMPORTANCE OF AGRICULTURAL FINANCE

Farm finance assumes vital importance in the agro-socio-economic development of the country both at individual/micro level and at aggregate/macro level. Its catalytic role strengthens the farming business and augments the productivity of scarce resources. For instance, new potential seeds, when combined with purchased inputs like fertilizers and plant protection chemicals in requisite proportions result in higher productivity of resources. Application of new technological inputs obtained through farm finance helps boost agricultural productivity. Accretion to farm assets and farm supporting infrastructure provided by large scale financial investment activities entail increased farm income levels, leading to overall improvement in the living standards of rural masses. Farm finance can also contribute to reduction in regional economic imbalances and is equally good at narrowing down the inter-farm asset and wealth variations. To quote Muniraj (1987): "Farm finance is the money extended to the farmers to stimulate the productivity of the limited farm resources. It is not a mere loan or credit or advance, it is an instrument to promote the well-being of the society. Farm finance is not just a science to manage the money, but is an applied science of allocating scarce resources to derive the optimum output. It is a lever with forward and backward linkages to the economic development both at micro and macro levels". Thus the role of farm finance in strengthening and development of both input and output markets in agriculture is crucial and significant. Indian agriculture is still traditional, subsistence and stagnant in nature, hence agricultural finance is needed to create the supporting infrastructure for adoption of new technology. Massive investment is needed to cary out major and minor irrigation projects, rural electrification and energisation, installation of fertilizers and chemical plants, execution of agricultural promotional programmes and poverty alleviation programmes in the country.

Farm Financial Management

An important component of agricultural finance which the financial manager aims at is acquiring, using and protecting the credit needed for his business. Decisions such as acquisition and use of credit are vital in financial management. This is a study concerning the financial analysis. Financial analysis deals with analysing requisite information and financial records in order to evaluate the past, present and future financial position of the business. Farm financial management mainly deals with the capital* acquisition and capital use in the farm business. Capital acquisition and capital use are important in every phase of farm management. Hence, financial management and farm management are synonymous and integrating (Nelson *et al.*, 1973).

Farm Financial Management Decisions

It has already been explained that farm financial management deals with acquisition and use of credit. We shall now examine financial management decisions which the farm financial manager takes in running his farm business. The decisions are as follows:

1) Decisions regarding requisite capital;
2) Decisions regarding sources of capital;
3) Decisions regarding allocation of capital among alternatives;
4) Decision-strategies to be adopted to counter risk and uncertainty; and
5) Decisions on the legal problems relating to farm organisation and operation.

Once a decision has been taken up to solve a problem, the farmer cannot remain complacent, for the decision problems are cyclical in nature and solutions are to be sought as and when they arise. This shows how crucial are the decisions of financial management in farm business.

1. Decisions Regarding Requisite Capital

As explained later in principles of financial management of the farm, any rational producer, under the situation of unlimited capital, continues the production till the marginal costs get equated with marginal returns in the short run. He has to increase the input application till this stage is reached, otherwise, he will be loosing the opportunity of getting greater returns than the costs incurred, which relates to the operation of farm business in stage I of law of diminishing returns. There is a possibility of coming across this situation when the farm business is operated under the capital constrained conditions. When the capital gap is made good through

---

*Capital is produced means of production. Karl Marx in his book 'Das Kapital' regards capital as "Crystallised form of labour". In the modern usage, money and capital are interchanged. But a clear distinction is sometimes made by the economists between money and capital. Money *per se* is not productive always. Capital is the money invested on physical items such as land, labour, fertilizers, etc.

borrowed funds from institutional and/or non-institutional agencies, the farmer can afford to operate the farm business in stage II of law of diminishing returns. If the farmer is still ambitious of getting greater output and returns in the presence of abundant capital, which has been raised through borrowings from various sources, then the third stage of diminishing returns sets in. Literature on the subject has amply revealed the pattern of overuse of fertilizers and pesticides by the farmers through borrowed funds and the precarious situation of farmers in not being able to realise adequate income for repayment of credit. Under such conditions the farmer attains the status of being stamped as a defaulter and his credit-worthiness is lost in the view of the banker and he confronts still more problems in securing funds from non-institutional sources too. Risk of equity capital is directly associated with the borrowed funds (debt capital). This is the underlying phenomenon in the principle of equity and increasing risk, which is explained in Chapter 4.

2. *Decisions Regarding Sources of Capital*

There are various sources, from which the farmer can raise the funds needed for farming. Basically, we have institutional and non-institutional agencies and it is quite evident that the non-institutional agencies charge higher rate of interest. But, these days, with the expansion of a wide net-work of institutional agencies, farmers are in a position to reduce the dependence on non-institutional agencies. Now, the pertinent question is that among the institutional agencies which is the best source that a farmer should opt for. Choosing a given financing agency basically depends upon two major criteria; one is the cost of credit and the other one is timeliness of credit. The significance of these two factors is that credit should not be too costly at the time of repayment of loan and if the loan amount is not disbursed in time, its productivity will be lost since the farmer fails to take up the farm practices as per the time schedule. Keeping these two factors in view, the farmer has to choose an appropriate agency.

3. *Decisions Regarding Allocation of Capital*

The farmer has alternatives for the profitable use of his limited resources. He may allocate the resources so that the enterprises bring revenue in the same year or he can also give weightage to the idea of investing funds on the enterprises which will not produce results immediately, but, reward the farmer suitably some time in future. In the first case of using limited capital, the financial principle which assists him is as follows:

Marginal return of capital = Marginal cost of capital.

Here the farmer can realise maximum income. Secondly, if the farmer thinks in terms of investing his limited funds on those enterprises, which can only bring returns in future, say after two or three years, analysis of time value of money serves as a basis for decision-making. He has to use compounding and discounting techniques (explained in detail in Chapter 8) in assessing the profitability of the enterprise. The allocation decisions guiding the farmer in obtaining the greatest profit under the situation of limited capital, are more common in Indian agriculture.

4. Decisions to Counter Risk and Uncertainty

No enterprise is free from risk and uncertainty, but by adopting certain possible and practicable strategies the farmers can offset losses. Following are certain measures which have relevance in this context:

(a) Enterprise Diversification: Among alternatives, choice should be made on those with mimimum variability in yields in the area. Also price behaviour of the alternative products need to be observed and preference given to the production of those products with relatively lesser variation. Decision of this nature can be a more safer one rather than opting enterprises capable of producing higher net incomes but, associated with violent oscillations in yields and prices.

(b) Flexibility: The crop planning should pave the way for flexibility depending upon the exigencies. If the crop programme warrants any changes, the farmers should prepare in adapting the needed changes.

(c) Insurance: It is a defensive device for a bad time. Every farmer should invariably opt for it, since it pulls them out of woods at least to certain extent. At present, this facility is not available to all the crops. Even if it is available for specified crops, borrowers of institutional agencies are only eligible to avail of this facility. Even among the eligible farmers, there is a sort of discontentment with the *modus-operandi* of the scheme. It needs the attention of the Government for evolving a procedure to benefit all the farmers, in general.

(d) Contractual Arrangements: A forward marketing contract provides means for sellers and buyers to exchange a commodity for an accepted price. In this way the farmer is able to anticipate a price that protects him from the future decrease in the price of the product. At times, he may be denied the future rise in price, however, risk can be reduced when colossal loss is in the offing.

(e) Production Management: Selection of appropriate recommended package of practices is likely to put the farmer on sound footing. This

is possible by following timely sowing of the required variety and quantity of seeds, recommended doses of fertiliser application, preventive and curative plant protection measures, etc.

(f) Back-up Management: The farm operator no doubt is a full time worker on the farm, but for any reason if he has to stay away from farming for a certain period of time, his absence will be surely felt in running the business by his children or spouse. Keeping this in view, the farmer has to involve his wife and children also in the business, whenever possible, so that even in his absence, the business can be run smoothly. There is a need for a stand-by in farming also.

5. *Decisions on the Legal Problems*
Legal aspects relating to acquisition, management and transfer of capital are studied here. We shall examine further the legal and other constraints associated with the different methods of resource use. For example, sharing of irrigation water from wells and canals, disputes over field bunds, etc.

Characteristics of Farm Financial Decisions

Financial decisions are basically divided into two categories, viz., organisational decisions and operational decisions. Organisational decisions relate to plans for developing the farm business by acquiring durable assets like machinery, implements, land, etc. Operational decisions involve factors like how much of land should be put under what crop, how much of finance is required for raising crops and livestock and the needed finance to be borrowed at lowest cost and the like. These decisions are to be modified or revamped more than once in executing the plans. Hence they are short run decisions.

Many characteristics are imparted to financial decisions, but listing of these is based on different criteria, which is beyond the scope of this book. However, an attempt is made to describe the important characteristics of decisions. These are: (1) Frequency; (2) Importance; (3) Imminence; (4) Revokability; and (5) Number of alternative decisions available.

(1) Frequency: Some decisions will occur once or twice in a year, like decisions on the choice of crops to be raised, decisions on the rearing of number and type of milch cattle in a year, etc. Some decisions are frequent in their occurrence and infact very little time is left to execute such decisions. For example: amount to be spent on each day for the purchase of livestock feed, use of labour and other routine decisions. Here, the financial manager must be careful of the errors that creep in executing such decisions. In this regard some thumb rules must be kept in view to overcome problems.

(2) Importance: Importance of the decisions should be gauged in terms of profit, loss and time required to execute the decisions. Decisions involving little investment would be preferred by risk-averse farmers, whereas, risk-takers would prefer decisions involving large amount of capital and time. Decisions which are executed in a routine manner are generally less expensive and require less time. Decisions like purchase of new land and potential breed of animals will definitely involve a large amount of capital. Then, careful analysis is necessary to examine the possible alternative decisions through budgeting.

(3) Imminence: Imminent decisions generally imply that these decisions are going to be taken up very soon. There will be some occasions for managers to take decisions inevitably to avoid losses. An example in this case is, investment on the plant protection measures to avoid and control incidence of pests on crops. Some decisions do not have any deadline in timing them and delays in this regard will not cause any loss to the farmer. For instance, decisions like whether or not to buy a new machine, purchase of land, etc. can be deferred. These will not come under the purview of imminent decisions. Time and expected loss are the main criteria to classify the decisions as imminent or deferred.

(4) Revokability: Some times there will be need for farm financial manager to alter the present decision and adopt altogether a new decision in its place. To cite an example, suppose the manager realises that spending on a particular brand of pesticide is futile, then he takes a decision of purchasing a new brand of chemicals, having the potentiality to control pests. Such characteristics of changing decisions or reversing them is called revokability. In many a situation, very little time is left for the managers to alter the decisions for avoiding loss, so that he needs to act quickly in the available time.

However, some decisions are not revokable or they can only be changed at a very high cost. Decisions, on sinking a new well or constructing a new farm building, etc. once executed cannot be reversed. Such non-reversible decisions, need sufficient time and thought.

(5) Number of Alternative Decisions Available: Some decisions have very limited options, say one or two, while, some have many more options. If the alternatives are many for executing a given decision, then it is not very easy and more time should be spent by the manager in analysing and selecting the best alternative. When there are restricted alternatives it is relatively easy for the manager to exercise the option.

Steps in the Process of Farm Financial Management

    (i)   Objective,
    (ii)   Problem recognition,
    (iii) Analysis,
    (iv) Decision making,
    (v)   Action,
    (vi) Accepting the consequences, and
    (vii) Evaluation.

(i) Objective: Every farm financial manager has a set of goals. He may contemplate achieving them immediately or some time in the future. Whatever may be the time period, mostly his goals revolve around effective management of limited financial input for increasing money inflows in the farm business. While setting the goals, the main underlying fact is that the financial manager should have the confidence of achieving them. For example, the objective of the farmer is to take up a perennial crop enterprise, which has been introduced in the area by some of his fellow-farmers. Then he must consider their experiences to achieve the objective.

(ii) Problem Recognition: Here the farm financial manager needs to identify the problems associated with the enterprise, proposed to be taken up. Till now, there are no serious production and marketing problems. But, the only major problem is large capital requirements of the enterprise. Since he does not possess the needed resource endowment base, he has to raise necessary funds through borrowings.

(iii) Analysis: The manager has to analyse the pros and cons of the enterprise based on the information already gathered from the farmers adapting the enterprise. He has to give a lot of thought at this stage. Suppose, he succeeds in his effort, everybody praises him and in case he fails, he may be ridiculed by other non-adopters, and another point is that since he is dependent heavily on borrowed sources, repayment of which may make his situation still worse.

(iv) Decision Making: Having analysed the problems from all the angles, he should now think seriously whether to opt for the enterprise or not. The farm financial manager finally decides to go ahead with his plan.

(v) Action: The financial manager puts his plan into action, i.e. he implements the decision.

(vi) Bearing Responsibility: He is fully convinced before implementation of the plan, hence, responsible for the events to follow,

whatever they may be. If the farm financial manager is successful, he is overwhelmed with joy and for any reason, if he receives a setback, he tries to come out of the tangle.

(vii) Evaluation: This refers to careful and continuous assessment of the changes that occur in the agro, socio and economic environment around the farmer.

Scope of Farm Financial Managment

Three basic economic activities constitute the managerial process of the farm. They are production activities, financing activities and marketing activities. Production activities comprise the decisions like what products to be produced, method of production and how much of each product should be produced. Financial activities relate to decisions of obtaining and use of credit. Marketing activities involve managerial decisions related to procurement of inputs and distribution and sale of output.

Financing decisions more often than not overlap the production and marketing decisions. For example, nature of enterprises and the quantum of the product determine the amount of capital and provide solutions to the decisions of how much capital should be used in the farm business. Evaluation and involvement of alternatives among enterprises is linked with the decisions of how products are produced. Analogously, marketing decisions are linked with financial decisions, because product marketing and selection of input marketing are often determined by the quantum of financing. Thus, we should recognise that production, financing and marketing decisions are concerned with financial acquisition and financial use depending upon the goals of financial manager. This clearly depicts that farm management and farm financial management are not altogether different and infact the latter is a part of former. Hence the concepts, principles, analytical tools, etc. which aid in the management of the farm are also applicable to farm financial management.

Classification of Loans or Credit

Loans are certain amount of money provided for certain purpose on certain conditions with some interest which should be repaid sooner or later. It is also referred to as credit. Credit is broadly classified based on various criteria (Fig. 1.1).

Based on Purpose

(1) *Production loans*: These loans are intended to increase the production of the crops. These are also called seasonal agricultural

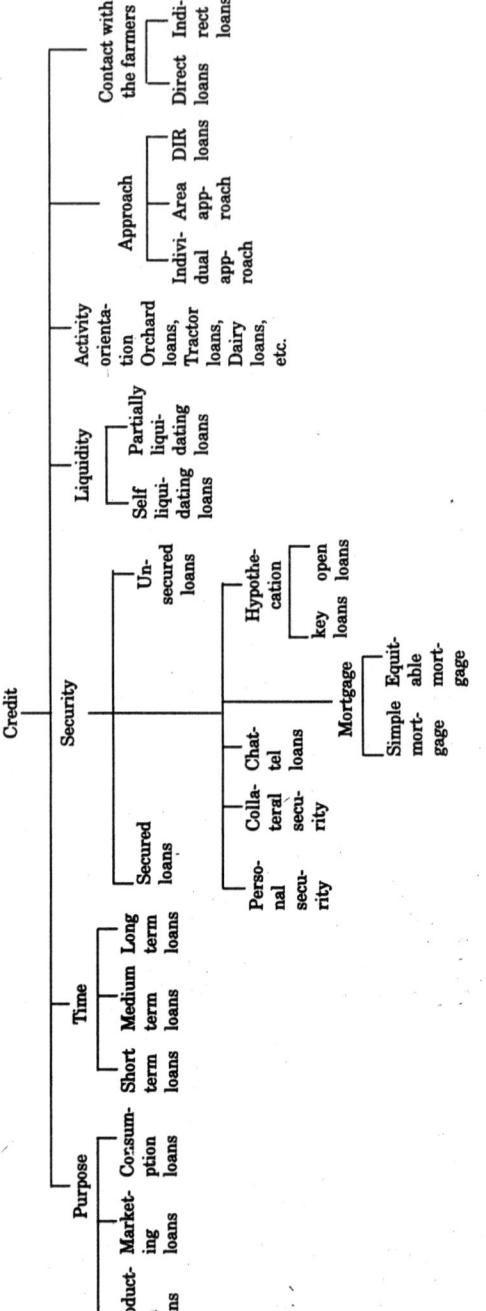

Fig. 1.1: Broad classification of Credit.

operations (SAO) loans or short-term loans or crop loans. These loans are repayable within a period ranging from 6 months to 18 months in lumpsum.

(2) *Marketing loans:* These are meant for helping the farmers to overcome distress sales and market the produce in a better way. Regulated markets as well as commercial banks, based on the warehouse receipt, are extending financial assistance to the farmers in this regard, by advancing 75 per cent of the value of the produce. This enables the farmers to clear off their loans and dispose the produce at remunerative prices.

(3) *Consumption loans*: Any loan advanced for the purpose other than production, is broadly categorised as consumption loan. It appears to be an unproductive loan but, in fact, it indirectly assists in more productive use of the crop loans and investment loans, averting to a greater extent the diversion of loans to other purposes. These are not very widely advanced and restricted to those areas which are hit by natural calamities. These loans are granted on group guarantee basis with a maximum of three members. The loan is to be repaid within five crop seasons or 2 ½ years whichever is less. The Branch Managers are vested with the discretion of sanctioning these loans upto Rs. 500 in each individual case. The rate of interest is around 11 per cent. This scheme is extended to:

i. IRDP beneficiaries,
ii. Small and marginal farmers,
iii. Landless labourers,
iv. Rural artisans, and
v. Other people of very small means such as carpenters, barbers, washermen etc. who form an integral part of village community.

Consumption credit is provided for the following purposes from 1976:

Medical expenses	Rs 500
Expenses related to marriage needs	Rs 500
Educational needs	Rs 200
Birth, funerals, etc.	Rs 150
Religious ceremonies	Rs 150
General consumption	Rs 150

Based on Time

This classification is based on the repayment period of the loan component.

(1) *Short-term loans*: These loans are to be paid back within a period ranging from 6 months to 18 months. All crop loans are said to be short-term loans, but, the length of the repayment period varies according to the duration of the crop. The farmer requires this type of credit to meet the expenses for the ongoing agricultural operations on the farm like sowing, fertiliser application, plant protection measures, payment of wages to casual labourers, etc. He is supposed to repay the loan from the sale proceeds of the crops raised.

(2) *Medium-term loans*: These loans are extended for a period varying from 15 months to 5 years. These loans are required by the farmer for bringing about some improvements on his farm business by way of purchasing implements, electric motors, milch cattle, sheep and goat, etc. The relatively longer repayment of these loans is due to their partial-liquidating nature.

(3) *Long-term loans*: These loans fall due for repayment over a long time ranging from 5 years to more than 20 years. These loans together with medium-term loans are called investment loans or term loans. These loans are meant for bringing about permanent improvements on the land, like levelling and reclamation, construction of farm buildings, purchase of tractors, raising orchards, etc. Since these activities require large capital, a longer period is required for the farmers to repay the loan, from additional returns obtained from these investment activities.

Based on Security

Based on security the loan transactions between lender and borrower are basically governed by the confidence in the borrower, the question of security may not arise at all in advancing loans. But, this assumption is confined to private lendings to certain extent, and institutional agencies do have their own procedural formalities in credit transactions. Hence, it is imperative to classify the loans under this category into sub-categories, viz. secured and unsecured.

(1) *Secured loans:* Loans advanced against some security by the borrower are termed as secured loans. Various forms of securities are offered in obtaining the loan which are as follows:

    i)   Personal security
   ii)   Collateral security
  iii)   Chattel loans
  iv)   Mortgage
       a) Simple mortgage
       b) Equitable mortgage

    v) Hypothecation
        a) Key loans
        b) Open loans

(i) Personal security: Borrower himself stands as the guarantor. It is advanced on the farmer's promissory note. Third party guarantee may or may not be insisted upon.

(ii) Collateral security: It is the property that is pledged to secure a loan. The movable properties of the individuals are offered as security. Examples are: LIC bonds, fixed deposit bonds, warehouse receipts, jewellery, machinery, livestock, etc. These are some of the properties accepted as collateral security by the institutional lending agencies.

(iii) Chattel loans: These are specific type of loans with particular category of lenders. Loans obtained from pawnbrokers by pledging movable properties such as jewellery, utencils made of various metals, etc., are the examples.

(iv) Mortgage: As against collateral security, immovable properties are presented for security purpose. For example, land, farm buildings, etc. There are two types of mortgages, viz. simple mortgage and equitable mortgage.
    (a) *Simple mortgage:* This is done by the banking institution, when the borrower's property is inherited from the ancestors. In this process the farmer-borrower has to register his property in the name of the banking institution as security for the loan obtained. This process entails registration charges to be borne by the borrower.
    (b) *Equitable mortgage:* This applies to self-acquired property. In this case there is no such registration because the ownership rights are clearly specified in the title deeds in the name of farmer-borrower. Hence, documents will be obtained from the borrower as security by the institutional agency.

(v) Hypothecation: This happens in the case of tractor loans, machinery loans, etc. Under such loans the borrower will not have any right to sell the equipment until the loan is cleared off. The borrower is allowed to use purchased machinery or equipment so as to enable him pay the loan instalment regularly. Hypothecated loans are further cetagorized into two types, viz. key loans and open loans.
    (a) *Key loans:* The agricultural produce of the farmer-borrower will be kept under the control of the lending institutions and the loan is advanced to the farmer. As and when the loan is repaid the produce will be handed over to the farmers. Such facility prevents the farmer from resorting to distress sales.

(b) *Open loans:* This is another name for hypothecated loans, in which the physical possession of the purchased machinery rests in the hands of the borrower, but, the legal ownership rights remain with the lending institution till the loan is cleared.

(2) *Unsecured loans*: Based on confidence between the borrower and lender the loan transactions take place. There is no mention of any type of security here.

Based on the Liquidity

Under this type, the loans are classified into self-liquidating loans and partially liquidating loans or non-liquidating loans.

(i) *Self-liquidating loans*: The income generated through these loans helps the farmer to repay the entire loan amount in the same season or year of obtaining loan. The productivity increase of the loan is direct in this case. Example—Short term loans or crop loans.

(ii) *Partially-liquidating loans or non-liquidating loans:* The income generated through these borrowings will help to pay part of the loan component only. In other words, these loans are cleared over a time period by the farmer-borrowers. These loans require relatively long time for realization of benefit. Example—Term loans.

Based on Activity Orientation

There is no other basis except the activities for which the loans are advanced by the institutional agencies. It is more a general type of classification. For example, if a loan is borrowed for sericulture, it is called sericulture loan. Similarly, tractor loans, dairy loans, orchard loans, loans for land development, etc., can be cited under this category.

Based on Approach

Under this, we have three categories :
1) Individual approach
2) Area approach, and
3) DIR loans

(1) *Individual approach*: This is advancing loans by the lending agency to any potential borrower for the purpose he needs. Examples–Crop loans, dairy loans, etc.

(2) *Area approach*: Here loans are advanced by selecting the contiguous area by a bank branch. 'Service area approach' followed by the banks

is an apt example.

(3) *DIR loans*: Loans are advanced to the weaker sections of the community at an interest rate of 4 per cent per annum.

Based on Contact with the Farmers

Based on contact by the institutional agencies, the loans can be categorised into: (1) Direct loans, and (2) Indirect loans.

1. *Direct loans:* These are advanced directly to the farmers by the institutional agencies. Examples–ST loans and Term loans.

2. *Indirect loans:* The institutional agencies directly do not finance the farmers, but indirectly benefit the farmers by financing enterprise activities. Examples—Financing fertilizer manufacturing companies, financing construction of warehouses, market yards, etc.

REFERENCES

Ghosal, S.N. *Agricultural Financing in India*, Asia Publishing House, 1966.

Kenneth, Duft D. *Principles of Management in Agribusiness*, Reston Publishing Company, Reston. 1979.

Muniraj, R. *Farm Finance for Development*, Oxford & IBH Publishing Co. Pvt. Ltd., New Delhi. 1987.

Murray, W.G. *Agricultural Finance*, 1953.

Nelson, A.G. Lee, W.F. and Murray, W.G. *Agricultural Finance*, Iowa State University Press, Ames., 1973.

Tandon, R.K. and Dhondyal S.P. *Principles and Methods of Farm Management*.

William G. Murray and Nelson Aaron G. *Agricultural Finance*, The Iowa State University Press, Ames, Iowa, 1960.

CHAPTER 2

AGENCIES OF AGRICULTURAL FINANCE

Though co-operatives are the pioneering institutional agencies in the sphere of agricultural credit, subsequently various institutional agencies made their entry into the field of agricultural finance. Particularly, after nationalization of commercial banks in 1969, there was remarkable growth in institutional credit to agriculture and some financial institutions were specially meant for specific group of rural people, in order to bring about improvement in their income, employment and standard of living. Knowledge and awareness of different institutional agencies are important for the farmers to formulate appropriate farm plans and take relevant decisions. Keeping this in view an attempt is made in this Chapter to present various institutional agencies which cater to the needs of agriculturists.

CO-OPERATIVE FINANCE

According to Calvert "Co-operation is a form of organisation, wherein persons voluntarily associate together as human beings on the basis of equality for the promotion of common economic interest of themselves." When co-operation is applied to agricultural credit, it has a great significance. If the co-operatives are rightly organised in the sphere of rural credit, they can thwart the domination of money lenders and rescue the farmers from their clutches.

If we look back into the history of the co-operative movement in the country, the first Co-operative Societies Act was passed in 1904. The scope of the Act was restricted to the establishment of primary credit societies and the non-credit societies were left out of its purview. The short-comings of the Act of 1904 were rectified by enacting another Co-operative Societies Act of 1912. This act gave provision for the registration of all types of co-operatives. This made the emergence of rural co-operatives both on credit front and non-credit front, but their growth was uneven spatially. This led to the appointment of the Sir Edward Maclagan Committee in 1914 to probe into the performance of the societies. The Committee came out with a report that the true co-operative spirit was lacking in respect of majority of societies and hence recommended for a limited area of operation for each society. The Indian Central Banking Enquiry Committee (1931) also highlighted the glaring lacunae, particularly with reference to undue delays and inadequacy of credit. Prof. D.R. Gadgil, heading the Agricultural Finance Sub-Committee appointed by the Government of India, recommended in 1944 the adoption of limited liability to the co-operatives, assessing credit worthiness based on the repayment capacity of the farmer, subsidising the cost of administration of small co-operative societies, linking of credit with marketing, etc., for improving the co-operative financial aspects. The All India Rural Credit Survey Committee appointed by Reserve Bank of India in 1951 under the chairmanship of Shri A.D. Gorwala brought out that the co-operative credit was unevenly distributed, inadequate and mostly lent to the asset-oriented large cultivators. The report observed that 'co-operation has failed in India but must succeed'. The Committee recommended an integrated scheme as a remedy to the existing situation, the salient features of which were, (1) State partnership in co-operative institutions at all levels, (2) Co-ordination between co-operative credit, marketing and processing, and (3) training of co-operative personnel at all levels. Later, the Committee on taccavi loans and co-operative credit under the Chairmanship of Sri B.P. Patel, in 1961–62 felt that the co-operatives should provide loans to the farmers for the agricultural operations and land improvements and taccavi loans should be confined to the farmers only under distressed conditions. Regarding the supervision of societies at grass-root level, i.e., Primary Co-operative Credit Societies, the Committee on Co-operative Administration, under the Chairmanship of Sri V.L. Mehta opined that the District Co-operative Banks should assume this responsibility. The All India Rural Credit Review Committee which was constituted in July, 1966 under the Chairmanship of Sri B. Venkatappaiah in its final report submitted in July, 1969, recommended the reorganisation of primary societies into viable units, rehabilitation of weak central co-operative banks, greater flexibility in the conversion of short term loans into medium term loans, simplification of application form and disbursal of part of the loan in kind.

Soon after Independence, the Government of India following the recommendations of All India Rural Credit Survey Committee (1951) felt that co-operatives were the only alternative to promote agricultural credit and development of rural areas. Accordingly co-operatives received substantial help in the provision of credit from the Reserve Bank of India as a part of loan policy and large scale assistance and encouragement from the Central and State Governments for their development. Many schemes of the Government with components of subsidies and concessions to the weaker sections were routed through the co-operatives. As a result, the co-operative institutions registered remarkable progress in the post-independence period. Co-operative structure was delineated into two types, i.e. three-tier structure and two-tier structure. Both co-operative credit societies and non-credit co-operative societies now have three-tier structure and two-tier structure in all the States except Bihar, Jammu and Kashmir, Maharashtra and Uttar Pradesh, where the structure is unitary. The co-operative credit structure in the country is shown in Figure 2.1.

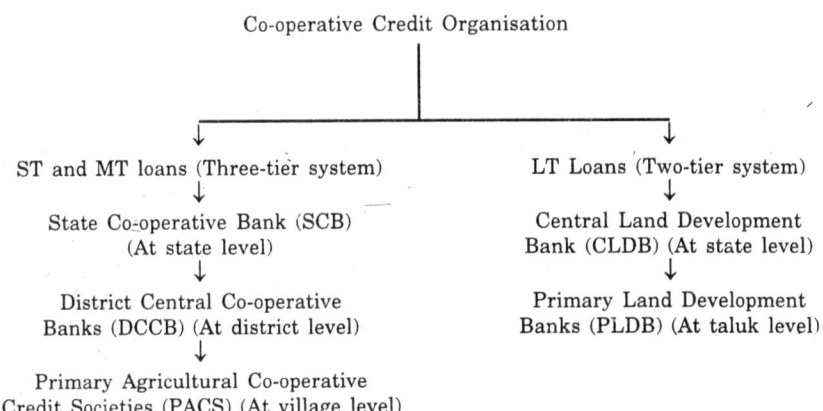

Co-operative Credit Organisation

ST and MT loans (Three-tier system)

State Co-operative Bank (SCB)
(At state level)

District Central Co-operative
Banks (DCCB) (At district level)

Primary Agricultural Co-operative
Credit Societies (PACS) (At village level)

LT Loans (Two-tier system)

Central Land Development
Bank (CLDB) (At state level)

Primary Land Development
Banks (PLDB) (At taluk level)

Fig. 2.1: Sketch of the co-operative credit structure.

STATE CO-OPERATIVE BANK (SCB)

These are the co-operative credit organisations present at the State capitals. DCCBs and PACS are the members of these banks. These institutions supervise activities of the member banks and mobilise and deploy the financial resources among the member banks. They serve as a link between the RBI and the PACS. The specific functions of the State Co-operative Banks are: (1) they help the State Governments in formulating development plans with regard to co-operative institutions; (2) they co-ordinate the policies of the co-operatives with the Government; (3) they formulate and implement uniform credit policies regarding co-operative development in the State; (4) they act as banker's bank to DCCBs , supervise, control and guide the activities of DCCBs; (5) they grant subsidies to DCCBs for the smooth functioning of co-operatives; and (6) similar to any commercial bank, they also perform normal banking operations.

DISTRICT CENTRAL CO-OPERATIVE BANKS (DCCBs)

These banks are, infact the link between State Co-operative Banks and PACS. They are basically meant to meet the credit requirements of PACS. They also undertake banking business such as accepting deposits from public, collecting bills, cheques, drafts, etc. and providing credit to the needy persons. The area of operation of the banks varies from the taluk to the district, but in most of the States their operations are confined to the taluk level. Membership is open to individuals and societies,working in its area of operation. Marketing societies, consumer societies, farming societies, urban banks and PACS are usually enrolled as members of the banks. The specific functions of the banks are: (1) they supervise and inspect the activities of PACS and help the credit societies run smoothly; (2) they maintain close and continuous contact and guide the primary societies and provide leadership to them; (3) they undertake non-credit activities like supply of seeds, fertilizers besides sugar, kerosine and other consumer goods; (4) they provide requisite funds to the societies under their control; and (5) they accept deposits from the member societies as well as from public.

Primary Agricultural Co-operative Credit Societies (PACS)

Consequent to the enactment of Co-operative Societies Act of 1904, PACS came into operation following the guidelines of the Raiffeisen model. The co-operative principles like limited liability, limited area of operation, honorary management, voluntary participation of villagers, etc., were framed for the smooth functioning of the societies. The societies are at the village level and directly meant for the farmers regarding provision of requisite short-term and medium term loans. Supply of agricultural inputs and other essential commodities is also taken up by these societies. In addition to these activities, PACS are also helping in formulating and implementing the agricultural development plans. They are also undertaking advisory and welfare functions for the members. The PACS are associated with the following functions: (1) they borrow adequate and timely funds from DCCBs and help the members in financial matters; (2) they attract local savings in the form of share capital and deposits from the villagers, thereby inculcating the habit of thrift; (3) they supervise the end use of credit; (4) they distribute fertilisers, insecticides, etc., to the needy farmers; (5) they provide machinery on hire basis to the farmers; (6) they associate with the programmes and plans meant for the socio-economic development of the village; (7) they also involve in the marketing of farm produce on behalf of the farmer-borrowers; (8) they provide storage facilities and marketing finance; and (9) they supply certain consumer goods like rice, wheat, sugar, kerosine, cloth, etc., at fair prices.

Central Land Development Bank (CLDB)

As an apex bank in the two-tier co-operative credit structure, it provides long-term finance to PLDBs and also to its affiliated branches working in the States. Branches of CLDBs, PLDBs and individual entrepreneurs are the members of the CLDB. NABARD* and Life Insurance Corporation (LIC) subscribe for its debentures in large amounts. Infact, NABARD is the refinancing agency to the CLDB. It acts as a link between NABARD and the Government in the long-term banking transactions. It supervises, inspects and guides the PLDBs in their banking operations. It floats debentures for raising necessary funds. It inculcates the spirit and practice of thrift among the member banks by mobilising savings and stimulating capital formation. The CLDB generally purveys loans to member banks for the redemption of old debts, improvement, reclamation and developments of land, purchase of agricultural machinery and equipment, and development of minor irrigation.

Primary Land Development Banks (PLDBS)

The establishment of Land Mortgage Bank on co-operative lines dates back to the year 1920 in Punjab. Later during the period 1920–29 many Land Mortgage Banks were established in Punjab, Madras, Mysore, Assam and Bengal. There was not much growth in the Land Mortgage Banks till 1945, however, an alround progress of these banks was witnessed during the post-independence period, i.e., 1948–53. During this period, only rich and affluent farmers derived benefit from the LMBs. Small and marginal farmers were hardly benefited. LMBs received massive support from institutional agencies like Reserve Bank of India, State Bank of India, Life Insurance Corporation and Agricultural Refinance Corporation. As a result the LMBs reoriented

---

* National Bank For Agriculture And Rural Development

their lending policies towards small and marginal farmers and much emphasis was given to agricultural development. In the year 1974, LMBs were renamed as LDBs in A.P. Primary LDBs are generally organised to serve the farmers at taluk level. The specific functions are: (1) they provide long term finance to the needy farmers for the development of land, increasing agricultural production and productivity of land; (2) they provide loans for minor irrigation and for redemption of old debts and purchase of land; (3) farmers interested in purchasing tractors, machinery and equipment are financed; (4) the banks also provide finance for construction of farm structure; and (5) they mobilise rural savings.

Single Window System

The farmers in Andhra Pradesh depended on PACS (in three-tier structure) for their short and medium-term credit requirements and on PLDBs (in two-tier system) for long-term credit needs till 1987, which means that the farmers had to obtain their total loan requirements from two different types of co-operative institutions and furthermore, the performance of PLDBs was not satisfactory. Regarding marketing of the farm produce, the farmers faced hardships in getting the services of marketing co-operative societies under three-tier system. To help co-operatives serve in a more useful way, the Government of Andhra Pradesh thought that it is appropriate to bring some organisational changes in the working of co-operatives in the State. Accordingly, a Committee under the Chairmanship of Sri Mohan Kanda was constituted to come out with meaningful and practicable alternatives in this regard. The Committee submitted its report in May 1985. It recommended for the establishment of 'single window system' and to this effect a bill was introduced and passed in Assembly in January 1987. The main idea of introducing this system is to supply all types of agricultural credit required by the farmers and provide processing and marketing facilities under one roof i.e., through PACS. The single window system is a three-tier structure in co-operative credit and two-tier structure in co-operative marketing. The organisational structure is sketched out in Figure 2.2.

Consequent to the introduction of single window system in A.P. 6,801 PACS were reduced to 4,257 and 218 Primary Co-operative Agricultural Development Banks (PCADBs) were merged with District Co-operative Central Banks and 125 Primary Co-operative Marketing Societies were amalgamated with DCMS.

Functions of PACS under single window system are: (1) to advance the ST, MT and LT loans; (2) to supply the needed farm inputs; (3) to

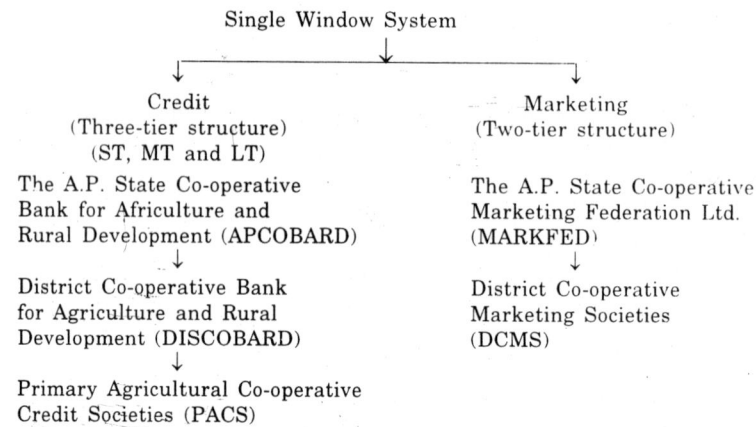

Fig. 2.2: Single Window System.

distribute essential commodities; and (4) to arrange the marketing of the farm produce of the farmer members.

Large-Sized Adivasi Multipurpose Co-operative Societies (LAMPS)

Akin to the objectives of FSSs, LAMPS were organised for the first time in December 1971 based on the recommendations of the Bawa team appointed by the Government of India in tribal areas of the country. According to its framed objectives, these societies are expected to provide through single window, all types of credit including consumption credit. Intensification and modernization of agriculture with appropriate technical guidance and improving the marketing of agricultural and forest products in the tribal areas, are their other objectives.

Membership and Area of Operation: All tribes can become members of the society on voluntary basis. Like FSSs, the area of operation of the society is larger than that of the PACS covering an area of block and some times covering an area, as big as a taluk.

Sources of Capital: Share capital of members and State Government, entrance fee, reserve fund, deposits collected from members and non-members and loans taken from co-operative institutions and Government are the various sources of capital.

Management of LAMPS: These are managed by a Board of Directors. In general, there are 11 members in the Board, of whom five come from tribal members, two from non-tribal members, two nominated by

Registrar of Co-operatives and two nominees from the lead bank of the concerned district. One of the nominees acts as the Managing Director of the LAMPS.

Farmers Service Societies (FSS)

Farmers Service Societies are well organised registered co-operative bodies, based on the principles of co-operation and governed by co-operative bye-laws. Since the Primary Agricultural Co-operative Credit Societies (PACS) are biased towards affluent sections of rural areas, the National Commission on Agriculture (NCA) strongly felt that separate societies for meeting the special needs of weaker sections in the rural areas are needed. Consequent to the recommendation of the Commission, FSS were organised in the year 1971, on the lines of co-operatives to provide integrated credit service to the weaker sections of the rural areas, viz., small farmers, marginal farmers, agricultural labourers and rural artisans. Following are the proposed functions of the FSS as suggested by the Commission: (1) to supply all types of loans to weaker sections, viz., crop loans, medium-term loans and long-term loans; (2) to provide adequate supplies of requisite inputs and technical guidance for the development of agriculture on timely and regular basis; (3) to encourage dairy, poultry, fisheries, farm forestry and other subsidiary occupations in rural areas; (4) to make arrangements for bringing about improvements in agricultural markets; and (5) to mobilise deposits and small savings from weaker sections through incentives.

Area of Operation: The societies have been launched in SFDA and MFAL districts. Each society has a jurisdiction of a block or a portion thereof. A district union of these societies is there at the district level to suggest ways and means of improving and organising the societies for executing specific activities. The membership of the societies is open to those who are eligible to receive assistance under SFDA/ MFAL programmes. Others may be associate members but they will not have any voting rights.

Sponsorship: The lead bank of the district generally sponsors the FSS in financial matters.

Capital Structure: The various financial sources for the society are: share capital, funds from various sources and loans. Share capital includes share capital contributed by members, lead bank and State Government. In the case of large-sized FSS the limit of the share capital is Rs one lakh but for a small society the same is Rs 50,000. Funds from different sources include the funds contributed by commercial banks, co-operative societies, subsidies from SFDA and MFALs and commissions accrued to the societies through the supply of essential inputs and interest on advances.

Management: Depending upon the size of the society, the number of Directors in the Board varies from 9 to 13. One full-time Managing Director is deputed by the lead bank. Among the remaining Directors, five will be elected from the members of the society of which three are from small and marginal categories and two from other farmers. The remaining Directors are representatives of financing institutions, Block Development Office, Department of Agriculture and Co-operative Societies.

Social Control and Nationalization of Banks

The private sector banks being predominantly urban-oriented and controlled by a few large industrialists were not properly equipped to help the achievement of the basic socio-economic objectives. The credit needs of agriculture, small-scale industries and also weaker sections such as small traders and artisans continued to be ignored. Though agriculture is the main occupation of the country for nearly three-fourths of the population and contributed to almost half of the gross national product, the total bank credit advanced to this sector was barely one per cent as on June 1967. The bulk of the deposits that was contributed by the public was being advanced to the organised sector of the industry and trade. In the absence of financial institutional protection, the agricultural credit scene was dominated by private money lenders who were charging exorbitant rates of interest. All these compelled the imposition of social control over banks in 1968 with the main objectives of achieving a wider spread of bank credit, directing a larger volume of credit flow to priority sectors and reducing the authority of the members of the Managing Committee, since they acted as the representatives of the industrialists, who strongly influenced the formulation of bank policies. Social control created the tempo of branch expansion as evident by the addition of 785 new offices during the first half of 1969. But this did not make any significant dent in reorienting lending activities of the banks in channelizing adequate credit requirements to the priority sector and weaker sections. In many banks, those who had been controlling their policies in the past continued to dictate terms in their functioning in one way or the other. Even the directions issued by the Government were ignored by many of the banks. This state of affairs created an impression in the Government that social control was not sufficient to make the commercial banking system a meaningful instrument of socio-economic development and hence, nationalisation was considered as the alternative solution. Accordingly on 19th July 1969, the Government of India promulgated an ordinance called the Banking Companies (Acquisition and Transfer of Undertakings) Ordinance 1969, under which 14 commercial banks which had deposits of not less than Rs 50 crore each were nationalized. The 14 banks together had 4,134 branches with deposits of Rs 2,626 crore and advances of Rs 1,813 crore. The 14 banks were:

1) Central Bank of India
2) Bank of India
3) Punjab National Bank
4) Bank of Baroda
5) United Commercial Bank
6) Canara Bank
7) United Bank of India
8) Dena Bank
9) Union Bank of India
10) Allahabad Bank
11) Syndicate Bank
12) Indian Bank
13) Bank of Maharashtra, and
14) Indian Overseas Bank

The objectives of nationalisation as set out by the Prime Minister, Smt. Indira Gandhi were: (1) removal of control of banking business by a few industrialists; (2) elimination of the use of bank credit for speculative and unproductive purposes, particularly to the extent that it is encouraged by the association of a few leading groups; (3) expansion of credit to priority areas which were hitherto grossly neglected such as agriculture and small industry; (4) giving a professional bent to the bank management; (5) encouragement of new classes of entrepreneurs; and (6) provision of adequate training as well as reasonable terms of service to bank staff.

The broad aims of nationalisation of banks as stated in the preamble to the Banking Companies Ordinance (Acquisition and Transfer of Undertakings Act 1970) were to control the peaks of the economy and to better serve the needs of development of the economy in conformity with national policy and objectives. It would be the responsibility of the commercial banks to allow the free flow of credit to the hitherto neglected "priority sectors" of the economy like agriculture and allied activities, cottage industries, individual business, artisans, etc.

Between June 1969 and June 1975, 8,455 offices were opened by public sector banks, of which 4,337 offices were in urban areas. The number of public sector bank offices went up from 6,596 in June 1969 to 15,077 in June 1975. The average population served per bank office declined markedly to 32,000 in June 1975 from 65,000 in June 1969. Out of 8,455 offices opened between June 1969 and June 1975, the rural areas accounted for 4,092 offices.

Credit was no longer to be provided only to those who could furnish security in the form of property and projects. No time was lost by the nationalised banks to effect organisational changes. Spurred by the success of first spell of nationalisation of 14 commercial banks, six more banks in the private sector, having deposits not less than Rs 200 crore were nationalised on 15 April 1980. The six banks were:

1) Punjab and Sind Bank
2) Andhra Bank
3) New Bank of India
4) Vijaya Bank
5) Oriental Bank of Commerce, and
6) Corporation Bank

Branch expansion received a further spurt between January 1979 and March 1984. Over this period the public sector banks opened 7,612 new offices, of which 5,384 offices were in unbanked centres. Priority sector advances of public sector banks at the end of June 1992 stood at Rs 44,995 crore, of which the share of agricultural advances was 16.2 per cent. The percentage of advances towards priority sector was 39.3 of net bank credit.

State Bank of India (SBI)

Imperial Bank of India was formed in 1921 by amalgamating Bank of Bengal (founded in 1809), Bank of Bombay (founded in 1840) and Bank of Madras (founded in 1843) as there was no Central Bank in the country at that time. Imperial Bank besides, issuing notes performed other functions of a Central Bank until the emergence of RBI as a Central Bank in 1935. Subsequently, in 1955 Imperial Bank of India was nationalised with other State Banks (subsidiary banks) converted into SBI. It is the largest commercial bank in India. The particulars of SBI and its associate banks are presented in Table 2.1.

TABLE 2.1

SBI and Its Associate Banks

Name of the Bank	Headquarters
State Bank of India	Bombay
State Bank of Bikaner and Jaipur	Jaipur
State Bank of Hyderabad	Hyderabad
State Bank of Patiala	Patiala
State Bank of Travancore	Trivandrum
State Bank of Mysore	Bangalore
State Bank of Saurashtra	Bhavnagar
State Bank of Indore	Indore

Specialised Branches

The commercial banks opened special bank offices to cater to the needs of weaker sections in the rural areas. In this context Agricultural Development Branches (ADBs), Agricultural Banking Divisions (ABDs) of SBI and its associate banks, Grama Vikas Kendras (GVKs) of Bank of Baroda, Rural Service Centres (RSCs) of Dena Bank, Farm Clinics (FCs) of Syndicate Bank, and Rural Credit and Development Division (RCDD) of Indian Overseas Bank need to be mentioned. These branches were established to overcome practical difficulties in lending activities, reducing the high cost of operations, strengthening follow-up measures, supervision, etc. The Branch Managers of these specialised branches have discretionary powers in respect of the sanctioning higher amounts of credit to farmer-borrowers, compared to the Branch Managers of Commercial Banks. Similar to RRBs, they have concessions in maintaining Statutory Liquidity Ratios (SLRs) and Cash Reserve Ratios (CRRs). They give half per cent more interest on the deposits over commercial banks. Analogous to FSSs, these branches are equipped with technical staff to provide technical guidance with regard to farming.

The Bank of Baroda has set up GVKs on the lines of ADBs of SBI group. The GVKs not only make advances to agriculture, but also extend credit facilities to business, retail sale, transport operations, etc. Multi-Service Agency (MSA) Cells are set up in those rural branches where full-fledged GVKs do not operate. At some places MSAs operate as independent rural branches.

Satellite offices are a micro feature of State Bank of Bikaner and Jaipur. They do not have independent existence and branches, but function as integrated parts of full-fledged branches. The officials of parent branches visit these centres through well intimated schedules.

Multi-Agency Approach

This concept was originated after the first spell of nationalisation of 14 commercial banks in 1969. Considering the magnitude of credit requirements to agriculture, no single financial agency can cater to the credit needs, so we have institutions like co-operatives, commercial banks, Regional Rural Banks and Farmers Service Societies purveying credit to agriculture. The All India Rural Credit Review Committee (1969) opined that though the co-operatives were the pioneering institutions in agricultural credit and increased their coverage (in terms of area, number of farmers and quantum of loans) since 1950s, in view of the growing demand for institutional credit in the field of agriculture, it is imperative to have other financial institutions in the form of commercial banks to act as supporting agencies. The report also mentioned that there should not be any room for conflicts among these institutions. Green revolution which flashed Indian agriculture during the late sixties also forced the need of providing adequate credit for the farmers to reap the benefits of technology. Though multi-agency approach was introduced for a good cause, some problems cropped up in practice. The most common problems were: (1) double financing, multiple financing, over-financing and under-financing; (2) unproductive use of credit; (3) failure of the financial institutions to formulate meaningful credit programmes; (4) problems in recovering loans; (5) greater diversity in the procedural formalities followed by the different financial institutions; (6) varying interest rates; and (7) unnecessary supervision charges.

Having noticed the problems that percolated with the introduction of multi-agency approach, RBI had appointed a Working Group under the Chairmanship of C.E. Kamath in August 1976 to probe into the problems that surfaced and suggest meaningful recommendations. The Committee submitted its report in 1978 with the following recommendations:

(1) Geographical Demarcation of Functions: The area of operation of each institutional agency needs to be demarcated.

(2) Prime Role of Co-operatives: Co-operatives were given the status of ideal institutions in view of their spread and accessibility. The other institutional agencies have to play a supplementary role to support and strengthen the co-operative sector.

(3) Respective Roles of Lending Institutions: The members of co-operative societies should not be financed by the commercial banks

and other institutional agencies. These banks can advance loans to the needy but without giving room to the element of competition.

(4) Uniformity in Rates of Interest: The Working Group expressed the view that there was a strong case for the adoption of a uniform pattern of interest rates by all the institutional agencies to avoid a feeling of dissatisfaction and discrimination among different types of borrowers in homogenous areas.

(5) Streamlining of Inspection Procedure: It should aim at meaningful and productive follow-up of advances.

(6) Agricultural Pass Book: Suggestion was made for the introduction of agricultural pass book, so that the present practice of insisting upon production of non-encumbrance certificate can be dispensed with. The improvement will successfully prevent the farmers from going for double finance. The other alternative use of pass book is that it avoids periodical verification of records like 10-1 and *adangal*.

(7) Inspection of the End Use of Loan: Here emphasis should be laid on quality of inspection rather than periodicity of inspection. In its absence there is a possibility of the loans being unproductive and in this process, repayment capacity of the farmer gets affected, leading to the poor recovery performance of the bank.

Branch Expansion

Simple earmarking of funds to the agriculturists will not serve the purpose of solving the credit needs of farmers, unless the distribution pattern of financial institutions is also examined. This emphasised that it is not enough, if we increase the number of branches of any institutional agency without considering the distribution aspect. The two important institutional agencies in multi-agency approach, viz., commercial banks and regional rural banks, which are only the supporting agencies to the co-operative institutions, should operate only where the co-operatives are ineffective owing to financial or managerial incompetence.

At the end of March 1992, there were 60,528 branches of commercial banks (including RRBs) in the country, of which 35,275 (58.3 per cent) were in rural areas. As a result of rapid branch expansion witnessed since 1969, the average population per bank office which was 65,000 at the time of nationalisation, came down to 11,000 (as per the 1981 census) at the end of March 1992. Of the 60,528 branches at the end of March 1992, 8,563 (14 per cent) belonged to the State Bank of India, 3,752 (6 per cent) to associate banks of SBI, 29,681 (49 per cent) to nationalised banks, 4,007 (7 per cent) to other commercial banks and 14,525 (24 per cent) to RRBs. Of the total number of 60,528 branches at the end of March 1992, 58.3 per cent was in rural areas as against 22.3 per cent at the time of bank nationalisation in July 1969.

Village Adoption Scheme

As per the guidelines of RBI, SBI had first conceived 'village adoption scheme' with an intention to do intensive financing in the rural areas, where there is lot of potential for agricultural development. The scheme aims at achieving full advantages from concentrated and coordinated efforts of banking activities. The scheme is not meant to serve the interests of few residents of a village but, instead it has to cover all farmers without exception in a phased manner through extensive financing. This does not preclude other banks to finance the villages adopted by a particular bank. It is for the adopted bank to take special interest in overall agricultural development of the village, it has adopted in co-ordination and co-operation of other financing agencies, functioning nearby the adopted village.

Lead Bank Scheme

The National Credit Council (NCC) had appointed a Study Group in 1969 under the Chairmanship of Prof. D.R. Gadgil to suggest an appropriate organisational framework for effective implementation of social objectives. The Study Group recommended an 'Area Approach' for the development of financial structure through intensive efforts. In the same year, RBI appointed Sri F.K.F. Nariman Committee to study this recommendation. The Committee endorsed the views of the Study Group on 'Area Approach' and recommended the formulation of 'Lead Bank Scheme'. The RBI accepted the recommendation and 'Lead Bank Scheme' came into force from 1969. As per the scheme specific districts are allotted to each bank which would take the lead role in identifying the potential areas for banking and banking development and in expanding credit facilities. Specifically the functions of the lead bank scheme are: (1) surveying the potential areas for development of banking in the district; (2) identifying the business establishments which were hitherto dependent upon non-institutional agencies and financing them so as to enable them to raise their resources and surpluses from the advances made by the bank; (3) examining the marketing facilities available for disposal of agricultural and industrial commodities and linking credit with marketing; (4) assisting other lending agencies; (5) developing contacts and maintaining liasion with Government and other agencies and (6) preparing District Credit Plans much ahead of the season with the help of technical committee.

The lead bank is not a monopolist in the banking business but acts as consortium leader for coordinating the efforts of all financial institutions operating in the district. Under the lead bank scheme in each district one of the commercial banks functions as a lead bank for providing branch network and deployment of credit under various areas of priority sector. This scheme covered all the 472 districts in the country by June 1992.

Regional Rural Banks (RRBs)

All India Rural Credit Review Committee (1969) pointed out that over large parts of the country small farms have been handicapped in having access to co-operative credit both for current inputs and investment. Therefore, a need arose for the establishment of institutional agencies. This led to first spell of nationalisation of banks with greater expectations. Though they did add to the institutional structure, they simultaneously created some problems too.

The subject was examined by Government of India and appointed a Working Group in 1975 under the Chairmanship of Sri M. Narasimham to go into the financial assistance fendered to the weaker sections in the rural areas. The Working Group came up with the recommendation of setting up of rural-based institutional agencies called 'Regional Rural Banks' after having identified shortcomings in the functioning of commercial banks and co-operatives. The Government of India accepted the recommendation and the RRBs came into existence through Regional Rural Banks Ordinance on 26 September, 1975 and initially five rural banks, sponsored by commercial banks were set up on a pilot basis in the country on 2 October, 1975. This ordinance of 1975 was immediately replaced by the Regional Rural Bank Act 1976. The major premises on which the establishment of RRBs recommended were that the existing credit institutions even after necessary restructuring and modifications cannot be expected to meet the varied and growing needs for rural credit. The purpose of introducing RRBs is to have an institutional agency with clear understanding of rural problems and local familiarity which the co-operatives possesed and the business outlook which the commercial banks were known for, to serve the rural community with much more dedication. These banks were conceived as low-cost ones to uplift the lot of rural economy by financing agriculture, trade and industry in general and small and marginal farmers, agricultural labourers, artisans and small entrepreneurs, in particular. RRBs were expected to play a vital role in mobilising the savings of the small and marginal farmers, artisans and agricultural labourers and initiate banking habit among the rural people. These institutions were also expected to plug the gap created in extending credit to rural areas by largely urban-oriented commercial banks and the rural co-operatives, which have the close contact with rural areas, but fall short in terms of funds.

List of RRBs

The list of RRBs first opened in the country is shown in Table 2.2.

TABLE 2.2

List of RRBs

Sl. No.	Sponsor Bank	RRB	Headquarters
1.	Syndicate Bank	Prathma Bank	Moradabad (UP)
2.	State Bank of India	Gorakhpur	Gorakhpur (UP)
3.	United Bank of India	Gaur Grameena Bank	Malda (WB)
4.	Punjab National Bank	Haryana Kshetriya Grameena Bank	Bhiwani (Haryana)
5.	United Commercial Bank	Jaipur Nagalur Anchalik Grameena Bank	Jaipur (Rajasthan)

The objectives assigned to RRBs were: (1) to develop rural economy; (2) to provide credit for agriculture and allied activities; (3) to encourage village industries, artisans, carpenters, craftsmen, etc.; (4) to reduce dependence of weaker sections on money-lenders; (5) to fill up the gap created by morotorium on borrowings from money-lenders; (6) to help the poor, financially for their consumption needs; and (7) to make backward and tribal areas economically better by opening new branches.

Characteristic Features of Regional Rural Banks

1) Sponsorship: RRBs are sponsored by scheduled commercial banks.

2) Jurisdiction: The operational area to be covered by each RRB varies from one to two districts for efficient functioning. The number of branches in the area covered by each RRB may range from 50 to 60, keeping in view operational and financial efficiency. Coming to the population to be served by each branch, it has been kept at 20,000 roughly. However, these are subject to changes as per the direction of the Central Bank of the country.

3) Management: The management of the bank is in the hands of a Board of Directors numbering eight, headed by a Chairman, who is an officer of the sponsoring bank. Of the eight Directors, three are nominees of the sponsoring bank, two from the State Government dealing with district developmental programmes and three from the Central Government. The Regional Rural Banks are sponsored by commercial banks, generally the lead bank in the district. In some areas State Co-operative Banks and private commercial banks are allowed to sponsor RRBs. The sponsoring bank provides assistance to RRBs for the first five years.

4) Share Capital: The authorised share capital of RRB has been fixed at Rs one crore and issued capital at Rs 25 lakh. This is contributed by the Central Government, State Government and the sponsoring bank in the ratio of 50, 15 and 35 respectively.

5) Functions: The main functions are, to grant loans and advances particularly to small and marginal farmers, agricultural labourers, co-operative societies, co-operative farming societies for agricultural purposes, artisans, small entrepreneurs etc., within the operational area of the RRB. They have been asked to extend other banking facilities like issue of drafts, collection of cheques, etc. They act as vital instruments in schemes, like IRDP, 20-point economic programme, etc.

6) Rate of Interest: The rate of interest on the loans charged is the same as collected by PACS. They have been allowed to offer 0.50 per cent interest more than that of commercial banks.

7) Special Concessions to RRBs: (1) Statutory Liquidity Ratio (SLR) to be maintained is fixed at 25 per cent as against 38 per cent by commercial banks; (2) Regional Rural Banks are allowed to pay half per cent higher interest to its depositors over the interest rate offered by commercial banks; (3) Cash-reserve requirements of 3 per cent to be maintained with RBI as against 10 per cent by commercial banks; (4) they are allowed to draw refinance from NABARD to the extent of 50 per cent or more depending upon the type of advance of the eligible outstanding loans at a concessional interest rate of 7 per cent per annum; and (5) the RRBs are registered as insured banks with Deposit Insurance and Credit Guarantee Corporation of India

(DICGC). All deposits up to Rs 30,000 in each bank are accordingly insured with the DICGC thus providing protection to the depositors.

By June 1986 there were 194 RRBs functioning in 343 districts with a network of 12,755 branches situated in rural areas that too mostly in remote areas. A survey conducted by RBI has shown that the deposits mobilised by these RRBs had moved on from Rs 252.85 crore at the end of June 1981 to over Rs 1,443.51 crore by the end of June, 1986. At the end of September 1989, 196 RRBs were functioning through 14,279 branches covering 370 districts in 23 States. Till 1991, while the number of RRBs remained unchanged at 196, the total number of districts covered by RRBs increased to 385. At the end of September 1991, RRBs had 14,531 branches. Among the States, U.P. had the highest number of RRB branches having 3,055. Aggregate deposits at the end of September, 1991 stood at Rs 5,141 crore. Aggregate advances at the same period were Rs 3,804 crore.

Based on the recommendation of Baldev Singh Working Group, the RRBs have simplified the procedural formalities in respect of agricultural finance. All RRBs use local languages in their dealings and financial operations. Their cost of operation is low as compared to commercial banks.

Differential Rate of Interest Scheme (DIR Scheme)

The Ministry of Finance instructed all the public sector banks to introduce DIR scheme on the recommendations of RBI Committee under the Chairmanship of Dr. B.K. Hazare.

It is being implemented since 1975 by all the commercial banks under the public sector. However, private banks too volunteered to participate in the scheme from 1977 onwards. Under this scheme loans are being extended to the weaker sections of the society, who do not possess tangible security, at a concessional rate of 4 per cent interest per annum. The scheme was originally applicable at selected branches located in 265 backward districts of the country. Later in 1971, the scheme was extended to cover all parts of the country. DIR Scheme is also expected to cover all backward districts including SFDA and MFAL areas. Eligible members for DIR scheme are marginal farmers and agricultural labourers, scheduled castes and scheduled tribes engaged in agriculture, people having rural industries and cottage industries, persons engaged in small business and service units such as tailors, road-side hotelliers, rickshaw pullers, cobblers, basket-makers, carpenters, physically handicapped persons, orphans and indigent students having higher education. The DIR loans are covered by Small Loans Guarantee Scheme of the Deposit Insurance and Credit Guarantee Corporation of India. Since 1981, the banks were allowed to route their advances under DIR scheme through RRBs in their area of operation on refinance basis which was taken into account by the sponsoring bank towards their lendings under the scheme. The amounts of loan advanced were up to Rs 3,000 and Rs 2,000 in urban or semi-urban and rural areas respectively. However, the restrictions on the loan amounts are relaxed for persons belonging to scheduled castes and scheduled tribes. The commercial banks are required to advance one half to one per cent of their aggregate lendings towards this scheme, and 40 per cent of the total amount available under the scheme should be made available to SC and ST borrowers. According to social justice the interests of the weaker sections should be safeguarded. DIR scheme is one such measure. This is based on the principle of negative taxation which means low-income groups must be subsidised in their borrowings.

At the end of June 1990, the outstanding advances by public sector banks under DIR scheme amounted to Rs 708 crore in 42.87 lakh borrower accounts and at the end of March 1992, outstanding advances of public sector banks amounted to Rs 727 crore. The Government of India had set up in April 1983 a Task Force to examine various provisions of the DIR scheme and make modifications, if any, considered necessary. After considering the recommendations of the Task Force, it has been decided that the DIR scheme, IRDP and Self Employment Programme for the Urban Poor (SEPUP) would be mutually exclusive. In other words, if a person is assisted under IRDP or SEPUP, he will not be eligible for the benefit under the DIR scheme. Furthermore, the benefit of DIR scheme will be available only to those borrowers within the prescribed eligibility criterion who are not assisted under any of the subsidy-linked schemes of Central/State Governments and State-owned corporations. Besides, the ceiling of family income of the borrowers under DIR scheme is revised from Rs 2,000 per annum in rural areas and Rs 3,000 per annum in urban and semi-urban areas to Rs 6,400 and Rs 7,200 respectively.

Farm Graduate Scheme

In order to enlarge the extent and scope of its lending activities and enable the agricultural graduates who have necessary technical expertise but lack financial sources to stand on their own feet, Farm Graduate Scheme was introduced by SBI.

Eligibility Criterion: Any one who has (1) proven integrity; (2) degree in Agriculture/Veterinary Science/Dairy Science/Agricultural Engineering; (3) the land either in his own name or jointly with others; (4) worthwhile project of agriculture/and allied activities; and (5) requisite technical ability to run the farm.

In exceptional circumstances, advances are also permitted to agricultural-diploma holders and to those who hold a degree in a subject other than agriculture, but have at least one year's training in agriculture.

The scheme is applicable to those who do not own land but want to join those who own land in partnership, subject to it being ensured that only *bona fide* ventures are financed under this scheme.

The scheme is intended to be made operative only at selected centres in areas which are most responsive and where extension of bank's activities results in substantial benefit.

Activities Covered: Production of food-grains and commercial crops including hybrid and high-yielding varieties of seeds and special farming activities such as poultry, dairy, piggery, fisheries, horticulture, etc. are being covered.

Quantum of assistance: Only those projects, where the total financial requirement is Rs 1 lakh are considered.

Margin: The applicant is required to offer as much as possible from his own resources, and in case he had no resources of his own, no margin is insisted upon.

DEPOSIT INSURANCE AND CREDIT GUARANTEE CORPORATION OF INDIA (DICGC)

The failure of two scheduled banks, viz. Palai Central Bank Limited (Kerala) and Laxmi Bank Ltd. (Maharashtra) in 1960 gave a rude shock to the stability of the banking system in the country. This forced RBI to frame legislative measures so as to arrest bank mortality and create confidence in depositors. In 1961, RBI formulated proposals for the establishment of Deposit Insurance Corporation (DIC) on the model of the Federal Deposit Insurance Corporation in USA. The Deposit Insurance Corporation bill was passed and the Corporation came into existence on January 1, 1962.

Role of the Corporation

(1) The Corporation gives protection to depositors particularly the small depositors, from the risk of loss of their savings in the event of a bank's failure; such protection increases the confidence of the

depositors in the individual banks and reduces the occurrence of panicky withdrawals of deposits; (2) the Corporation contributes to the stability and orderly growth of individual banks as well as collectively of the banking system; and (3) it plays an active role in developing the banking habits of the people and ensures a larger mobilisation of their savings.

The Corporation has a paid up capital of Rs one crore which was contributed by RBI. The insurance scheme has been made compulsory for all banks. Till December, 1967, the amount of insurance cover provided by the corporation was Rs 1,500 per account in each bank. From January 1968, the cover had been raised to Rs 5,000 and at present it is Rs 10,000. The increased cover is certainly a welcome measure.

In order to provide safety to the banking system from risks involved in lending to priority sectors, Government of India established Credit Guarantee Corporation of India Limited (CGCI) in 1971. The CGCI is associated with Credit Guarantee Organisation (CGO) set up in 1960 to provide guarantee in respect of lending to small scale industries. Subsequently, in 1978 CGCI and CGO were merged with Deposit Insurance Corporation of India (DIC) and a new institution by the name of Deposit Insurance and Credit Guarantee Corporation of India (DICGC) was established.

Service Area Approach

After the first spell of nationalisation of banks in 1969, to reach agriculturists and those involved in allied activities, village adoption scheme was introduced by many of the banks. But, there was no bar for entry by the other banks in an area operated by a particular bank in extending credit facilities. This liberal entry of several banks created innumerable problems in a planned approach. To emphasise the planned approach to the rural areas the 'Service Area Approach' was proposed in 1988, which is not an altogether a new concept from Village Adoption Scheme, but it has certainly some merits. It is aimed at improving the productivity of bank credit in the rural areas. Scattered lendings over wide areas diluted the quality of lending and also post-disbursement supervision was inadequate. Hence, increased attention is being paid by each rural branch in lending activities within a compact area.

At the instance of RBI, the chief executives of the nationalised banks evaluated the rural credit delivery system in 88 districts of 21 States in November 1987. The reports submitted by the executives were discussed in a seminar held on 9th and 10th of January 1988 which was addressed by the then Union Minister of Finance. One of the recommendations that emerged out of this was to assign a specific service area to each bank branch. Thereafter, a committee was set up under the Chairmanship of Dr. P.D. Ojha to examine operational aspects in implementation of 'Service Area Approach'. After getting convinced about the recommendation, the RBI implemented the 'Service Area Approach' for bank branches in 1989.

Need for Service Area Approach: This is based on the following aspects: (1) to ensure planned development of villages by qualitative lending, i.e., to make credit much more productive, (2) to make Branch Managers responsible for developing villages under their jurisdiction, and (3) emphasizing grass-root level planning involving Branch Managers, and block/village level officials of the Government.

The following stages are involved in the 'Service Area Approach': (1) identification and allocation of service areas for each branch of commercial banks in rural and urban areas, (2) a survey to identify the scope of lending, (3) preparation of branch credit plans, (4) co-ordination between different agencies for development, and (5) a continued system of monitoring the performance under credit planning, branchwise or bankwise.

Objectives of Service Area Approach: The objectives are: (1) to make the area of operation of the bank compact and accessible; (2) to improve the quality of lending in rural areas; (3) to envisage systematised credit planning and supervision; and (4) to remove regional imbalances in credit lending.

The special feature of the 'Service Area Approach' is that the Branch Manager is made responsible for the preparation of credit plans of the villages attached to his bank. The distinguishing features of 'Service Area Approach' from that of 'Village Adoption Scheme' are presented in Table 2.3.

CROP LOAN SYSTEM

Though All India Rural Credit Survey Committee 1954 and the V.L. Mehra Committee on Co-operative Credit (1960) recommended the adoption of crop loan system in all the States, for one reason or the other it was not implemented in several States of the country immediately. After a lapse of five years this was introduced in the country during 1965 and in Andhra Pradesh from kharif, 1966. The scheme has been implemented with the twin objectives of treating crop as security instead of landed property and fixing the scale of finance depending upon the actual farm expenditure.

TABLE 2.3

Differences between 'Village Adoption Scheme' and 'Service Area Approach'

Sl. No.	Particulars	Village Adoption Scheme	Service Area Approach
1.	Identification of villages	According to the will of the Branch Manager based on potentiality of business the villages were identified.	According to criteria such as proximity, contiguity, dominant share, IRDP allocation etc., the villages are identified.
2.	Operation	Operation was not strictly within the adopted villages.	Operation is strictly within the assigned villages only.
3.	Basis for development	Detailed surveys were not conducted for implementation of all relevant schemes.	It entails a detailed village survey for deciding potentiality for various schemes by the Branch Manager.
4.	Coverage of families	There was no firm commitment about provision of credit to all the needy families.	All the families needing credit facilities would be covered in a phased manner.
5.	Accountability	The Branch Manager was not accountable for full development of villages	The Branch Manager is fully accountable for providing need-based credit to villagers.
6.	Integration	There was no integration between, credit and non-credit activities.	Perfect integration is expected between credit and non-credit activities.
7.	Involvement of agencies	There was no involvement/ commitment of other agencies.	There is involvement of other agencies.
8.	Forum for coordination	There was no forum for coordination.	The forum for coordination is Block Level Bankers, Committee (BLBC).

Salient Features of the System

(1) the credit requirements of the farmers are to be based on the cost of cultivation (variable costs) of the crop; (2) the eligibility to receive the loan is not gauged by the ownership of the land, but by the factor that he is a *bona fide* farmer who needs credit for cultivation; (3) the crop loan should be given based on the hypothecation of the crop; (4) the disbursement and recovery of loan are to be made in accordance with the crop production schedule; (5) the loan should be given both in cash and kind, and kind component is related to quantum of factors

total inputs required for production of a particular crop; (6) the quantum of loan should be fixed according to the variety and the season in which it is grown and type of crop i.e., irrigated or rainfed; (7) crop loan should be recovered with tie-up arrangement i.e., linking credit with marketing; and (8) crop loan is fixed by the District Consultative Committee which consists of experts from fields of agriculture, animal husbandry, banking, etc.

District Credit Plans (DCPs)

Scattered lendings over a large area do not create any desired impact of institutional finance on agricultural development. However, the impact of bank finance can be achieved if the lendings are advanced in a compact area. The District Credit Plans introduced through the 'Lead Bank Scheme' have become instruments for the Government to implement the developmental activities, identify the priority sectors and reduce the imbalances in the operational area. The 'District Credit Plans' are prepared keeping in view the credit requirements for agriculture and allied activities and small industries. Regulating the flow of funds as per the plan priorities is the main objective of District Credit Plans. It is a blue print of bankers containing the technically viable and economically feasible schemes which will be implemented by the collective efforts of all institutional agencies. According to the original scheme, these plans used to be prepared by Lead Bank Officers covering a period of 3 to 5 years based on the development plans of various participating agencies and conveniently phased into 'Annual Action Plans' for smooth implementation. However, with the implementation of 'Service Area Approach', the bank branches are required to prepare their Branch Credit Plans for each financial year, which are aggregated at district level into 'Annual Credit Plan' by the Lead Bank Officer. With the introduction of 'Service Area Approach', the method for preparation of 'Annual Action Plans' at district level has undergone a sea change. According to the new method, Branch Managers are required to prepare branch credit plans, which after finalization by Mandal Level Bankers' Committee/Taluk Level Bankers' Committee, are aggregated at joint mandal level/taluk level and district level. Till now the exercise used to be top-down while hereafter it will be bottom-up.

District Consultative Committee (DCC)

It is formed at the district level. Lead Bank Officer is the Convener and district collector/district magistrate the Chairman. The participants are Chief Executive Officer of Zilla Parishad, Project Director of DRDA, Executive Officers of SC/BC Corporation, General Manager of District Industries Centre, District level functionaries of agricultural/animal husbandry/sericulture, Regional Managers of the participating banks, representatives of NABARD, RBI and representatives of Co-operative Institutions.

Functions of DCC: The functions are: (1) identifying potential areas for development and formulation of bankable schemes for inclusion in DCP/AAP; (2) discussing and finalising DCP/AAP/IRDP plans; (3) reviewing the implementation of the plans and identifying unbanked areas for branch expansion; (4) reviewing advances made by all institutional agencies to various sectors; (5) reviewing the recovery performance and rendering necessary help for recovery of overdues; (6) reviewing the progress achieved in implementation of various Governmental sponsored programmes; (7) reviewing the problems faced by the banks and Governmental agencies (officials) in implementing various Governmental programmes; and (8) considering the security arrangements and other infrastructural facilities for rural branches.

HIGHER FINANCING AGENCIES

World Bank

It is officially known as International Bank for Reconstruction and Development (IBRD). It is a specialized agency of the United Nations. Its affiliate bodies are International Monetary Fund (IMF, 1945), International Finance Corporation (IFC, 1956) and International Development Association (IDA, 1960). Its main focus is laid on loans and advances and technical assistance to promote the balanced growth of international trade and economic development. The World Bank along with its affiliate agencies popularly known as the World Bank Group (WBG) is the unique and remarkable lending agency in international development.

Member countries can avail loan facilities and loans can be made to private firms, if member Governments will guarantee repayment to bank. Projects like agriculture, mining, irrigation, communications, transportation and general industrial development are being considered by the World Bank for grant of loans. The repayment period ranges from 10 to 35 years. Interest rates for the poorest countries are almost negligible or zero but a service charge of 0.5 to 1 per cent is included. For private firms and industrial development projects interest rates are nearer to commercial lending rates. Regarding technical assistance, the bank's technical mission along with personnel of FAO (Food and Agricultural Organization) assist in surveying, evaluation and setting up of projects in the member countries. Its headquarters is in Washington, D.C., USA. The Chairman and Board of Governors (20) meet once in a year to determine policies. The quantum of loans is decided based on the voting on loans which is related to subscription of capital paid by member countries.

1) International Monetary Fund (IMF)

It was established on 27 December, 1945 as an independent international organization and began its operations on 1 March 1947 with headquarters in Washington D.C. Its relationship with the UN is defined in an agreement of mutual co-operation which came into force on 15 November 1947. The capital resources of the Fund come from Special Drawing Rights (SDRs) and currencies that the members pay under quotas calculated for them when they join the Fund.

The Fund is authorised under its 'Articles of Agreement' to supplement its resources by borrowing. In January 1962, a four year agreement was concluded with 10 industrial members (Belgium, Canada, France, Federal Republic of Germany, Italy, Japan, Netherlands, Sweden, UK and USA) which undertook to lend the Fund up to $ 6,000 million in their own currencies. Switzerland subsequently joined the group. These arrangements, known as the General Arrangements to Borrow (GAB) have been extended several times and the most recent five-year renewal ended in December 1993.

Purposes: The purposes are as follows: (1) to promote international monetary co-operation, the expansion of international trade and exchange rate stability; (2) to assist in the removal of exchange restrictions and the establishment of a multi-lateral system of payments, and (3) to alleviate any serious disequilibrium in members, and international balance of payments by making the financial resources of the fund available to them.

Activities: Each member of the Fund undertakes a broad obligation to collaborate with the Fund and other members to ensure the existence of orderly exchange arrangements and promote a system of stable exchange rates. In addition, members are subject to certain obligations relating to domestic and external policies that can affect the balance of payments and the exchange rates. The Fund makes its resources available, under proper safeguards to its members to meet short-term or medium-term payment difficulties.

2) International Finance Corporation (IFC)

The International Finance Corporation (IFC) is a specialized agency of the United Nations that is closely associated with the World Bank. It was established in July 1956 to provide capital for private enterprises in its member-countries, particularly less developed countries. The IFC invests in private enterprises when sufficient private capital is not available. It also serves as a clearing house to bring together investment opportunities, foreign and domestic private capital and experienced management. It is authorised to borrow from the World Bank and to sell its own bonds to the public. The Corporation helps finance new ventures, and it also assists established enterprises to expand, improve or diversify their operations. On 30 June 1988, IFC had approved investments amounting to $ 10,500 million in over 90 countries.

3) International Development Association (IDA)

IDA concentrates its assistance in those countries with an annual per capita gross national product of less than $ 790 (at 1983 rate). Its resources consist mostly of subscriptions, general replinishments from its more industrialized and developed members, and special contributions and transfers from the net earnings of the bank.

The IDA, instituted in September 1960, is an affiliated organization of the International Bank for Reconstruction and Development (World Bank). Its members must also be the members of the World Bank (total membership of the countries stands at 120). The IDA extends credit to developing nations on terms that are easier and more flexible than those of the bank. IDA borrowers, may repay their loans over a period of 50 years with a service charge of less than one per cent instead of interest. Loans are for the purpose of stimulating investment and economic development and encouraging foreign trade. By 1981, IDA credit totalled $ 16.7 billion for 74 member countries. It had committed over $ 43,307.7 million for 1,699 development projects in 83 countries by 30 June 1987.

RESERVE BANK OF INDIA (RBI)

The Reserve Bank of India was established in 1935 under the Reserve Bank of India Act, 1934. The bank was set up to regulate issue of bank notes and keeping up resources with a view to securing monetary stability in the country and operate the currency and credit system to its advantage. When examined, the role of RBI in the sphere of agricultural credit, the creation of Agricultural Credit Department (ACD) comes to light. The primary functions of ACD were to co-ordinate the functions of RBI with regard to agricultural credit with other banks and State Co-operative Banks, to maintain expert staff to study all questions of agricultural credit and be available for consultation by Central Government, State Governments, Scheduled Commercial Banks and State Co-operative Banks and to provide legislations to check private money-lendings and checking malpractices. All India Rural Credit Survey Committee (AIRCSC) in 1954 suggested several recommendations with regard to activities of RBI in the sphere of rural credit. Subsequently two funds were established after amending the RBI Act, viz., the National Agricultural Credit (Long Term Operations) Fund and the National Agricultural Credit (Stabilization) Fund. The National Agricultural Credit (Long-Term Operations) Fund was set up in 1955 with an initial contribution of Rs 10 crore and a sum of Rs 5 crore was to be further added every year from the profits of the RBI in the first five years. In May 1960, as per the recommendations of the Committee on co-operative credit, the RBI was authorised by Government of India to credit Rs 15 crore to the Fund annually as against Rs 5 crore contemplated to be added earlier. This Fund was meant to provide long-term loans to various State Governments with a view to enabling them to contribute to the share capital of different types of co-operative societies including Land Mortgage Banks. Loans and advances out of this fund are made to State Governments for periods not exceeding 20 years, for purchasing debentures of State Land Development Banks and for providing funds to the Agricultural Refinance and Development Corporation for periods not exceeding 20 years. Since the creation of this fund, medium-term loans are provided by the RBI only out of this fund.

The second fund, viz., National Agricultural Credit (Stabilization) Fund was established in June 1956 with an initial contribution of Rs 1 crore and subsequent annual contributions of Rs 1 crore. The fund is utilized for the purpose of granting medium-term loans to State Co-operative Banks, specially during the times of famine, drought or other calamities, when they are not able to repay their short-term loans to RBI. This fund is also used for converting short-term loans which are due to RBI from the Central Co-operative Banks in areas affected by natural calamities. The State and Central Co-operative Banks, and Primary Agricultural Co-operative Credit Societies in turn provide a similar facility to the farmer-borrowers regarding short-term production loans taken for the crops affected by natural calamities. This makes them eligible for further agricultural finance at the same time reducing their burden of repaying the loans.

The role of RBI in the sphere of rural credit can be seen under three aspects, viz., provision of finance, promotional activities, and regulatory functions.

1) Provision of Finance

RBI provides necessary finance needed by agriculturists through commercial banks, co-operatives and Regional Rural Banks. It advances long-term loans to State Governments for their contribution to the share capital of the co-operative credit institutions, i.e. apex and district banks. Refinance facility is extended to RRBs only, to an extent of 50 per cent of their outstanding advances.

2) Promotional Activities

The RBI's efforts on this front can be seen in the appointment of study teams in organising and running the co-operative credit institutions in the country. It conducts a number of studies and surveys pertaining to rural credit aspects in the country. Like the All India Rural Credit Survey, All India Rural Debt and Investment Surveys etc., can be cited as the most comprehensive ones. The Committees which need special mention are: The Committee on Co-operative Land Development Banks (1974), the Committee on Integration of Co-operative Credit Institutions (1976), and Committee to Study the Interest Rates Spreads in Agricultural Lending Sector. The RBI felt that co-operatives are the major force in the sphere of agricultural credit and accordingly the following policies were made for strengthening the co-operatives:

  a) Reorganisation of the State and Central Co-operative banks on the principle of one apex bank for each State and one central bank for each district.
  b) Rehabilitation of those Central Co-operative banks which are financially and administratively weak for reasons such as mounting overdues, inadequacy of internal resources, untrained staff, poor management, etc.
  c) Strengthening of PACS to ensure their financial and operational viability and
  d) Arranging suitable training programmes for the personnel of co-operative institutions.

3) Regulatory Functions of RBI

Apart from lending aspects, RBI is concerned with efficiency of channels through which credit is purveyed to rural sector. Banking Regulation

Act 1966 of RBI enables it to exercise effective supervision over co-operative banks and commercial banks. The co-operative banks should get prior authorisation from RBI for providing finance beyond a certain limit as per the Credit Authorisation Scheme of 1976. Based on institutional demand for credit, credit limits are fixed. The Cash Liquidity Ratio (CLR) and Cash Reserve Ratio (CRR) are fixed by RBI for co-operatives, FSSs, RRBs and ADBs at lower level than those fixed for commercial banks. For these banks the bank rate is 3 per cent less than that of commercial banks. They are permitted by RBI to pay ½ per cent higher rate of interest on their deposits.

Credit Control or Credit Squeeze

The term refers to the regulation by monetary authority (RBI) of the volume and direction of credit (loans and advances) of the banking system, particularly the commercial banks. In times of inflation, credit control operations aim at contraction of credit, while during deflation, they aim at expansion of credit. Credit control is meant for price and exchange stability avoiding business fluctuations, halting the gold drain, ensuring full employment and to accelerate development of the economy. Different devices or levers used for this process are: (1) the RBI can raise or reduce bank rate; (2) RBI can engage in the open market operations in the Government Securities market to absorb or increase the supply of funds; (3) it can raise or lower the level of reserves that commercial banks must maintain; and (4) RBI can set limits on the credit terms offered in loans on securities, mortgages and consumer credit.

The first three levers or methods augment or limit the volume of money supply to commercial banks for credit expansion. They also exert an indirect impact on the price, interest rate charged for new credit, and influence indirectly the size and quantum of new loans that can be made by the banks. Only the specific controls on securities, mortgages and consumer credit can be called credit rationing. Fiscal policies are also a sort of credit control.

Fiscal Policy

This refers to the use of Government's spending and revenue producing activities in order to achieve specific objectives of full employment with price stability. When Government taxes to a greater extent than it spends, it causes a net reduction in the flow of income, thereby reducing the aggregate demand. When it spends a greater amount of money than it receives, it raises national income and aggregate demand. Budget deficits or surpluses are the tools of fiscal policy meant for regulating the economic stability and growth. The instruments of credit control are:

1) Discount rate or bank rate
2) Open market operations
3) Rationing of credit
4) Direct action
5) Variation of cash reserves
6) Regulation of consumer credit
7) Regulation of margin money
8) Minimum secondary reserves, and
9) Moral suasion or publicity.

Credit Rationing

This refers to the art of rationing loans by non-price means in situations of excess demand for credit by financial intermediaries. It may assume two forms.

    (1)   Variable portfolio ceiling: This is the system under which RBI fixes a ceiling or maximum amounts of loans and advances for every commercial bank.

    (2)   Variable capital asset ratio: This refers to the system by which RBI fixes the ratio, which the capital of commercial banks should have to the total assets of banks.

If the loan ceiling to commercial banks is fixed with reference to total amount, it is quantitative control, but if it is done with reference to specific type of credit, it assumes a qualitative character.

Credit rationing also refers to the power of RBI to allow only a fixed amount of accommodation to member banks by means of rediscount.

AGRICULTURAL REFINANCE AND DEVELOPMENT CORPORATION (ARDC)

Prior to independence long-term credit requirements for agricultural development were by far met by money lenders and to a small extent by the State Government. Considering this, All India Rural Credit Survey Committee (1951) and Committee on Co-operative Credit in 1960 stressed the inadequacy of term finance for investment in agriculture and suggested the establishment of an institution at the apex level. The Standing Advisory Committee of RBI on agricultural credit had also supported the recommendations. Consequent to their recommendations, Parliament through an Act of 1963 provided for the establishment of Agricultural Refinance Corporation (ARC) from 1 July 1963. It was basically a refinancing agency, meant for promotion and development of agriculture through long-term financial assistance. Considering its developmental and promotional role, it was renamed as Agricultural Refinance and Development Corporation (ARDC). Ever since its inception it is providing term finance which includes medium-term and long-term loans for major agricultural development projects, which were hitherto not financed by existing credit agencies. The corporation was primarily meant to refinance, assist and guide the State Co-operative Land Development Banks. But later, it extended its financial assistance to scheduled commercial banks and State Co-operative Banks. On 30 June 1980, a provision to the Act of ARDC was promulgated to provide short-term refinance facility. The broad functions of ARDC were as follows: (1) to help commercial banks for their participation in investments in agricultural development in a big way; (2) to extend needed assistance to the Governmental agencies in the formulation of technically feasible and economically viable projects; (3) to offer needed strength to the member banks in the aspects pertaining to operation and finance; (4) to provide greater assistance to the small farmers; (5) to diversify its lending activities to achieve overall growth in the nation's economy; (6) to play a role as an effective development bank; and (7) to strive hard for reducing regional inequalities in growth and development by concentrating assistance in backward and under-developed areas.

The range of refinance facilities in respect of agricultural development projects provided by the corporation was very wide and the following were the specific investment projects:

(1) Afforestation programmes.
(2) Horticultural development and plantation crops like cardamom, pepper, cloves, coffee, tea, rubber, etc.
(3) Minor irrigation in the form of tube-wells, dug wells, installation of filter point pumpsets, energisation of wells, etc. Minor irrigation claimed a lion's share in corporation's refinance.
(4) Soil conservation, reclamation and dry farming programmes.
(5) Infrastructural development projects like development of market yards, warehouses, cold storage facilities, etc.
(6) Dairy, sheep-breeding and rearing, fisheries, poultry, sericulture, shrimps, etc.
(7) Selective farm mechanisation, agro-service centres, etc.

Of all the above, 80 to 90 per cent of the refinance of the corporation goes to minor irrigation, land development and farm mechanisation activities.

As a development banker, the corporation made earnest efforts to remove regional imbalances by instructing commercial banks and other financial institutions to formulate bankable projects in the areas where co-operatives were weak. All community development blocks in the country were covered by one scheme or the other in a phased manner under the guidance of the corporation. The corporation provided special concessions to small and marginal farmers in the SFDA, MFAL and IRDP areas with relatively lower rate of interest at 9½ per cent. A longer repayment period was allowed with concessions in repayment. Increased quantum of refinance facility at the rate of 90 per cent of the total disbursement of the loans was made to commercial banks functioning in these areas. It rendered specific assistance to all the banks in these areas in drawing up of bankable projects in collaboration with State Governments and other authorities concerned with the development of weaker sections. Generally, it provided 75 per cent of the bankable projects through refinance in developed regions, but in the backward regions, to eliminate the regional imbalances in development, it extended refinance to an extent of 90 per cent of the bankable projects. In the year 1982, ARDC was merged with NABARD.

Sources of Capital

The authorised share capital of the corporation was Rs 25 crore with a paid-up share capital of Rs 5 crore. The share of the ARDC was guaranteed by the Government of India. The sources of funds were share capital, issue and sale of bonds guaranteed by the Government of India and loans from RBI.

Management

It was managed by a Board consisting of 9 members with Deputy Governor of RBI as the Chairman. Managing Director was appointed by RBI and one more Director was also nominated by RBI. Three directors were nominated by the Government of India. Three more directors were elected from among share-holders of State Co-operative Land Development Banks, State Co-operative Banks, scheduled commercial banks, Life Insurance Corporation of India and other insurance companies.

NATIONAL BANK FOR AGRICULTURE AND RURAL DEVELOPMENT (NABARD)
GENESIS

ARDC has not made much headway in the field of direct financing and delivery of rural credit against the massive credit demand for rural development. Its role to meet the challenges of integrated rural credit through institutional buildings, training, research, policy making, planning and providing expertise in the diverse disciplines of finance was inadequate and insufficient. As a result, many Committees and Commissions, viz., Banking Commission (1972), National Commission on Agriculture (1976) and Committee to Review Arrangements for Institutional Credit for Agriculture and Rural Development (CRAFICARD) in 1979, under the Chairmanship of B. Sivaraman, former member of Planning Commission, recommended the setting up of a national level institution called NABARD for providing all types of production and investment credit for agriculture and rural development. In pursuance of their recommendations, NABARD came into existence in July 1982. The then existing national level institutions such as Agricultural Refinance and Development Corporation (ARDC), Agricultural Credit Department (ACD) and Rural Planning and Credit Cell (RPCC) of RBI were merged with NABARD.

Objectives

As an apex refinancing institution, NABARD purveys all types of credit needed for the farm sector and rural development. It is also vested with the responsibility of promoting and integrating rural development activities through refinance. The bank is also providing direct credit to any institution or organisation or an individual, subject to the approval of the Central Government. It has close links with RBI for guidance and assistance in financial matters. As an effective catalytic agent for rural development and in formulating appropriate rural development plans and policies, its role is remarkable.

Functions

(1) It helps in planning, in operational matters relating to credit for agriculture, allied activities, rural artisans, village industries and other rural developmental activities as a development policy; (2) it extends refinance to commercial banks for term loans in relation to agriculture and rural development; (3) it provides short-term credit to State Co-operative banks, RRBs and any other financial institutions notified by RBI for a period not exceeding 18 months by way of refinance for

agricultural operations, marketing of crops, and marketing and distribution of agricultural inputs. For short-term loans, it gives a concession of 3 per cent in the bank rate; (4) it makes direct loans by way of refinance to all eligible institutions for a period not exceeding 25 years; (5) it provides finance for production and marketing activities of rural artisans, cottage industries, small scale industries, handicrafts, etc., in the rural areas; (6) it facilitates all the eligible financial institutions for conversion of production loans into term loans in times of adverse situtations arising out of natural calamities, wars, etc., by providing needed finance; (7) it contributes to share capital and securities of eligible institutions and State Governments concerned with agriculture and rural development. It also helps State Governments to contribute to the share capital of eligible institutions working for rural development; (8) it offers advice and guidance to State Governments, Federation of Co-operatives and National Co-operative Development Corporation (NCDC) and functions in close contact with RBI and Government of India pertaining to agriculture and rural development; (9) it co-ordinates and monitors all agricultural and rural lending activities with a view to tie them up with extension and planned development activities in rural areas; and (10) it conducts training, consultancy and research relating to credit for agricultural and rural development.

Purposes for which Refinance is available are:

(1)	Pilot rainfed farming projects	(100%)
(2)	Waste land development schemes	(100%)
(3)	Non-farm sector schemes (outside the purview of IRDP)	(100%)
(4)	Agro-processing units	(75%)
(5)	Biogas	(75%)
(6)	All other schemes including IRDP	(70%)
(7)	Farm Mechanisation	(50%)

(Note: Percentage figures in parentheses indicate extent of refinance provided by NABARD)

Board of Management

All the directors in the Management Board are appointed by the Central Government in consultation with RBI. The Board is envisaged with the role of providing direction, management and supervision of various financial affairs of NABARD. The Chairman and the Managing Director are the two major top level executives. The Managing Director is the chief executive of NABARD and he is primarily responsible for the various operations and performance of the bank

In addition to Chairman and Managing Director, the Board consists of 13 other directors and these directors form an Advisory Council of NABARD. Of the 13 directors two are experts in rural economics and rural development. Three directors are representatives of co-operatives and three from commercial banks. Three directors are officials of Government of India and two belong to State Governments.

Sources of Funds

Authorised Share Capital of NABARD   Rs 500 crore
Issued and paid up capital   Rs 100 crore
Other sources are:

(1) Borrowings from the Government of India and any institution approved by the Government of India
(2) Issue and sale of bonds by the Government of India
(3) Borrowings from RBI
(4) Deposits from State Governments and local authorities and
(5) Gifts and grants received

During 1989–90 (July–March) NABARD sanctioned short-term credit limits of seasonal agricultural operations (SAO) aggregating Rs 2,807 crore. During 1989–90 (July–March) State Co-operative Banks/Central Co-operative Banks were sanctioned credit limits of Rs 91 crore to convert short-term agricultural loans (including rephasing and rescheduling of loans) granted to farmers into medium-term loans, due to the occurrence of widespread crop failure following drought, floods and other natural calamities. During the financial year 1989–90 (April–March) long-term credit limits amounting to Rs 37 crore were sanctioned to State Governments for contribution to the share capital of co-operative credit institutions. During the year 1991–92, NABARD sanctioned 6,706 schemes involving refinance commitments of Rs 2,236 crore. The refinance for supporting activities and IRDP accounted for the largest share of refinance disbursement, followed by minor irrigation and farm mechanisation.

AGRICULTURAL FINANCE CORPORATION (AFC)

In view of the inexperience of the commercial banks in financing agriculture, a need was felt to set up an institutional agency at the national level to take care of this aspect. Accordingly, the Agricultural Finance Corporation was promoted by the Indian Banks' Association. It was incorporated on 10 April 1968 under the Indian Companies Act 1956, with an authorised share capital of Rs 100 crore and issued share capital of Rs 10 crore. Basically AFC is a consortium of commercial banks and consultancy agency of member banks in the formulation of projects for agriculture and rural development. Scheduled Commercial banks numbering 37, notified under the RBI Act of 1934 had subscribed to the share capital of the corporation.

The Corporation has two distinct roles, viz., financing the individuals/institutions/organisations involving agricultural development and promoting commercial bank advances for agricultural development.

(i) Financing Role

In order to gain experience in financing, only certain projects and areas are selected and farmers are financed for these projects. If the projects are successful, its experience in financing will be passed on to commercial banks. In this regard the corporation formulates projects, works out the economics and invites the commercial banks to join with it in financing the projects. Top priority is being given by the corporation to the following projects.
(1) sinking and deepening irrigation wells and energiging the same; (2) production, distribution and marketing of agricultural inputs such as seeds, fertilisers, insecticides, implements and machinery; (3) construction of storage structures for foodgrains and fertilisers, and (4) establishment of agricultural service units, etc.

(ii) Promotional Role

This is indeed a challenging task for AFC. It provides expertise in the formulation of appropriate projects to all commercial banks working under its guidance and advancing loans. To increase the credit absorbing capacity in agriculture for modernising agriculture, it suggests the following steps to be taken by the commercial banks. (1) Commercialisation and industrialisation of agriculture; (2) development of requisite infrastructure for rapid agricultural development; (3) formulation of potential projects financed by commercial banks; (4) removal of various difficulties and handicaps experienced by the commercial banks and the farmer-borrowers; (5) simplification and streamlining the procedures in sanctioning the loans, and (6) development of co-operation, coordination and consortium arrangement among different lending agencies and co-operatives involved in agricultural financing.

A national level consultative committee for bringing out co-ordination among the different lending agencies has already been set up by the corporation. Besides being a financing agency the corporation has emerged as a consultancy organisation to the State Governments in the block level planning.

It organizes seminars, workshops and training programmes to bank staff. Its association with FAO and World Bank is also significant.

OUTLINES OF RECOMMENDATIONS OF KHUSRO COMMITTEE AND NARASIMHAM COMMITTEE

Two committees viz., Khusro Committee and Narasimham Committee examined the formal agricultural credit system in India and recommended certain important changes regarding modifying rural banking structure, interest rates policy and co-operative credit structure. The Agricultural Credit Review Committee (ACRC) under the Chairmanship of A.M. Khusro was appointed by RBI in August 1986 and it submitted its report in August, 1989. Later the Committee on financial systems which was appointed by Government of India in August, 1991 submitted its report in November 1991. The outlines of the recommendations of the two committees are briefed hereunder.

Khusro Committee's Report

Its recommendations pertained to the co-operative credit system, RRBs and commercial banks. It estimated the gross interest margins and suitably recommended lending rates to these institutions. The ceiling for the lending rate for commercial banks towards agricultural lendings was fixed at 15.5 per cent, whereas in the case of PLDBs it was 5 per cent and 8.65 per cent for RRBs. The Committee recommended that any shortfall in the interest earnings may be made good to the credit institutions by the Government. The committee did not thoroughly examine the margins required for improved measures in lending rates. It made two broad recommendations on the structure of agricultural credit institutions in India. Firstly, it recommended the merger of RRBs into sponsoring commercial banks. This is very essential in areas where the performance of RRBs is not economically viable. Secondly, it recommended the creation of National Co-operative Bank to function as national apex bank for all co-operative institutions in the country.

Narasimham Committee's Report

The first set of recommendations related to the extent of directed investment and directed credit programmes. These are: (1) to cut the Statutory Liquidity Ratio (SLR) from 38.5 per cent to 25 per cent over five years; (2) to reduce Cash Reserve Ratio (CRR) progressively; (3) to bring down the priority sector credit target to 10 per cent of the total bank credit (here priority sector is defined in terms of small and marginal farmers, small business and transport operators, village and cottage industries, rural artisans and other weaker sections); and (4) left out priority sector should be made eligible for preferential refinance.

Second set of recommendations related to Bank of International Settlement (BIS) standards of capital adequacy in a planned manner.

Third set of recommendations pertained to: (1) ruling out further nationalisation of banks, abolition of branch licensing, and increasing the operational autonomy of the banks and financial institutions, (2) creating four-tier structure comprising three to four large banks with international character, eight to ten national banks with country-wide universal banking, and (3) increasing competition between commercial banks and financial institutions, etc.

Programmes of Rural Development—Small Farmers Development Agency (SFDA) and Marginal Farmers and Agricultural Labourers Development Agency (MFAL)

Many of the small farmers did not reap the benefits from the nationalisation of commercial banks due to cumbersome loaning procedures and their inadequacy of tangible securities in obtaining loan, undue delays in the disbursement of loans and high cost of credit. As a result, small farmers depended mostly on the money-lenders for their credit needs paying usurious rates of interest. Hence, there was a need to develop and uplift the small and marginal farmers in the rural areas. All India Rural Credit Review Committee (1969), keeping this in view, recommended the establishment of SFDA and MFAL in areas where there was scope for development. SFDA and MFAL came into operation in 1971. In general, marginal farmers are not potentially viable, hence depend upon agricultural wages and subsidiary occupations. To help them come out from the abject poverty, the Government formulated a pilot project for marginal farmers and agricultural labourers and this project was implemented by an agency called Marginal Farmers and Agricultural Labourers Development Agency (MFAL). These projects were sponsored by the Government of India and executed in selected districts of different States with substantial financial assistance. These agencies were created primarily to provide employment avenues in rural areas and foster rapid increased agricultural production by helping the small and marginal farmers. These agencies were expected to coordinate with the credit institutions in the matter of disbursal of loans to weaker sections. It was pointed out that these agencies were resorting to undue delays in releasing the subsidy amount to deserving farmer-borrowers. As a result, the credit institutions were in irksome position with regard to sanctioning timely credit to these farmers. Several schemes like minor irrigation, dairy, poultry, sheep rearing etc., which were being implemented by these agencies were meant to raise the standard of living of the small and marginal farmers. But many of the schemes could not be implemented in time due to lack of supporting infrastructure, consequently granting of loans for small farmers was delayed. Most of the loaned founds by the agencies to small farmers were misutilised due to lack of supervisory mechanism and inadequacy of the staff.

Functions of SFDA

Following were the functions of SFDA: (1) to identify eligible small farmers and their problems; (2) to arrange for the services and supplies of various inputs; (3) to arrange for developing irrigation sources in the area through finacing schemes like digging of wells, deepening of wells, installation of motors, etc., (4) to promote production activities in the given area; and (5) to help small farmers in securing facilities of storage, transportation, processing, marketing, etc.

Functions of MFAL

The functions of MFAL were: (1) to identify eligible marginal farmers and agricultural labourers; (2) to investigate their problems and offer relevant solutions to such problems; (3) to formulate economic programmes for providing gainful employment; (4) to promote rural industries in the given area; (5) to evolve adequate institutional, financial and administrative arrangements for implementing various programmes; (6) to organise labour contracts required for farming; (7) to construct and develop minor irrigation structures; and (8) to establish facilities for storage, etc. These agencies gave subsidies at the following rates to the individual beneficiary.

Small farmers were eligible to receive 25 per cent of the total investment while marginal farmers and agricultural labourers* $33\frac{1}{3}$ per cent.

INTEGRATED RURAL DEVELOPMENT PROGRAMME (IRDP)

A number of programmes and agencies have been started in the country during the past two decades for the improvement of economic conditions of the rural poor. But these programmes did not create the expected impact in the rural areas. The reasons behind this state of affairs

---

* A small farmer is one with 2 ha of dryland or 1 ha. of wetland. Marginal farmer is one whose holding is 1 ha of dryland or 0.5 ha of wetland or less. A person without any land holding but having a homestead and deriving more than 50 per cent of his wage income from agriculture is called agricultural labourer.

were that none of these programmes covered the entire country, frequent overlapping of the schemes in the same area, lack of co-ordination and enthusiasm among these agencies, lack of earnest efforts and motivation from the officials of these agencies, etc. In essence these programmes and agencies, by far remained as subsidy-giving programmes rather than development oriented ones. Hence, it was decided to replace all the programmes and agencies by one single integrated programme, which aims at poverty alleviation and rural development. This programme was named as Integrated Rural Development Programme (IRDP) and launched during 1978–79 by the Ministry of Rural Reconstruction with the twin objectives of eliminating poverty and unemployment in rural areas. Basically, it is an action-oriented and time-bound programme. Under this programme hitherto existing programmes like SFDA, MFAL, Drought Prone Area Programme (DPAP), Command Area Development Authority (CADA), National Rural Employment Programme (NREP), Training of Rural Youth for Self Employment (TRYSEM), etc., have been merged.

IRDP is popularly known as an anti-poverty programme. Under this programme, in addition to small and marginal farmers, agricultural labourers, landless workers, share-croppers, artisans, scheduled castes and scheduled tribes and others living below the poverty line* are being covered. For implementing the IRDP at the district level, District Rural Development Agencies (DRDAs) have been set up in all the districts of the country. Initially IRDP covered 2,000 blocks in the country. Later it was extended to all 5,011 blocks in the country in the year 1980.

Specific Objectives

IRDP aims at achieving the following specific objectives: (1) increasing the productivity of land by providing the needed inputs in required quantities at right time, thereby raising the productivity and production in agriculture; (2) creating tangible assets for the rural poor to improve their economic conditions; (3) augmenting the resources and income levels of weaker sections; (4) diversifying agriculture through poultry, dairy, fishery, sericulture etc.; and (5) providing infrastructural facilities like processing, storage, organised marketing, milk chilling and collecting centres, artificial insemination centres, etc.

Identification of Beneficiaries

Those people living below the poverty line are eligible to be covered under this programme. Income is the criterion to decide the poverty

---

* A family of 5 members is said to be below poverty line, if it earns an annual income of less than Rs 11,600 in rural areas and Rs 12,800 in urban areas.

line. The different categories of people falling under the purview of the scheme besides those falling below the poverty line are small and marginal farmers, agricultural and non-agricultural labourers, rural artisans and scheduled castes and scheduled tribe families.

Subsidies

The subsidy in the case of small farmers is 25 per cent while for marginal farmers, agricultural labourers, and non-agricultural labourers it is $33\frac{1}{3}$ per cent, and for scheduled tribes 50 per cent.

Progress of IRDP

The total number of beneficiaries covered during the period from 1980 to 1985 was 16.56 millions as against the target of 15 millions. Of the beneficiaries covered, 6.46 millions belonged to SC/ST categories. During the period from 1985 to 1990 the target to be covered was put at 20 million households and for the period (1985–86 to Dec 1988) the number of families assisted was 4 millions. During the year 1991–92 (April–March), under IRDP, banks assisted 25.17 lakh beneficiaries and an amount of Rs 1,133.27 crore was distributed as loan and Rs 800.99 crore as subsidy. Out of these beneficiaries, 12.78 lakh belonged to SCs and STs and 8.33 lakh were women. Loans and subsidy disbursed during the Seventh Plan amounted to Rs 5,373 crore and Rs 3,316 crore respectively. The proportion of recovery to demand of public sector banks under IRDP loans was 41.4 per cent during 1990–91.

Merits of IRDP over Earlier Programmes

Most of the earlier programmes, viz., SFDA, DPAP, CAD etc., were implemented by Government on an basis with specific objectives and time framework. Since no extra staff was given to implement these programmes they have become part and parcel of the work of the officials involved in the development programmes. Contrary to these programmes IRDP is an integrated and permanent development programme with accepted objectives and action-oriented programme with direct involvement of the officials. Hence the staff of the programme takes keen interest in implementation of the programme. IRDP has efficiently combined and strengthened both area and beneficiary approach. Compared to the earlier programmes IRDP distinguishes itself in identifying target group and variations in the amount of subsidy under various development programmes. Overall it is a poverty alleviation programme meant for improving the standard of living of families falling below the poverty line.

COMPREHENSIVE CROP INSURANCE SCHEME (CCIS)

Agricultural Production is fraught with risk and uncertainty conditions. Risks are very many and generally measurable, whereas uncertainty situations are not amenable to measurement. This general distinction is lost in the modern usage and hence, both terms are used interchangeably. Weather uncertainty, price risk and production risks are the major types confronting Indian agriculture. However, risks also emanate from institutional changes along with natural hazards like flood, drought, hail, cyclones, hurricanes, earthquakes, etc. Natural hazards cause widespread devastation and grave loss to the properties of humans and their lives. Under such situations, disaster management programmes will be implemented by the Government with large-scale help coming both from the people and the Government.

Market risks arise from the fluctuations in demand and supply situations of goods and over-indulgence of middlemen in the market system. Vegetable products, fruits, commercial agricultural products, etc., do have substantial market risk, sometimes forcing the producer into helpless distress sales situation like dumping, etc. Strategies like storage, processing, hedging, etc. are being resorted to overcome such situations.

Risks that are associated with the weather aberrations such as changes in the rainfall distribution, quantum of rainfall, floods, droughts, etc., result in heavy losses of crop and livestock products. Inefficient management of the farms due to illiteracy, ill-health and ignorance along with institutional risk also causes losses in production of crops and allied products. The production risks in dryland agriculture due to these factors are not only higher in magnitude but also more frequent. Hence, the farmers in these regions have developed risk averse attitudes. Many management strategies have been evolved over time to combat production risks. They are practices of improvement of soil moisture holding capacity through bunding, levelling, mulching, strip cropping, mixed cropping, coupled with other agronomic practices and tenancy practices. Crop insurance, oflate is being given prime importance by Government of India primarily with the idea of safeguarding the farmers against crop losses during drought and flood years.

Origin of Crop Insurance Scheme

The desire to introduce two pilot schemes, viz., crop insurance scheme and cattle insurance scheme with the objective of protecting the farmers from the heavy losses of crop and livestock by the Government of India, dates back to 1948, soon after the independence. But, none of the State Governments agreed to implement the schemes due to paucity of funds. In the year 1970, an Expert Committee on crop insurance under the Chairmanship of Dharamnarain was appointed by the Government of India to examine and analyse administrative and financial implications of the scheme with a view to introducing it. In his report he ruled out the possibility of implementing the scheme in India. Contrary to this report, Prof. Dandekar strongly defended the implementation of the scheme. In 1973, the Government of India had set up General Insurance Company (GIC) to carry out all types of insurance business throughout the nation with four subsidiary insurance companies.

At the instance of the Government of India, GIC first introduced the crop insurance scheme in 1973 on experimental basis as a pilot scheme in selected centres of Gujarat. Only H4 cotton was considered for implementation of the scheme. Later, the same was extended to West Bengal, Tamil Nadu and Andhra Pradesh for the cotton crop and the scheme was in operation till 1979 except the year 1977.

Area based crop insurance scheme was subsequently introduced from 1979 by GIC on a pilot basis in selected areas. If the actual average yield of the crop in the selected area was less than the guaranteed yield of the crop, then the indemnity would become payable to all the insured farmer-borrowers. Sum assured was 100 per cent of the crop loan but a ceiling was imposed with regard to payment of indemnity, i.e., Rs 5,000 per farmer-borrower in the case of dryland and Rs 10,000 per farmer-borrower in the case of irrigated areas. This scheme was implemented by 12 States in India up to 1984.

In the year 1985, Comprehensive Crop Insurance Scheme (CCIS) was introduced by GIC in all the States. The scheme covers all farmers availing crop loans and it is limited to cereals such as rice and wheat, millets, oilseeds and pulses. Two percent of the sum insured is fixed as premium for rice, wheat and millets, whereas for the oilseeds and pulses it is one per cent. Sum insured is 150 per cent of the crop loan. Indemnity is calculated based on the following formula:

$$\text{Indemnity} = \frac{\text{Shortfall in the yield of the crop}}{\text{Threshold yield of the crop}} \times \text{Sum insured}$$

Eighty per cent of the average annual yield of the crop in a given area (block level) over the last previous five years is considered as threshold yield in that area. Shortfall in the yield of the crop is the difference between threshold yield of crop and actual yield of the crop in a particular area in the year under reference. The scheme is applicable only to farmer-borrowers.

The following are the specific advantages of the present scheme which is now in operation in all the States since 1985.

Advantages of Crop Insurance

(1) it stabilizes the farm business during the period of crop failure, (2) the farmer can act much more confidently in farm business as there is protection against hazards of farming, (3) the necessary payment of premium inculcates a habit of thrift among the farmers, (4) it prevents the farmers to approach non-institutional agencies during the periods of crop failure, (5) it enhances the use of modern inputs to boost the productivity in agriculture, and (6) in high-risk areas crop insurance serves as a catalyst in bringing areas under cultivation which otherwise remained uncultivated.

Certain suggestions were made by the eminent economists regarding satisfactory functioning and improvement of the crop insurance scheme. The important suggestions among them are: (1) all crops and all farmers should be brought under the purview of the scheme; (2) the premium rates should vary with the nature and index of crop production in different areas; (3) the defined unit area for paying indemnity should be a village or group of villages as against block, as is being considered at present; (4) threshold yield should be worked out by considering indices of crop production over a 10-year period as against five-year period, etc.

REFERENCES

1. *All India Rural Credit Survey Report*, Vol. I.
2. *Banks since Nationalisation*, Economic Research Division, Birla Institute of Scientific Research, Allied Publishers Pvt. Ltd., 1981.
3. Bansil, P.C., *Agricultural Problems of India*, Vikas Publishing House Pvt Ltd., New Delhi, 1977.
4. Choubey, B.N., *Principles and Practice of Co-operative Banking in India*, Asia Publishing House, Bombay, 1968.
5. Jain, M.K., *Rural Banks and Rural Poor*, Printwell Publishers, Jaipur, 1989.
6. Mamoria, C.B. and Saksena, R. D., *Co-operation in India*, Kitab Mahal, Allahabad, 1973.
7. Mukhi, H.R., *Co-operation in India and Abroad*, New Heights Publishers, New Delhi, 1983.
8. Narendra Kumar (Ed), *Bank Nationalization in India, A Symposium*, Lalvani Publishing House, Bombay, 1969.
9. *Report of the Co-operative Planning Committee*, 1952. Ministry of Food and Agriculture, Government of India, New Delhi.
10. *Report on Rural Debt and Investment Surveys*, Bombay, 1962.
11. Tokhi, M.R. and Sharma, D.P. (Ed.), *Rural Banking in India*, Oxford & IBH Publishing Co. Pvt Ltd., New Delhi, 1983.
12. Vasant Desai, *A Study of Rural Economics–A Systems Approach*, Himalaya Publishing House, Bombay, 1983.
13. Vyas, M.R., *Evolution and Management of Regional Rural Banks*, Arihant Publishers, Jaipur, 1990.

CHAPTER 3

ECONOMIC PRINCIPLES APPLIED TO FINANCIAL MANAGEMENT OF THE FARM

The decisions on the use of finance on the farms are profitably made by applying economic principles. Each principle has a bearing on the nature of financial management decisions taken by the farmers. A direct application of these principles is the principle of combining enterprises which provides the framework needed for deciding upon the exact combination of enterprises that the farmer can take up so that the financial use on the selected enterprises brings in the maximum profit. Another example which can be cited here is the principle of least cost combination, which guides the farmers to minimise the financial outlay required in obtaining a given level of output. Equity percentage on the farms in general is low, so to make good the capital requirements, the farmers borrow. Here too, the economic principles come to the fore, in helping the farmers to select the appropriate financial agency and the amount to be borrowed from the selected sources. In fact, all economic principles are at the disposal of the manager, either as a financial manager or a farm business manager. The objective of this Chapter is to help clarify the applications and importance of economic principles in financial management of farms.

IMPORTANCE OF ECONOMIC PRINCIPLES IN THE FARM FINANCIAL MANAGEMENT

Management is basically aimed at making choices and decisions. In a prudent management and planning process, the most profitable alternative among the possible and feasible activities will be selected. In this process, economic principles form a basis for making correct and wise decisions. In fact, economic principles are applied not only to the management of resources such as land and labour, but also, to the most important and crucial input, i.e., finance. The principles, thus, are universally important in all aspects of management. The only variation is with respect to their application to a particular resource. In the ensuing discussion, the basic economic principles applied to farm financial management are briefly explained with farm data as examples.

LAW OF DIMINISHING RETURNS

In economic analysis, this law assumes considerable importance from both theoretical and practical points of view. It has much relevance particularly in decisions like raising the marginal productivity of resources. It forms the basis for the entire framework of marginal analysis. It has economic significance in the use of scarce resources.

The term 'diminishing returns' relates to physical production, i.e., the total physical product (TPP), average physical product (APP), and marginal physical product (MPP). These values of the products eventually decline after some point when more and more variable inputs are used along with one or two fixed inputs in the production process. In the words of Alfred Marshall: "An increase in the capital and labour applied to the cultivation of land causes in general a less than proportionate increase in the amount of produce raised, unless it happens to coincide with an improvement in the art of agriculture."

The law is expressed in terms of marginal physical product, but not in terms of total production, and it has practical significance in denoting the optimal input level as well as optimal output level. In the optimisation of inputs, the concern is, as to how much input to use for maximisation of profit. Given the goal of profit maximisation, the manager must select from all possible input levels, the one which will result in the greatest profit. The three stages of the law of diminishing returns are depicted in Figure 3.1

In Figure 3.1 stage I ends where MPP = APP. Stage II ends where MPP is zero and correspondingly TPP is maximum.

In stage I adding additional units of finance causes APP to increase, hence adding another unit of finance increases the productivity of all previous units. It is reasonable to add the additional units of finance up to that level, which gives the highest profit. Since a rational producer aims at profit maximisation, the addition of financial input must be continued further. Keeping in view the above logic, stage I is not considered to be a rational zone.

Similarly, stage III is also not a rational zone from the point of view of profit maximisation, because further addition of units of finance results in negative marginal product. This leaves stage II alone as a rational zone of production. Profit maximising input level is presented in Table 3.1

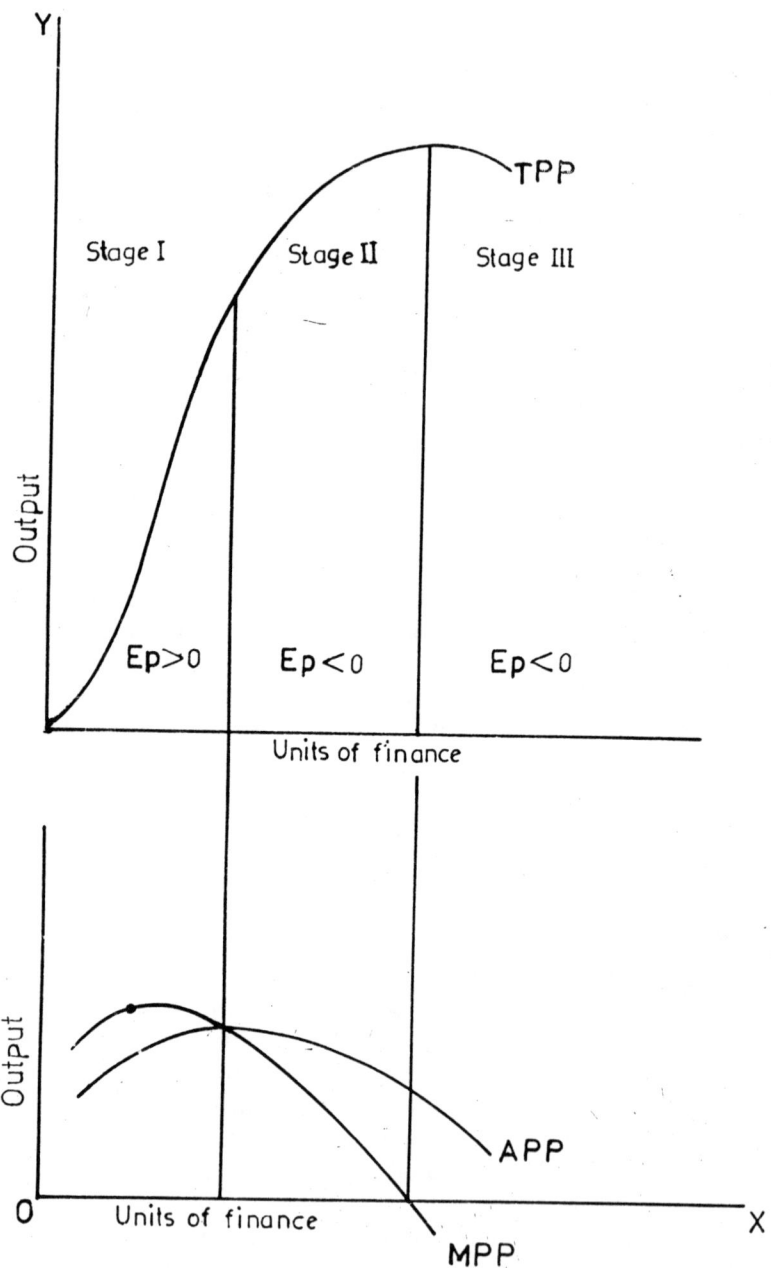

Fig. 3.1: Graphical illustration of law of diminishing returns.

TABLE 3.1

Marginal Value Products, Marginal Input Costs and the Optimal Financial Input Levels

Each financial input is Rs 100.00
Unit price of output is Rs 10.00

Units of finance in '00 Rs	TPP	MPP	TVP	MVP	MIC
0	0		0		
		14		140	100
1	14		140		
		21		210	100
2	35		350		
		13		130	100
3	48		480		
		11		110	100
4	59		590		
		10		100*	100*
5	69		690		
		4		40	100
6	73		730		
		−3		−30	100
7	70		700		
		−2		−20	100
8	68		680		
		−6		−60	100
9	62		620		
		−8		−80	100
10	54		540		

*Optimum input level.

Two additional columns are essential to work out optimal input level. They are MVP (Marginal Value Product) and MIC (Marginal Input Cost) which are presented in Table 3.1. MVP is the additional income received from using additional unit of financial input. It is derived from the following expression:

$$MVP = \frac{\Delta\ TVP}{\Delta\ \text{Financial input level}^*}$$

MIC is defined as the change in the total input cost by using an additional unit of financial input. The relevant expression is as follows:

$$MIC = \frac{\Delta\ \text{Total input costs}}{\Delta\ \text{Financial input level}}$$

Decision Rule

MVP and MIC values in the table are used to determine the optimal financial input level. In the first four rows of the table MVP is greater than MIC. At the fifth financial input level MVP and MIC are exactly equal. At this point the additional income and the additional financial

---

*Any input or factor of production which is purchased with money.

input are equal in their values. Beyond fifth unit of financial input MVP is less than MIC, implying profit reduction as more financial inputs are applied. The profit maximising financial input level is, therefore, at the point where MVP = MIC. The following decision rule can be deduced from the foregoing analysis: When MVP > MIC, the marginal output enhances profit; conversely, if MVP < MIC, the marginal output decreases the profit. At the output level where MVP = MIC, profit is at its highest level. This principle has the following implications for the financial manager: When MVP > MIC, he should increase the present level of financial input use, i.e., it should be relative to the optimum input level. The present level of input use will be higher than the optimal input level when MVP < MIC. Hence there is a need for reduction in the present level of input use (Finance).

In the aforesaid table, the hypothetical data gave exact equality between MVP and MIC but, in practice, this is not possible, when actual data are given. Hence, there is a need for estimating production functions and finding out optimum output or through cost function approach (dealt in Chapter 6).

PRINCIPLE OF MARGINALISM

This principle is postulated by the traditional theory to describe the behavioural rule in the decision making process of the farm. Under perfect competition, short-run profits are maximised at the intersection of MC and MR curves. This applies to the profit maximisation process in the short-run period, but, with the assumption that the temporal decisions are independent. This principle also implies profit maximisation of the farms in the long run.

Mathematical Derivation of the Principle of Marginalism

Assume that the objective of the farm is to maximise profits in the short-run period under perfect competition; then its profit π is defined by the equation (3.1).

$$\pi_t = R_t - C_t \qquad\qquad\qquad ...(3.1)$$

Where,

π_t = Profit in rupees of the farm in the tth period (short run period)

R_t = Total revenue in rupees in t^{th} period

C_t = Total cost in rupees in t^{th} period

We know that R_t is a function of output, i.e., (X)

$R_t = f_1(X)$ and similarly, cost is a function of output, i.e.,

$C_t = f_2(X)$, and given the price P.

Profit equation in terms of revenue and cost functions is expressed in equation (3.2).

$$\pi = f_1(X) - f_2(X) \qquad \qquad ...(3.2)$$

Applying the first order condition of the profit maximisation to the above equation (3.2) i.e., the first derivative* with respect to X is equal to zero.

Differentiating the total profit function and equating it to zero, we get the equations

$$\frac{\partial \pi}{\partial X} = \frac{\partial R}{\partial X} - \frac{\partial C}{\partial X} = 0 \qquad \qquad ...(3.3)$$

$$= \frac{\partial R}{\partial X} = \frac{\partial C}{\partial X} \qquad \qquad ...(3.4)$$

The term $\frac{\partial R}{\partial X}$ in equation (3.4) is the slope of the revenue curve,

i.e., marginal revenue (MR). Similarly, $\frac{\partial C}{\partial X}$ is the slope of the total

cost curve, i.e., the marginal cost (MC). Thus, the first order condition for profit maximisation gives

$$MR = MC \qquad \qquad ...(3.5)$$

Since MR is equivalent to P, i.e., price per unit of output, the first order condition may be written as

$$P = MC \qquad \qquad ...(3.6)$$

The second order condition for maximum profit requires that the second derivative of the total profit function is less than zero and expressed as

$$\frac{\partial^2 \pi}{\partial X^2} = \frac{\partial^2 R}{\partial X^2} - \frac{\partial^2 C}{\partial X^2} \qquad \qquad ...(3.7)$$

$$= \frac{\partial^2 R}{\partial X^2} - \frac{\partial^2 C}{\partial X^2} < 0 \qquad \qquad ...(3.8)$$

$$= \frac{\partial^2 R}{\partial X^2} < \frac{\partial^2 C}{\partial X^2} \qquad \qquad ...(3.9)$$

In equation (3.9), $\frac{\partial^2 R}{\partial X^2}$ is the slope of the MR curve, whereas the

term $\frac{\partial^2 C}{\partial X^2}$ is the slope of the MC curve. This means that the slope of

---

* For its meaning and application please refer Appendix A.

MR is less than slope of the MC curve. This confirms the theory that the MC curve must have a positive slope and rising and it must intersect MR curve from below, but in pure competition* the MR curve is a straight line implying that the slope of the MR curve is zero. Hence, the second order condition for profit maximisation is simplified and expressed as:

$$0 < \frac{\partial^2 C}{\partial X^2} \text{ or } \frac{\partial^2 C}{\partial X^2} > 0 \qquad \qquad ...(3.10)$$

which means the MC curve must have a positive slope and also rising. This situation is represented in the Figure 3.2.

Decision Rules

The following decision rules are drawn from the principle of marginalism.

(1) If $MC < MR$, profits are not maximised; so, it is desirable for the farm to expand its production in the short-run.

(2) If $MC > MR$, the profits will be reduced; consequently, the farm has to cut down the present level of production.

(3) If $MC = MR$, profit is maximised and input application is at its optimal level.

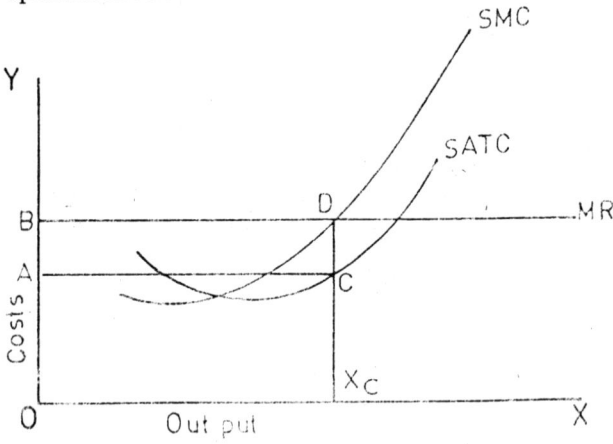

Fig. 3.2: Short run cost curves

SMC　=　Short run marginal cost curve with positive slope and rising trend
SATC　=　Short run average total cost curve with 'U' shape
MR　=　Marginal revenue curve with 0 slope
X_C　=　Optimal output
BACD　=　Profit

---

* It refers to the market structure with the assumptions such as presence of large number of sellers and buyers, product homogeneity, free entry and exit of firms, profit maximisation and absence of government intervention in the market through tariff and rationing of products.

PRINCIPLE OF SUBSTITUTION OR FACTOR-FACTOR RELATIONSHIP

The problem of input choice assumes vital importance, particularly when alternatives of producing a given product are available. Most of the agricultural products are produced with two or more crucial inputs. In this context, substitution of one input for the other with least cost, to produce a given output, forms the basis for most of the decision-making problems. In livestock, grain ration is substituted for forages, and in crop production herbicides are substituted for human labour, fertilizers for FYM, etc. The managerial problem here is to find out the least cost combination of inputs for producing a given output. The first step lies in finding out the substitution ratio of the two inputs in question. Substitution ratio is determined from the following expression.

$$\text{Substitution ratio} = \frac{\text{Quantity of input replaced}}{\text{Quantity of input added}} = \frac{\Delta X_2}{\Delta X_1}$$

If there is a constant rate of substitution between the inputs, corresponding isoquant will be a straight line (Figure 3.3).

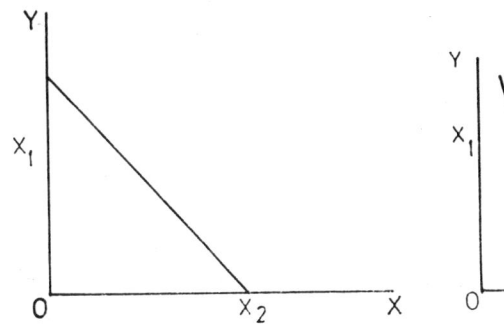

Fig. 3.3: Linear Isoquant   **Fig. 3.4:** Convex Isoquant

In the diminishing rate of substitution the isoquant* is convex to the origin as shown in Figure 3.4.

In Leontief isoquant the substitution ratio is fixed and isoquant takes the shape of a right angle triangle as observed in Figure 3.5.

---

*Isoquants and indifference curves exhibit similarity to a large extent. Various combinations of two inputs for producing a given amount of output are shown on isoquant, while indifference curve shows various combinations of two consumable goods that yield a given amount of satisfaction. Keeping in view this similarity, isoquants are frequently addressed as production indifference curves. The slope of the isoquant is negative and its absolute value indicates the marginal rate of technical substitution (MRTS). Isoquants are convex to origin

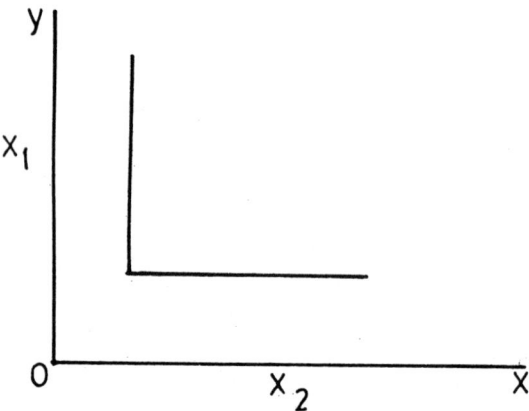

Fig. 3.5: Leontief Isoquant

In order to find out the optimal level of input combination the ratio of input prices is compared with the substitution ratio. Price ratio is defined as follows:

$$\text{Price ratio} = \frac{\text{Price of input being added}}{\text{Price of input being replaced}} = \frac{P_{X_1}}{P_{X_2}}$$

The least cost combination of inputs will be at a point, where substitution ratio and inverse price ratio are equal. The least cost principle is shown with the help of livestock data in Table 3.2 and its diagrammatic representation in Fig. 3.6. This principle helps the financial manager in allocating the limited finance in purchasing two important substitutable inputs.

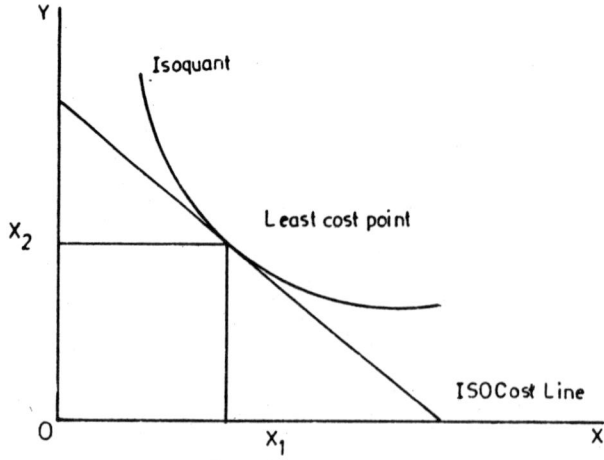

Fig. 3.6: Least cost combination of two inputs.

TABLE 3.2

Selecting Least Cost Feed Ration for Producing 25 kg Body Weight

Price of grain (X_1) = Rs 4/kg

Price of hay (X_2) = Rs 1.90/kg

Feed combinations	Grain (kg)		Hay (kg)		MRTS	Price ratio
	(X_1)	ΔX_1	(X_2)	ΔX_2	X_1 for X_2	
A	500		2190		2.5	2.10
		50		125		
B	550		2065		2.44	2.10
		50		122		
C	600		1943		2.36	2.10
		50		118		
D	650		1825		2.20	2.10
		50		110		
E	700		1715		2.10	2.10*
		50		105		
F	750		1610		1.96	2.10
		50		98		
G	800		1512		1.74	2.10
		50		87		
H	850		1425		1.52	2.10
		50		76		
I	900		1349		1.20	2.10
		50		60		
J	950		1289		1.12	2.10
		50		56		
K	1000		1233			

* Optimal combination.

Costs are at minimum point, where, input substitution ratio is equal to inverse price ratio. From the table it is found at the feed combination 'F'. Substitution ratio will remain the same over time, provided physical/biological relationships do not change. The price ratio changes if relative input price change. In the hypothetical example, it is assumed that prices will not change. As the price of one input increases compared to another, the existing least cost combination tends to change.

Decision Rule

If the substitution ratio is greater than price ratio, the total cost of feed ration can be reduced by moving downwards to the succeeding ration in the table. If the substitution ratio is less than price ratio, the converse holds good.

PRINCIPLE OF COMBINING ENTERPRISES OR PRODUCT-PRODUCT RELATIONSHIP

Here the problem lies in finding out the combination of enterprises that gives greatest net income. When resources are limited, this principle assumes greater importance in selecting combination of enterprises. The problem in this principle primarily depends upon the inter-relationship between enterprises, i.e., whether they are independent, joint, complementary, supplementary or antagonistic.

TABLE 3.3

Combination of Output of Crops Y_1 and Y_2 with Rs 10,000 of Financial Input

$(Py_1 = \text{Rs. } 4.2,\ Py_2 = \text{Rs. } 6.00)$

Product combination				MRS of Y_1 for Y_2	Price ratio (PY_1/PY_2)
Output of crop (quintals)		Output of crop (quintals)			
Y_1	ΔY_1	Y_2	ΔY_2		
0		60			
	20		4	0.2	0.70
20		56			
	20		6	0.3	0.70
40		50			
	20		9	0.45	0.70
60		41			
	20		11	0.55	0.70
80		30			
	20		14	0.70*	0.70*
100		16			
	20		16	0.80	0.70
120		0			

*Optimum enterprise combination.

Competitive Enterprises

When resources are limited enterprises compete with each other for their use. The two relevant questions in this context are which enterprise should be included in the farm business and how large should it be? The rate of subsitution of one enterprise for another takes place when an increase in one enterprise receives larger and larger reduction in other enterprise. Increasing rate of substitution is most common in agriculture because of diminishing marginal productivity of enterprises. Constant rate of substitution is possible when constant amount of one enterprise is replaced by other enterprise. An example of enterprise combination is provided in Table 3.3.

Optimal Enterprise Combination

Profit maximising enterprise combination lies in knowing the trade-off between the enterprises and price ratio. This trade-off line is called production possibility curve (PPC)*. Since this curve (PPC) assumes a fixed level of finance or any other crucial input, it is also called iso-resource curve. Price ratio is given by the slope of the isorevence line.

---

*Production possibility curve represents all possible combinations of two products that could be produced with a given quantity of inputs.

Substitution ratio (MRS) and price ratio are to be compared for knowing
the optimum enterprise combination which is defined as follows:

$$\text{Substitution ratio (MRS)} = \frac{\text{Quantity of output lost}}{\text{Quantity of output gained}}$$

$$\text{Price ratio} = \frac{\text{Unit price of output gained}}{\text{Unit price of output lost}}$$

Profit is maximised at the point where substitution ratio is equal
to inverse price ratio, i.e.,

$$\frac{\Delta Y_2}{\Delta Y_1} = \frac{Py_1}{Py_2}$$

In the hypothetical example, it occurs at 6th combination. The
optimum combination of the two enterprises is illustrated in Figure 3.7.

Decision Rule

The procedure for determining profit maximisation is basically
analogous to that of least cost principle, but with one exception. For
enterprise combination when substitution ratio is less than the price
ratio, substitution should continue by moving downwards to the right
on the PPC. Conversely, when substitution ratio is greater than price
ratio, it would mean too much substitution taking place and adjustment
should be upwards, i.e., to the left of PPC.

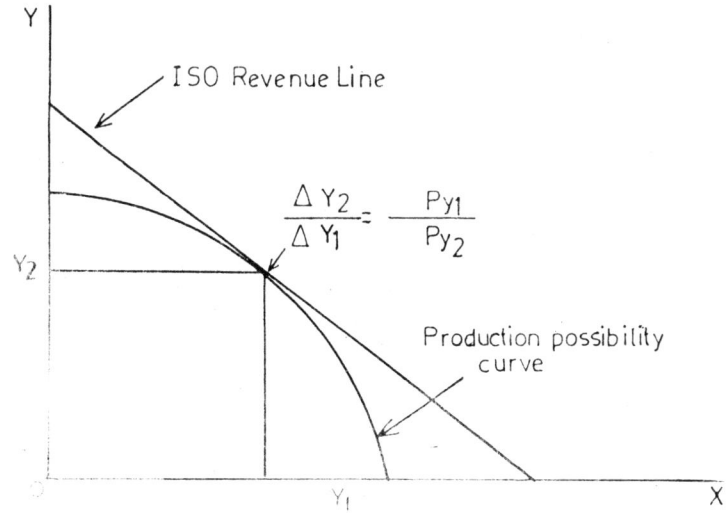

Fig. 3.7: Optimum combination of two enterprises

When enterprises have constant rate of substitution, the PPC assumes a straight line touching the axes (Fig. 3.8).

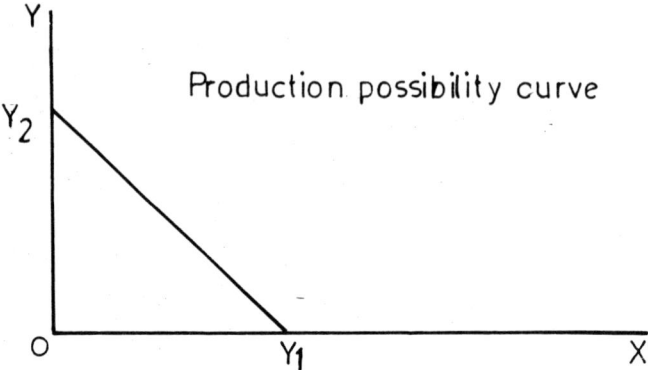

Fig. 3.8: Enterprises substituting at constant rate.

Here the profit maximisation solution will be to produce one of the enterprises but not a combination of enterprises. An increasing substitution ratio will result in combination of enterprises. The combination depends upon the current price ratio. Any change in the price ratio of the output will affect profit maximising enterprise combination.

The shape of the PPC curve will differ when other types of enterprise combinations are considered. These could be complementary relationship or supplementary relationship, which are shown in the Figures 3.9 and 3.10 respectively.

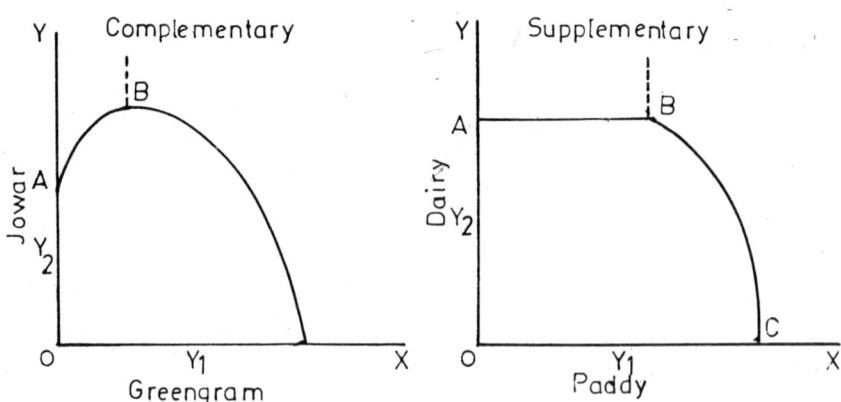

Fig. 3.9: Complementary relationship.

Fig. 3.10: Supplementary relationship.

Two enterprises are said to be complementary if the increase in production of one enterprise leads to the increased production of other enterprises (Fig. 3.9). In the diagram on PPC, up to the point 'B' greengram is complementary to jowar and beyond point 'B' it becomes competitive.

The enterprises are said to be supplementary if the production of one enterprise can be increased without affecting production of other enterprise. In Fig. 3.10 up to the point 'B' paddy enterprise is supplementary to dairy enterprise. Beyond point 'B' the two enterprises become competitive.

Enterprises are not usually complementary for all combinations and hence they become competitive after certain degree of combinations.

Mathematical Derivation of Optimal Enterprise Combination

Resources can be allocated to produce two or more products. Let us assume a single variable input (capital in units of '00 Rs) is used to produce two products Q_1 and Q_2. By definition production possibility curve indicates different combinations of two products Q_1 and Q_2 that can be produced with a fixed level of capital input, i.e., 20 units. To draw the production possibility curve, we assume two production functions Q_1 and Q_2 as dependent variables and X_1 variable the independent variable i.e., capital input.

Therefore, $Q_1 = f(X_1)$ ...(3.11)

$Q_2 = f(X_1)$ ...(3.12)

Further we assume that the available capital with the farmer is $X°_1 = (20)$. This is given by the equation as:

$X_1^0 \geq X_1Q_1 + X_1Q_2$ ...(3.13)

According to equation (3.13) the sum of the capital input should not exceed $X°_1$.

The rate of product transformation (RPT) is the marginal rate of substitution of one product for the other, i.e., Q_1 for Q_2 or Q_2 for Q_1. And this is measured from the ratio of the first derivatives of equations (3.11) and (3.12).

Algebraically RPT is defined as:

$RPT = MP_1 Q_1 / MP_1 Q_2$

Let us assume the estimated production functions (3.11) and (3.12) as:

$$\hat{Q}_1 = 15 X_1^{0.4}$$ ... (3.14)

$$\hat{Q}_2 = 20 X_1^{0.5}$$ ... (3.15)

Then $RPT = 15 \times 0.4 X_1^{-0.6}/20 \times 0.5 X_1^{-0.5}$

Let P_{Q_2} = Rs 415 and P_{Q_1} = Rs 250

Inverse price ratio of products $= \dfrac{415}{250} = 1.66$

Assume $Q_1 = 20$, then X_1 level is obtained by substituting $Q_1 = 20$ in euqation (3.14)

$$\hat{X}_1 = 2.04$$

The remaining of X_1 capital invested in production of
$Q_2 = 20.00 - 2.04 = 17.96$

Using X_1 levels in the production of Q_1 and Q_2 in equations (3.14) and (3.15) we can derive RPT.

$$RPT = \frac{dQ_1}{dX_1} \div \frac{dQ_2}{dX_1}$$
$$= 15 \times 0.4 \ (2.04)^{-0.60}/20 \times 0.5 \ (17.96)^{-0.5}$$
$$= 6 \times (0.6519)/10 \times (0.236)$$
$$= 3.917/2.36$$
$$= 1.6573$$
$$= 1.66$$

Since RPT is equal to the inverse price ratio of the products, the optimal levels of products Q_1 and Q_2 áre 20 quintals and 84.76 qtl respectively. Q_2 level is obtained by substituting X_1 level. i.e., 17.96 in equation (3.15).

PRINCIPLE OF EQUI-MARGINAL RETURNS

When financial input is a limiting constraint, the farm manager must prudently decide as to how available finance should be allocated or used among many possible alternatives. Decisions are to be made on the best allocation of limited financial input among many acres of crops, different types of livestock, etc. The equimarginal principle provides guidlines and ensures that allocation is done in such a way that profit is maximised. The principle is stated as follows. A limited input (finance) should be allocated among alternative uses in such a way that the marginal value products of the last unit of input is equal in all uses. In Table 3.4 the application of equimarginal principle, on the use of limited financial input unit is provided as an example.

Decision Rule

The limited availability of financial input must be allocated among the three crops in the following manner using MVPs. First three units should be allocated to sugarcane and one unit each to cotton and paddy which gives the maximum income (Rs 11,900) vide

Table 3.4. Diagrammatic representation of the principle is found in Figure 3.11.

TABLE 3.4

Principle of Equi–Marginal Returns

Financial input in '000 Rs	Marginal value products per unit of '000 Rs		
	Paddy	Sugarcane	Cotton
1	1,800 *	3,000 *	2,000 *
2	1,200	2,800 *	1,600
3	1,000	2,300 *	1,200
4	900	1,400	800
5	800	1,000	600

*Total income = Rs 11,900 (3,000 + 2,800 + 2,300 + 2,000 + 1,800).

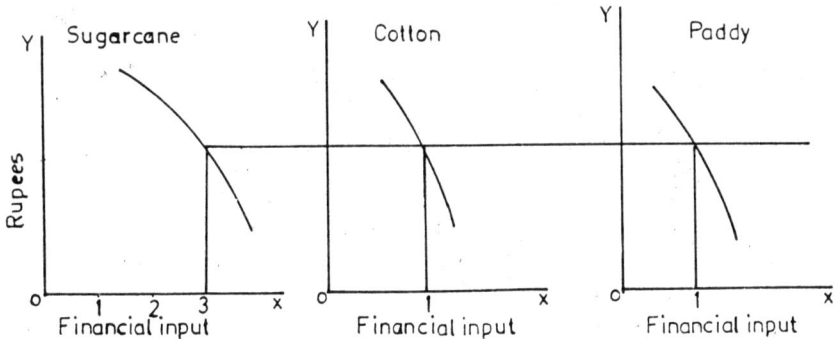

Fig. 3.11: Principle of Equimarginal Returns

PRINCIPLE OF COMPARATIVE ADVANTAGE

It is true that some crop enterprises can be raised over diversified soil types and climatic conditions, but with different yields and production costs. This difference in the yield levels and production costs leads to specialisation. We observe that wheat farming is predominant in the Indogangetic plains and rice farming in the coastal belt and apple production confined to the Himalayan region. Thus, regional specialisation in the production of crops and livestock is better explained by the principle of comparative advantage.* This principle affirms that areas of certain category will tend to specialise in the production of those commodities for which a comparative advantage

---

*It states that individuals or regions will tend to specialise in the production of those commodities for which their resources give them a relative or comparative advantage. Relative yields, costs and profits are considered in this principle.

exists. The differences in the relative yields, costs and benefits are to be considered as the criteria for explaining this principle.

Consider two competing crops namely paddy and groundnut in two regions, namely region I and region II, in Rayalaseema irrigated belt of Andhra Pradesh. Region I has an absolute advantge* in the production of both the crops (vide Table 3.5).

TABLE 3.5

Yields Per Hectare in Quintals

Crops	Region I	Region II
Paddy	58	38
Groundnut	25	20

Region I must give up 2.32 quintals of paddy for every quintal of groundnut, while region II has to sacrifice 1.90 quintals of paddy to get one quintal of groundnut. Region II has an absolute disadvantage in the production of both the crops, but in the case of groundnut it has a comparative advantage because it sacrifices less paddy for a quintal of groundnut. Thus, the concept of opportunity cost principle is taken to explain the principle of comparative advantage.

To explain the principle, we have to hypothesise area under these crops and prices of these products. Let us assume that regions I and II have 200 ha of land each, for these crops to grow. If the entire 200 ha are allotted to the cultivation of paddy in region I and 200 ha in region II to the production of groundnut, then the gross income from these crops would be Rs 34,80,000 and Rs 36,00,000 respectively (Table 3.6).

TABLE 3.6

Assumption of Allotment of Entire Area Under Paddy and Groundnut in Respective Regions

Particulars	Region I (Paddy)	Region II (Groundnut)
Production	11,600 qtl	4,000 qtl
Price/qtl	Rs 300	Rs 900
Gross returns	Rs 34,80,000	Rs 36,00,000

Decision Rule

In order to know the comparative advantage of regions in production of crops, we have to use the following decision criterion. Under the

---

*It means that regions will specialise in the production of those crops for which their resources give them higher yields only. Here, only principal yields are considered.

assumption of 50 per cent area under these crops in each region, the total production of paddy is 9,600 qtl. and from groundnout 4,500 qtl. (Table 3.7).

TABLE 3.7

Assumption of Equal Area under Paddy and Groundnut in Regions

Particulars	Region I		Region II	
	Paddy	Groundnut	Paddy	Groundnut
Production	5,800 qtl	2,500 qtl	3,800 qtl	2,000 qtl
Price/qtl	Rs 300	Rs 900	Rs 300	Rs 900
Gross income	Rs 17,40,000	Rs 22,50,000	Rs 11,40,000	Rs 18,00,000

Gain in paddy production is 2,000 qtl and loss in groundnut production due to specialisation is 500 qtl. So, the decision criterion is: as long as income from additional paddy production is more than the income lost from groundnut production, specialisation will increase the total value of crop production. Since gain from additional paddy production is more than the income lost from groundnut production, it is advantageous to have region I in paddy production and region II in groundnut production (refer Ta le 3.8 for detailed information). In the above example only yield levels and prices, excluding other inputs and costs, are considered. If other inputs and their costs are also taken into account the decision criterion becomes complicated, because, each input availability coupled with its costs complicates the decision criterion and hence the principle will have limitation in the choice of specialisation process. The manager then has to seek the help of programming models in this regard.

TABLE 3.8

Assumption of Equal Area under Paddy and Groundnut in Regions

Region I			Region II		
Crop	Acreage (ha)	Yield (qtl)	Crop	Acreage (ha)	Yield (qtl)
Paddy	200	11,600	Groundnut	200	4,000
Paddy	100	5,800	Goundnut	100	2,000
Groundnut	100	2,500	Paddy 100	3,800	
Difference in 11,600 – 9600			Difference in	4,000 – 4,500	
Paddy yield (5,800 + 3,800)			Groundnut yield (2,500 + 2,000)		
	= 2,000		= – 500		
	2,000 qtl		– 500 qtl		

OPPORTUNITY COST PRINCIPLE

The farm financial manager has got many choices regarding the use of inputs. If an input is used in a particular production process, it has no alternative use at that particular point of time. This means that the input will be loosing the income from the alternative use and this income foregone by this input from its alternative use is called opportunity cost. By definition, opportunity cost is the income that could have been received if the input had been used in its most profitable alternative use. Alternatively, it is the value of product not produced because the input was used for another purpose. The concept of opportunity cost will have a bearing on the decision-making process of farm manager, particularly in decisions related to input use. The opportunity cost in economics is referred to as the real cost of an input. Real cost of an input is not the purchase price of the input. It is the income earned by the input in its alternative use, which is the next best opportunity. Apart from the input use decisions, opportunity cost principle is a useful device in selecting the most profitable enterprise combination. In the decision-making process of selecting the enterprises, the farm financial manager has to consider all the enterprises suited to his farm situation and resource endowment. The income from all the next best alternative enterprises is given importance, following the principle of opportunity cost and the most profitable enterprise is selected by the farm financial manager. This selection process is similar to the procedure followed by the principle of equimarginal returns. Input use decisions and decisions of most profitable enterprise selections are indeed based on opportunity cost principle or the principle of equimarginal returns. But, working out the opportunity cost of capital assets entails problems. One such problem is regarding the determination of value of services provided by the land, machinery, farm buildings, livestock, etc., in their alternative uses. Before arriving at the values of the services, determination of fixed costs involves many problems. Once the problems associated with the value determination of the assets in the next best alternative use are solved, this principle then can be conveniently used. To simplify the complexities involved in value determination, some times crude approximations to these values were resorted to by the economists and researchers in the past, when there was a constraint of time and data limitation. These approximations include giving 2 to 3 per cent depreciation to farm structures and interest rate on capital equal to return on savings or cost of borrowed capital. So, this principle is not that simple as it appears for application to all types of farm financial decisions.

COST PRINCIPLE

In all types of markets, costs play an important role in the determination of price. Costs also help in the explanation of the behaviour of the farms. In pure market situations, the shapes of the cost curves determine the optimal output so long as the slope of the marginal cost curve is smaller than the slope of the marginal revenue curve. Profit maximising situation of the farm is determined by the MC = MR rule, which is known as "principle of marginalism". Thus, cost curves are the important components in the price-output decisions. Costs also play an important role in determining the bargaining power of the farmers and their managerial behaviour. Direction of the growth of the farm is determined by the cost considerations. The shape of the cost curves has several implications for the farms. For instance, if the long-run cost curve is U-shaped, it implies that the farm has exhausted all the available economies of scale. Cost considerations are also important for the entry and exit of the farms and regulation of the agricultural industry.

In economic theory we have two important costs, viz. short-run costs and long-run costs.* Costs related to short-run period are called short-run costs. In this period, only some factors of production are fixed, for example, size of the farm and management. Similarly, the costs incurred over a period long enough to permit changes of all the factors of production are called long-run costs. In fact, nothing is fixed in the long-run, all factors are allowed to vary including the size of farm and management.

The total costs of the farm are conveniently split into two broad groups, viz., total fixed costs and total variable costs, i.e., $TC = TFC + TVC$. Fixed costs generally include the costs that are incurred even if, output is not produced or inputs are not used. Fixed costs remain invariant to the level of production in the short run, but respond to the level of production in the long run. Hence, in the long run there are no fixed costs and these exist only in the short run. They are not under the control of the manager in the short run. Fixed costs are the summation of several types of costs, viz., depreciation of machinery, insurance, taxes, interest on fixed capital, rental value of owned land, land revenue, etc. Straight line method is generally followed in working out depreciation. Annual depreciation is computed

---

*The short-run period is that period of time during which, one of the factors of production, such as land size is fixed. Long-run is defined as the period of time during which the quantities of all necessary factors of production including the size of land are subject to change.

using the following equation.

$$\text{Annual depreciation} = \frac{\text{Cost} - \text{junk value}}{\text{Useful life}}$$

Here, cost of the machinery is purchased price, useful life is the number of years a machinery is expected to be used, and junk value is the expected value of the asset, at the end of the useful life.

Money invested in the purchase of machinery and equipment has an opportunity cost, which is the interest accrued on the investment capital. It is not correct to charge the interest on the purchase price of the implement or machinery.

$$\text{Interest on fixed capital} = \frac{(\text{Cost} + \text{junk value})}{2} \times \text{Interest rate}$$

In order to give the average value of the machinery over its life time, cost and salvage value are divided by two, because the asset decreases its value over time. Repairs are not included in general as fixed costs, because of the difficulties in dividing the total repair costs between fixed costs and variable costs. Mostly repairs are considered as variable costs.

Fixed costs, if expressed as an average per unit of output, they become average fixed costs and computed by the equation.

$$AFC = \frac{TFC}{\text{Output } (X)}$$

Total fixed cost curve is a straight line parallel to horizontal axis as shown in Figure 3.12.

Graphically, AFC is a rectangular hyperbola which implies that at all the points on the curve, the level of TFC remains the same (Fig. 3.13).

Variable costs are those over which the farmer has control at a given point of time i.e., they can be increased or decreased

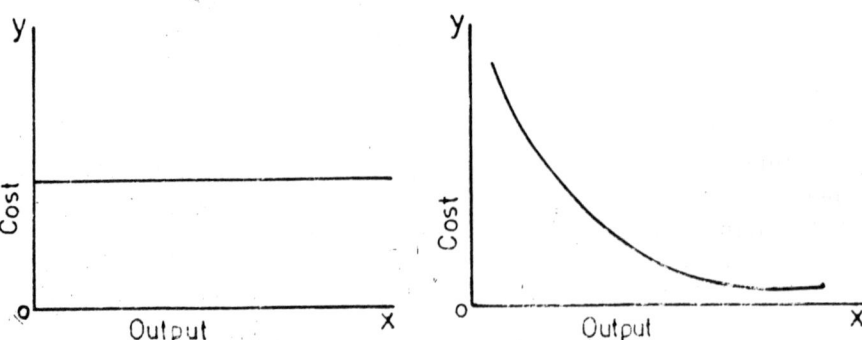

Fig. 3.12: Total fixed cost curve   Fig. 3.13: Average fixed cost curve

as per his discretion, on items such as seed, fertilizers, pesticides, feed, etc., However, in the short run, the gross returns must cover the variable costs, for the farmer to be in the farm business. If the variable costs are not covered by the gross returns, the farmer will have no option but to quit the production of that particular crop enterprise. Total variable costs are obtained by summing up individual variable costs and the average variable costs are calculated from the following equation.

$$AVC = \frac{TVC}{\text{Output}(X)}$$

Graphically TVC has inverse 'S' shape (Fig. 3.14).

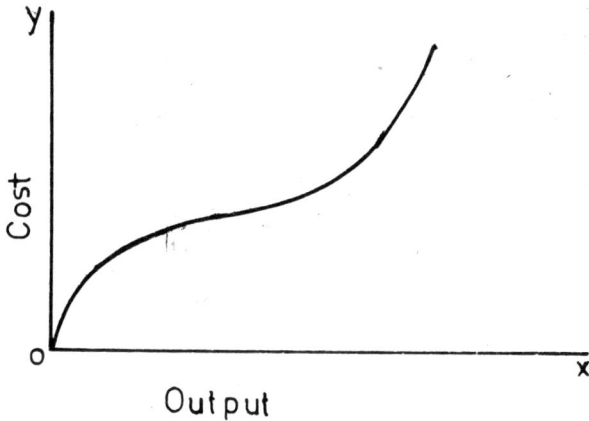

Fig. 3.14:   Total variable cost curve

AVC curve is U-shaped and represented in Fig. 3.15.

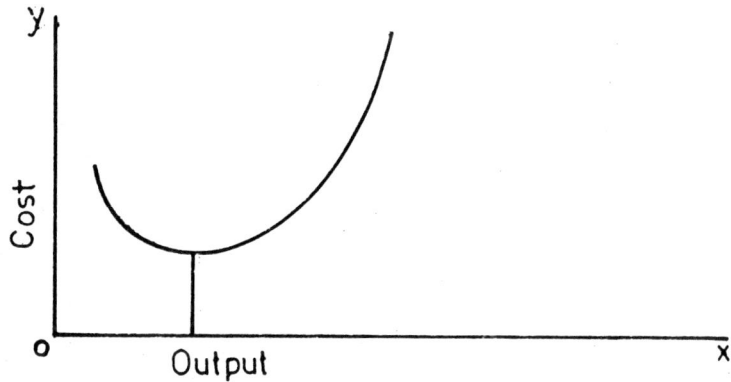

Fig. 3.15.   Average variable cost curve

Total cost is the summation of total fixed costs and total variable costs. TC increases as TVC increases, irrespective of the planning period.

$$TC = TFC + TVC$$

TC curve is drawn in Figure 3.16.

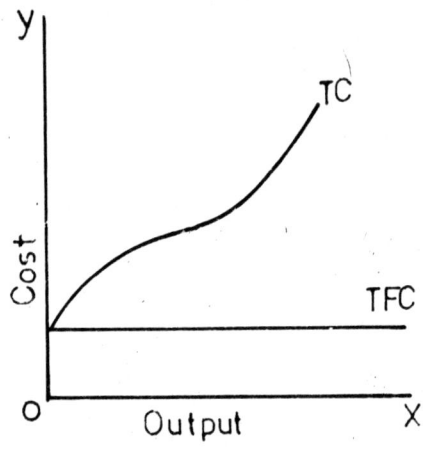

Fig. 3.16:   Total cost curve.

Average total cost (ATC) is computed by dividing the total costs by the output and shown in Figure 3.17.

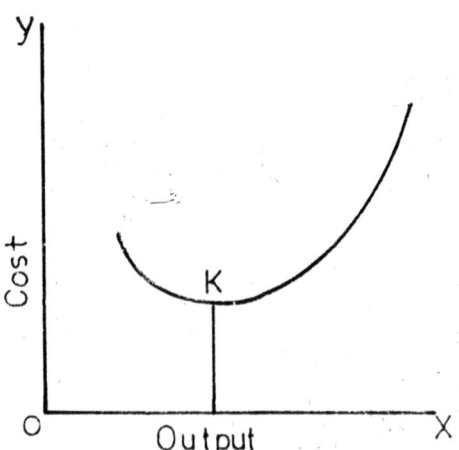

Fig. 3.17:   Average total cost curve.

$$ATC = \frac{TC}{Output\ (X)} \ or \ \frac{TFC + TVC}{Output\ (X)} \ or \ AFC + AVC$$

Marginal cost (MC) is the change in TC which results from an unit change in output.

$$MC = \frac{\Delta TC}{\Delta X}$$

Graphically it is of the following form (Fig. 3.18).

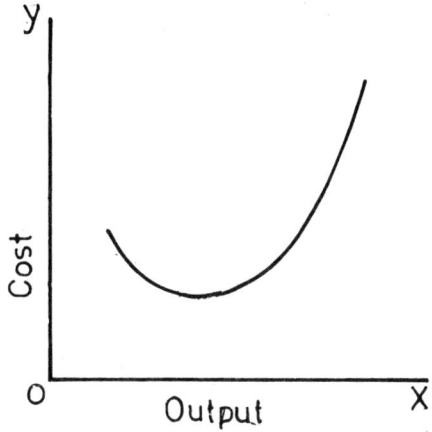

Fig. 3.18: Marginal cost curve

Relationship among Costs

TFC is constant and unaffected by output level. TVC is always increasing first at decreasing rate, later at increasing rate. The TC curve has the same shape as that of the TVC and it is always higher by a vertical distance equal to TFC. These curves are represented in Figure 3.19.

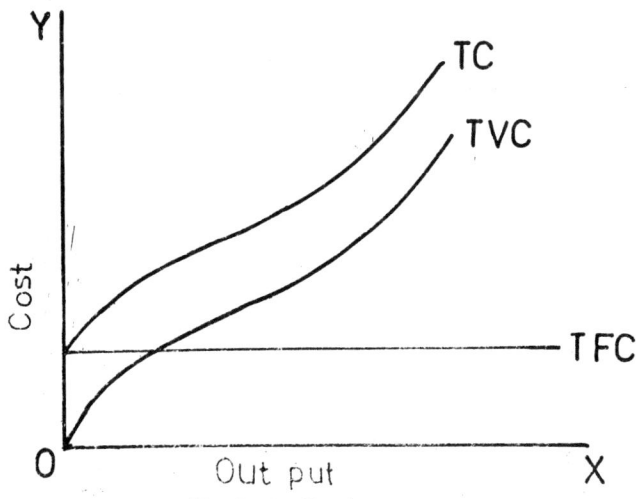

Fig. 3.19: Total cost curves

The shapes of the average and marginal cost curves are furnished in Fig. 3.20. *AFC* is an hyperbola and always declining at decreasing rate as said earlier. The other two average costs, i.e., *AVC* and *ATC* are 'U'-shaped, declining first, reaching a minimum and increasing at higher levels of output. Observe that the distance between the two, i.e., *AVC* and *ATC* is not equal. The vertical distance between them is equal to *AFC* and hence their minimum points are at two different output levels.

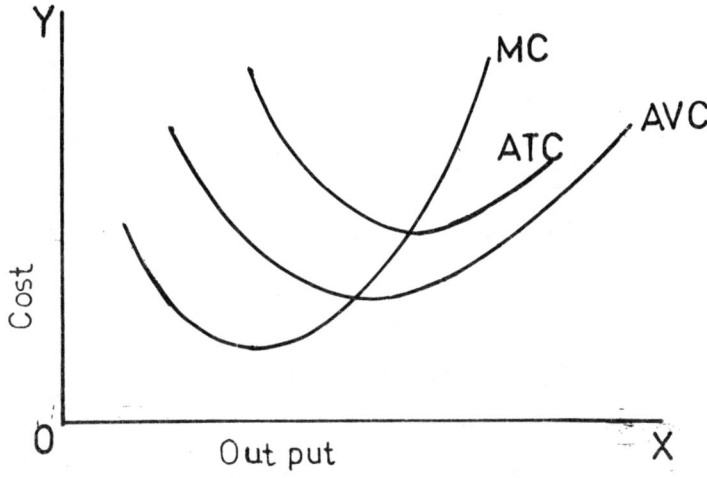

Fig. 3.20: Average and marginal cost curves.

MC curve first decreases and then starts increasing continuously. Note that the *MC* curve crosses both *AVC* and *ATC* at their minimum points. The above graph indicates the said relationship.

REFERENCES

1. Dwivedi, D.N., *Managerial Economics*, Vikas Publishing House Pvt Ltd. 1980.
2. Handaker, J.B., Lewis, J.N. and G.C. McFarlane, *Farm Management and Agricultural Economics–An Introduction*. Angers & Robertson Ltd., Sydney, 1970.
3. Heady and Jenson, *Farm Management Economics*. Prentice-Hall of India (Private) Limited, New Delhi. 1964.
4. Milton M. Snodgrass and L.T. Wallace, *Agriculture economics and Resource Management*. Prentice-Hall of India, New Delhi. 1970.

CHAPTER 4

TESTS OF FARM CREDIT PROPOSALS

The technological break-through which revolutionised Indian agriculture made it capital-intensive. In our country most of the farmers are capital-starved necessitating the institutional agencies to provide the needed capital base through credit. The farmers need the credit at the right time from the right agency to derive maximum productivity out of it. This is from the farmers', point of view. In the view of the bankers, on the other hand, when a farmer approaches an institutional agency with a proposal for loan, the banker should be convinced about the economic viability of the proposed investment. In this connection, some guidelines are essential for the banker to ponder over, for, each investment activity is different from the other in terms of productivity. Keeping this in view, various farm credit proposals including the details of repayment plans are furnished in this Chapter.

ECONOMIC FEASIBILITY TESTS OF CREDIT

When we take up this issue, three basic financial aspects are assessed by the banker:

(1) If the loan is advanced, will it generate returns more than the costs;

(2) Will the returns have surplus, to repay the loan when it falls due, and

(3) Will the farmer stand up to risk and uncertainty in farming. These three aspects are popularly known as 'Three Rs' of credit, which are as follows:

(1) Returns from the investment;

(2) Repayment capacity the investment generates, and

(3) Risk-bearing ability of the farmer-borrower.

Returns from the Investment

This is an important measure in the credit analysis. The banker needs to have an idea about the extent of returns likely to be obtained from the proposed investment. The farmer's demand for credit can be accepted only when he will be able to generate returns that will enable him to tide over the costs. Returns depend upon the decisions like what to grow, how to grow, how much to grow, when to sell, where to sell, etc., which the farmers take in their production activities. The main concern here is that the farmers should be able to generate incremental income when they go for the additional costs to be made good by the borrowed funds. To estimate the additional returns from the borrowed funds, we can apply partial budgeting technique as presented in Table 4.1.

By getting a loan amount of Rs 4, 500 and Rs 4,600 in kharif and rabi respectively, the farmer can switch over from improved varieties of paddy to high yielding varieties in both the seasons. The borrowed fund is quite productive in generating an incremental amount of Rs 5,700 per hectare of land. It is an important positive factor in favour of the farmer to present his claims for the loan amount from the institutional agency.

Repayment Capacity

This simply means the ability of the farmer to clear off the loan obtained for production purposes within the time stipulated by the bank. The loan amount may be productive enough to generate additional income to the borrower, but it may not be productive enough to repay the loan. Hence, the necessary condition here is that the loan should not only be profitable but also have potential for effecting repayment. Then only the farmer has a favourable point on his side. The above condition emerges out of the fact that repayment capacity not only depends upon returns, but also several other factors as given below

$$Y = \frac{f(X_1, X_2, X_3, X_4}{\underset{\text{variables}}{\text{Quantitative}}} \underset{\text{variables}}{\frac{X_5, X_6, X_7)}{\text{Qualitative}}}$$

Where,

Y = Repayment capacity (in Rs)

X_1 (+) = Gross returns from the enterprise for which loan was taken during a season/year (in Rs)

X_2 (−) = Working expenses (in Rs)

X_3 (−) = Family consumption expenditure (in Rs)

TABLE 4.1

Partial Budgeting Technique

Season/Crop	EXISTING PLAN				Season/Crop	ALTERNATIVE FARM PLAN			
	Area (ha)	Gross returns (Rs)	Costs (Rs)	Net Income (Rs)		Area (ha)	Gross returns (Rs)	Costs (Rs)	Net income (Rs)
Kharif Paddy (Improved)	1.0	7,000	3,500	3,500	**Kharif** Paddy (H Y V)	1.0	11,500	5,200	6,300
Rabi Paddy (Improved)	1.0	7,400	3,900	3,500	**Rabi** Paddy (H Y V)	1.0	12,000	5,600	6,400

A. i) Added costs = 5,200 + 5,600 = Rs 10,800
   ii) Reduced returns = 7,000 + 7,400 = Rs 14,400
   Total of A = Rs 25,200

B. i) Added returns = 11,500 + 12,000 = Rs 23,500
   ii) Reduced costs = 3,500 + 3,900 = Rs 7,400
   Total of B = Rs 30,900

Incremental income = 30,900 − 25,200 = Rs 5,700

$X_4(-)$ = Other loans due (in Rs)

$X_5(+)$ = Literacy

$X_6(+)$ = Managerial skill

$X_7(+)$ = Social status

The signs in parentheses are apriori expected signs based on the past studies.

Though the returns are encouraging, other factors may offset the returns reducing the farmer to a helpless condition with regard to repayment capacity. The estimation of repayment capacity varies from crop loans (self-liquidating loans) to term-loans (non-liquidating loans or partially-liquidating loans). In the case of self-liquidating loans the repayment capacity is as follows:

For simplicity only quantitative variables are taken into consideration.

Repayment Capacity = Gross income − (working expenses excluding crop loan + family living expenses + other loans due + miscellaneous expenditure + crop loan).

An hypothetical example is presented in Table 4.2 which is generally practiced by the bankers.

TABLE 4.2

Estimation of Repayment Capacity for Self-liquidating Loans

Particulars	Amount (in Rs)	
	Without loan	With loan
Gross returns	28,000	40,500
Working expenses excluding crop loan	8,800	8,800
Family living expenses	10,000	10,000
Other loans due	4,000	4,000
Miscellaneous expenditure	600	600
Loan taken	—	5,000
Repayment capacity	4,600	12,100

It is evident from the table that the farmer has generated gross income of Rs 40,500 with a loan amount of Rs 5,000. His repayment capacity stood at Rs 12,100 after clearing the loan which indicates his credit-worthiness.

In respect of partially liquidating loans or non-liquidating loans, the repayment capacity is estimated in the following manner.

Repayment Capacity = Gross income – (Working expenses including short term loans + family living expenses + other loans due + miscellaneous expenditure + annual instalment due for term loan)

Another hypothetical example for partially-liquidating loans is given in Table 4.3.

TABLE 4.3

Estimation of Repayment Capacity for Partially Liquidating Loans

Particulars	Amount (in Rs)	
	Without loan	With loan
Gross income	38,000	54,000
Working expenses including short term loan	18,600	23,600
Family living expenses	10,000	10,000
Other loans due	4,000	4,000
Miscellaneous expenditure	600	600
Annual instalment due for term loan	—	5,617
Repayment capacity	4,800	10,183

The particulars in Table 4.3 reveal that the farmer has taken an investment loan of Rs 20,000 which is payable in 5 equated annual instalments of Rs 5,617 each. In this case also the term loan is productive enough to augment gross income to clear off annual instalment quite comfortably. The repayment capacity stood at Rs 10,183 after deducting the annual instalment.

Causes for poor Repayment Capacity: Following are the causes for poor repayment capacity of the Indian farmers.

(1) Small size of land holdings; (2) low productivity and production; (3) low prices and fluctuations of prices for agricultural commodities; (4) high family expenditure; (5) using farm credit for unproductive purposes; (6) low farmer's equity; (7) lack of adoption of improved technology; and (8) poor management of farm resources.

Measures to Strengthen Repayment Capacity: Following are the measures to be adopted to strengthen the repayment capacity of the farmers.

(1) Increasing net income by proper orgnanisation and operation of the farm business; (2) adopting the potential technology for increasing production and reducing the farm expenses; (3) removing the imbalances in the resource availability; (4) scheduling the loan

repayment plans according to the flow of income; (5) strengthening networth of the farm house-holds; (6) diversifying the farm enterprises; (7) adopting the risk management strategies like crop insurance/cattle insurance/machinery insurance, hedging to control price variations, etc.

Risk Bearing Ability: It is the ability of the farmer to withstand the risks that arise due to financial loss. Risk can be quantified through statistical techniques like Co-efficient of Variation, Standard Deviation, Programming Models, etc.

Probabilities can be estimated and ascribed to the measurement of uncertainty phenomenon. Most of the Indian authors use the terms risk and uncertainty synonymously. Some of the types or sources of risk in farming are:

(1) Production risk;

(2) Technological risk;

(3) Risk caused by illiteracy and ignorance;

(4) Inefficiency by sickness of the farmer (personal risk);

(5) Institutional risk;

(6) Weather uncertainty;

(7) Price uncertainty; etc.

The farmer may satisfy the banker with regard to returns and repayment capacity, but yet another factor to be fulfilled is risk-bearing ability. This is vital because at times our estimates go awry and the expected output may not be forthcoming because of the risks enumerated above may stand in the way. Consequently our plans turn topsy-turvy. Here what we wish to know is whether the farmer has got shock-absorbing capacity to withstand the onslaught of the unforeseen events or not. How is the risk-bearing ability estimated under such situations? The productivity of any enterprise or investment activity is gauged by its past performance. Similarly, in estimating the risk-bearing ability, we need to find out what has been the variation in the yields or returns from the given enterprise over the past 5 or 10 years. This variation can be computed using coefficient of variation technique (we have confined ourselves to simple statistical tool here). The gross returns are deflated to the extent of variability of income (CV). For example, if the CV of paddy yields in a given area is 15 per cent, the expected gross returns are deflated by 15 per cent to arrive at the corrected yield or income. From this income so arrived at, the repayment capacity is estimated. In this exercise if the farmer comes out successfully, his credit worthiness is cent per cent endorsed.

Repayment capacity under risk = Deflated gross returns – (Working expenses excluding proposed loan + family living expenses + other loans due + miscellaneous expenditure + crop loan).

An hypothetical example pertaining to this can be seen in Table 4.4. Suppose the gross income expected is Rs 48,000 and the variability in gross income is 15 per cent, then the deflated gross income is Rs 40,800 i.e., [48,000 – (48,000 × 0.15)]

TABLE 4.4

Estimation of Risk Bearing Ability or Repayment Capacity under Risk

Particulars	Amount (in Rs)	
	Without credit (in Rs)	With credit (in Rs)
Deflated gross returns	28,000	40,800
Working expenses excluding crop loan	8,800	8,800
Family living expenses	10,000	10,000
Other loans due	4,000	4,000
Miscellaneous expenditure	600	600
Loan taken	—	5,000
Repayment capacity under risk	4,600	12,400

After allowing the possible reduction in gross income the repayment capacity is also increased with the loan amount. It infers that the farmer has the risk bearing ability in using the borrowed funds. His is a very sound case for consideration for extending loan by the banker.

Measures to Strengthen Risk Bearing Ability

These are: (1) developing owner's equity which is the backbone of risk bearing ability, (2) developing moral character i.e., honesty, integrity, dependability, feeling responsibility, etc., which are also called good credit rating, (3) reducing farm and family expenditure, (4) taking up stable and reliable enterprises, (5) providing ability to borrow in both good and bad periods, particularly during the bad periods, the farmer should get the funds, (6) creating ability to earn money and save money, i.e., an individual farmer may be very good in farming but part of the earnings should be saved to meet uncertainty, and (7) taking up crop and other insurance, etc.

'FIVE Cs' OF CREDIT

Next to the 'Three Rs', the other tests that can be applied to study the economic viability of a scheme or investment activity are the 'Five Cs', viz.

(1) Character

(2) Capacity

(3) Capital

(4) Condition, and

(5) Commonsense

(1) Character

The basis for credit transactions is the trust, the trust that the banker has on his borrowers. No doubt the bank insists upon security for any loan, even then, the element of trust has greater say in the mind of the banker, before he takes a decision in considering the proposal of a prospective borrower. The confidence which the institutional agency keeps is influenced by the moral qualities like honesty, integrity, commitment, hard work, promptness, etc., which the borrower exhibits. In essence it means the mental as well as moral characters of the borrower. Generally, people with good mental and moral character will have good credit character.

(2) Capacity

This is related to the capacity of an individual to clear loans when they fall due. It is synonymous with repayment capacity. It largely depends upon the income obtained in the farm business, i.e., $C = f(Y)$, where, C = Capacity and Y = Income.

(3) Capital

Capital implies availability of money with the farmer-borrower, when character and capacity proved to be inadequate. It represents the net worth of the individual. It is related to repayment capacity and risk-bearing ability.

(4) Condition

This refers to conditions needed for obtaining a loan from the financial institutions (presented in detail under the topic procedural formalities followed in obtaining a loan).

(5) Commonsense

This relates to perfect understanding between the lender and the borrower in credit transactions. This is in fact a prima facie requirement for obtaining credit for the borrower.

'SEVEN Ps' OF CREDIT

The role of financial institutions in the light of the technological changes that have been brought in, on the agricultural front, lies in evolving principles of farm finance which are expected to bring not only commercial gains to the bankers but also social benefits. The principles thus evolved by the institutional agencies are supposed to have universal validity. These are popularly known as 'Seven Ps' of credit which are listed and explained hereunder:

(1) Principle of productive purpose;
(2) Principle of personality;
(3) Principle of productivity;
(4) Principle of phased disbursement;
(5) Principle of proper utilization;
(6) Principle of payment; and
(7) Principle of protection.

(1) Principle of Productive Purpose

When owned capital is a limiting factor on the farms, the credit needs of the farmers are many and varied. The requirements of credit commence right from short-term loans to term loans. This capital limitation is visible on all the farms but more pronounced on small and marginal farms. The farmers of these tiny holdings require another type of credit, which the large farmers do not need i.e., the consumption loan. In the absence of consumption loans for the small and marginal farmers, the crop loans advanced may not be as productive as they are expected to be, because of their diversion for other purposes. But inspite of this known fact, the consumption credit is relegated to the backseat by the institutional agencies. When the loan is diverted for other purposes, the productivity of the loan receives a setback and the desired results will be a far cry. But the principle of productive purpose says that loan disbursed to any borrower should be capable of generating incremental income. If one wants the principle of productive purpose, to hold good, the short-term loans of small and marginal farmers can be made productive, if they are provided with other income augmenting assets through term loans. The income generated from these productive assets will add to the income obtained from farming. In this process, the term loans not only turn out to be productive assets but also help in enhancing the productivity of crop loans taken by these categories of farmers. To cite some of the assets for which term loans are required are dairy animals, sheep and goat (grazing or stall-feeding), poultry, installation of pumpsets on group action, etc.

(2) Principle of Personality

The 'Three Rs' which were explained earlier are the sound indicators of credit-worthiness of the farmers. Credit-worthiness of the farmer makes him eligible for the loan he desires from the institutional agencies. Over years of experience in lending, the bankers have identified an important factor in credit transactions, i.e., the trust-worthiness of the borrower. It has relevance to personality of the individual. When the farmer-borrower fails to repay the loan in the event of natural calamities, his is a case of non-wilful default. He has to be bracketed in the category of defaulters, not by his own fault, but by the natural forces that influence farming, which are beyond the control of human beings. But a large farmer who profitably uses the loan, and still falls in the category of defaulters means, his is a case of sheer wilful default. This character is born out of the dishonesty of the individual. When this habit becomes perpetual with large farmers, who borrow substantial funds, the very functioning of the institutional business gets crippled. Thus, the safety element of the loan is not totally dependent upon the security of the loan alone, but also on the personality (character) of the borrower. The growth and progress of the lending institutions have dependence on this major influencing factor, i.e., personality. The personality of the individual and growth of the financial institutions, thus are inter-linked.

(3) Principle of Productivity

This principle stresses that the credit which is advanced is not just meant for increasing production from that enterprise alone, but should be able to increase the productivity of other factors employed in the enterprise. For example, for taking up any enterprise we need resources (factors of production), but the resource productivity (marginal value productivity) of the factors employed exhibit a varying trend among the enterprises choosen. To cite few more examples in crop enterprises, preferring HYV to improved variety among the competing crops, choosing the one which gives relatively higher returns and in livestock, selecting the breed which is superior among alternatives. Here what we understand is that by our above decisions of varietal preference in crops, better competing crops and superior breeds, not only increase the returns by themselves, but also augment the productivity of other complementary factors employed in the respective production activities. The main concern here is that since we are using scarce borrowed capital resources no leaf should be left unturned in realising as much productivity as possible from each resource employed. Thus, this principle is centred around the point of making the resources as productive as possible by choosing the most appropriate enterprises.

(4) Principle of Phased Disbursement

Ensuring the end-use of the funds is the most vital aspect of institutional lendings. No enterprise or investment activity needs all the required funds at a time and the funds requirement is spread over a period of time. In paddy crop enterprise the need for capital is felt over 4 or 5 months for different operations, for sugarcane over an year and investment activities like digging a well or installation of pumpsets require an altogether different time schedule. Relevant to this situation, the principle of phased disbursement underlines that the loan amount need to be distributed in phases or spells to make it productive and the banker can also make himself doubly sure about the end use of the borrowed funds. This procedure holds good in perennial crops and investment activities, where the phased disbursal of the loan helps to overcome the misuse or diversion of funds, but the demerit of this system is that it will make the cost of credit on the higher side.

(5) Principle of Proper Utilization

Proper utilisation implies using the borrowed funds for the purposes for which they have been advanced. It sounds pretty good because every banker by heart and soul wishes-this particular aspect for the mutual benefit. This, to certain extent, depends upon the climate prevailing in the rural areas. Explaining this a bit further, this means whether the farmers are getting the type of resources they need at the right time and in right quantitties. Are the resources like seeds, fertilizers, pesticides, etc. free from adulteration to guarantee the farmer to take full advantage of their use? Whether the techincal advice is available with regard to production problems that crop up from time to time? Whether infrastructural facilities like storage, transportation, marketing, etc. are available? Is the price stability in existence to help the farmer plan the cropping pattern for effective use of funds? Proper utilization of funds is possible, when the suitable conditions for investment of funds exist.

(6) Principle of Payment

This principle deals with the fixing of repayment schedules of the loans advanced by the institutional agencies. As far as the investment credit is concerned, say, irrigation structures, tractors, etc., the annual repayments are fixed over a given number of years depending upon the incremental returns that are supposed to be obtained after duly accounting for consumption needs of the farmers. With reference to crop loans (barring perennial crops) the loan is to be repaid in lumpsum because he gets the output only once. Two to three months are allowed after the harvest of the crop to enable the farmer to get a reasonable price for his produce, otherwise, he will resort to distress sales. Whenever the crop fails due to unfavourable weather conditions, the repayment is not insisted upon immediately, and the repayment period is extended besides assisting the farmer with another fresh loan to enable him carry on the farm business.

(7) Principle of Protection

In view of unforeseen calamities striking farming more often than not, banks cannot abstain themselves from extending loans to the farmers. Instead, what they do is that they demand the security for the advances they make, otherwise, the overdues resulting due to non-payment of loans by the farmers owing to the natural calamities, affect the recycling of bank funds adversely. To tide over the situation of this nature, the institutional agencies resort to safety measures, viz., (i) insurance coverage, (ii) linking credit with marketing or tie up arrangement, (iii) provision of finance on production of warehouse receipt, (iv) covering credit under small loan guarantee scheme of Deposit Insurance and Credit Guarantee Corporation of India, and (v) taking securities.

(i) *Insurance Coverage:* The loans for certain crops and investment activities like poultry, dairy, piggery, irrigation structures, etc., are insured. Suppose any eventuality breaks out and brings colossal loss to the farmers, it is beyond their capacity to repay the loan, more so if the affected happen to belong to small and marginal categories. Under such situations, the insurance agencies estimate the losses and indemnity is paid to the farmer, from which banks recover their dues.

(ii) *Linking Credit with Marketing or Tie-up Arrangement*: By linking credit with marketing the banker is quite safe in recovering the loan. Let us take the case of a sugarcane grower-borrower who supplies cane to the factory as per the agreement. The loan particulars of the sugarcane farmer are let known to the sugar factory. As soon as the crop is harvested it is supplied to the factory. The factory will not pay the proceeds of the entire cane received, but deducts the loan component and the balance is paid to the grower. The loan amount so deducted will be credited to the bank against the loan amount taken by the farmer.

(iii) Provision of Finance against the Warehouse Receipt: When the prevailing product prices are not acceptable to the farmers, they need not submit to the situation. They can store the produce in the warehouse and based on the warehouse receipt, the financial institution advances loans to the extent of 75 per cent of the value of the produce. It is a symbiotic process wherein the bank can recover loans and the farmers can derive price benefits when they sell after the glut period is over.

(iv) Credit Guarantee: When the banks fail to recover the loans advanced to the weaker sections, Deposit Insurance and Credit Guarantee Corporation of India (DICGC) reimburses the loans to them.

(v) Taking Surities: The banks advance loans either by hypothecation or mortgage of assests.

Acquisition of Capital

By all possible means, farm financial manager has to raise the needed capital for running the farm business. The sources through which he can raise the capital are savings that have been generated in the previous year or years and borrowings. For many farming households in our country, credit (non-equity capital) is a *sine-quo-non* in runing the farm business. As far as possible, credit transactions are maintained with the institutional agencies. In the utilization of non-equity capital risk is an associated factor. This can be clearly explained with the principle of equity and increasing risk.

PRINCIPLE OF OWNER'S EQUITY AND INCREASING RISK

The principle hinges upon the fact that the risk in farming tends to increase at an increasing rate, as the owner's equity decreases. When owned capital (equity capital) is limited with the farmers, borrowings will become necessary to raise needed capital for production. We have to mention here the concept of leverage, which is nothing but the ratio of debt to equity. The leverage will be higher on the farms using more and more of non-equity capital. As the leverage stands higher and the farmers get expected returns, it contributes to the prosperity of the farm business. The non-equity capital is productive, when every thing goes right on farms, but it is equally destructive when the

TABLE 4.5

Principle of Equity and Increasing Risk.

Sl. No.	Items	Farms				
		A	B	C	D	E
1.	Owned capital (Rs) (equity capital)	5,000	5,000	5,000	5,000	5,000
2.	Borrowed capital (Rs) (non-equity capital)	—	2,500	5,000	7,500	10,000
3.	Owned + borrowed capital (Rs) (Total capital)	5,000	7,500	10,000	12,500	15,000
4.	Leverage ratio	0	0.5	1.0	1.5	2.0
5.	Gain @ 15% on total capital	750	1,125	1,500	1,875	2,250
6.	Interest to be paid to the institutional agency @ 12%	—	300	600	900	1,200
7.	Owned capital at the end of year (Rs)	5,750	5,825	5,900	5,975	6,050
8.	Gain on owned capital in %	15.0	16.5	18.0	19.5	21.0
9.	Loss @ 15% on total capital	750	1,125	1,500	1,875	2,250
10.	Interest to be paid to the institutional agency @ 12%	—	300	600	900	1,200
11.	Owned capital at the end of the year (Rs)	4,250	3,575	2,900	2,225	1,550
12.	Loss on owned capital %	15.0	28.5	42.0	55.5	69.0

farmer's expectations go topsy-turvy. The borrowed capital which earlier brought prosperity to the farmers now spells doom.

Statement of the Principle

As the debt-equity ratio or leverage increases, the borrower runs a greater risk of loosing owned capital. This principle is clearly explained with the example presented in Table 4.5. Before that, we should know the formula of percentage of equity.

$$\text{Percentage of equity} = \frac{\text{Owned capital}}{\text{Owned capital} + \text{borrowed capital}} \times 100$$

We have considered five farms with an identical owned capital of Rs 5,000 each. Barring farm A, the other four farms have borrowed an amount of Rs 2,500, Rs 5,000, Rs 7,500 and Rs 10,000 respectively.

Consequently the total capital available with A, B, C, D and E farms exhibited an increasing trend. Assuming that a gain of 15 per cent uniformly on all the five farms, the resultant profit would be Rs 750, Rs 1,125, Rs 1,500, Rs 1,875 and Rs 2,250 on the corresponding farms.

After paying the interest to the lending agency, owned capital increased in ascending order for the respective farms in question. The percentage gain on owned capital too, exhibited a similar trend. Now let us assume that there is a 15 per cent loss uniformly on the five farms. Analogous to the profit trend, the loss calculated too reveals an increasing trend on farms A, B, C, D and E respectively. The position of owned capital after the loss resulted in progressive decline leading to increased percentage loss on owned capital on the above farms. An overview of the particulars in Table 4.5 infers that, as the borrowed funds increase the percentage of equity gets reduced under the condition of losses. No doubt borrowed capital is productive as long as there is no setback, but in the context of any eventuality, it is equally destructive to the farmer. This amply demonstrates that credit is a double edged knife and hence the requisite amount only, need to be borrowed by the farmers.

PROCEDURAL FORMALITIES IN SANCTION OF FARM LOANS

The financing bank is vested with the powers either to accept or reject the farmer's loan application. This is a sequel to an objective appraisal of farm credit proposals and procedures and formalities followed in the processing of loans. Here an attempt is made to explain the set of procedures and formalities required in processing of a farm loan application. The processing procedure is detailed under the following sub-heads.

1. Interview with the farmer;
2. Submission of loan application by the farmer;
3. Scrutiny of records;
4. Visit to the farmer's field before sanction of loan;
5. Criteria for loan eligibility;
6. Sanction of loan;
7. Submission of requisite documents;
8. Disbursement of loan;
9. Post-credit follow-up measures; and
10. Recovery of loan.

(1) Interview with the Farmer

A banker studies the farmer-borrower in the interview regarding his credit characteristics such as honesty, integrity, frankness, progressive thinking, indebtedness, repayment capacity, etc. The banker explains to the farmer the terms and conditions under which the loan is going to be sanctioned. Interview helps the banker to understand the genuine credit needs of the farmer. So interview is more than a mere formality, as it facilitates the banker to study the farmer in detail and assess his credit requirements.

(2) Submission of Loan Application by the Farmer

After getting satisfied with the credentials of the farmer, the banker gives a loan application form to him. Details regarding the location of the farm, purpose of the loan, cost of the scheme, credit requirements, farm budgets, financial statements, etc., as required in the form are filled in by the farmer. Certificates such as 10-1 (indicates ownership of the land or title deeds) and Adangal (Statement showing cropping pattern adopted by the farmer-borrower), farm map, no objection certificate from the co-operatives, non-encumbrance certificate from Sub-Registrar of Land Assurances, affidavit from the borrower regarding his non-mortgage of land elsewhere are appended to the loan application. A passport size photograph is affixed to the loan application form.

(3) Scrutiny of Records

The ownership and extent of land as indicated in the relevant certificates are verified by the bank officials with village karanams or village revenue officials.

(4) Visit to the Farmer's Fields before Sanction of Loan

After verifying the records the Field Officer of the bank pays a visit to the farm to verify the particulars given by the farmer. The pre-sanction visit is expected to help the banker to identify the farmer and guarantor, locate the boundaries of land as per the map and assess the managerial capacity of the farmer in farming and allied enterprizes and the farmer's attitude towards latest technology. Details on economics of crop and liverstock enterprizes, feasibilities for implementing proposed plans, farmer's loan position with the non-institutional sources are ascertained in the pre-sanction visit. Thus, pre-sanction visit of the bank officials is very important to verify credit-worthiness and trust-worthiness of the farmer-borrower. While appraising different types of loans, different aspects should be verified. For example, to advance loan for well-digging, the location of proposed well, ground water availability, distance from the nearly well, rainfall, command area of the well, etc., are verified in the pre-sanction visit.

Similarly, for other loans, the pertinent aspects are verified. All these aspects are included in the report submitted to the Branch Manager for taking up final decision in the sanction of the loan.

(5) Criteria for Loan Eligibility

The following aspects are considered in judging the eligibility of a farmer-borrower to receive loan.

(a) He should have sound character and financial integrity,

(b) His dealings with friends, neighbours, financial institutions etc., must be proper (He should not be a defaulter in the past)

(c) He must have progressive outlook and be receptive to modern technology,

(d) He should sincerely implement the proposed scheme and ensure proper use of credit,

(e) The security provided by the farmer must be free from any sort of encumbrance and litigation.

(6) Sanction of Loan

After examining all the aspects presented in the pre-sanction farm inspection report, the Branch Manager takes a decision whether to sanction the loan or not. Before sanctioning, the Branch Manager considers the technical feasibility, economic viability and bankability of proposed projects including the repayment capacity, risk-bearing ability and surities offered by the farmer-borrower. If the loan amount is beyond the sanctioning power of the Branch Manager, it is forwarded to the Regional Manager or Head office of the bank, incorporating his recommendations. The authorities at the respective offices take the final decision on the proposed projects, and communicate their decision to the Branch Manager for further action.

(7) Submission of Requisite Documents

After sanctioning the stipulated amount to the farmer-borrower the following documents are obtained.

(a) Demand promissory note;

(b) Deed of hypothecation;

(c) Guarantee letter;

(d) Instalment letter;

(e) Authorisation letter regarding the payments of loan from the marketing agencies or intermediaries on behalf of the farmer; and

(f) Mortgage deeds.

Title deeds are examined by the legal officer of the bank and his opinion with regard to clear, marketable and unlitigated title is sought.

Simple mortgage is followed in the case of acquired property and equitable mortgage or registered mortgage in respect of ancestral property. However, the opinion of the bank's legal officer is obtained in this regard. Mortgage of land is done prior to obtaining non-encumbrance certificate and sanction of loan.

(8) Disbursement of Loan

As soon as the execution of documents is completed, the loan amount is credited to the borrower's account. The loan amount is disbursed in a phased manner, that too after ensuring that the loan is used by the farmer-borrower properly. A realistic repayment plan is framed and given to the farmer keeping in view the income flow of the proposed project.

(9) Post-credit Follow-up Measures

The Branch Manager or Agricultural Officer pays a visit to the farmer to ascertain the proper use of the credit. This also benefits the farmer, for, they can get the technical advice if any needed from the Agricultural Officer in the implementation of the scheme. These visits are also meant for developing a close rapport between the farmer and the banker. These visits are more informal than formal, which are supposed to inculcate the feeling of friendliness and underlying the obligation of the farmer to repay the loan when it falls due. Such visits also facilitate in assessing any further requirement of supplementary credit to complete the scheme.

(10) Recovery of Loan

The bank reminds the farmer-borrower in advance about the repayment of loan in time. If needed recovery camps, special drives, village meetings, etc. are organised at an appropriate time. All appropriate measures are taken to persuade the farmer-borrower to repay the loan in time. In the case of failure, the reasons for the same are ascertained to find out whether the borrower is a deliberate defaulter or not. If the reason is genuine, the borrower is further helped by extending finance to accelerate farm production. In such situations, a closer supervision is necessary. If the bank officials find that the borrowers are wilful-defaulters stringent measures are initiated to recover the loans through court of law. In all possible cases the bank officers make tie-up arrangements, i.e., the recovery of the loan is linked with marketing. Rephasing of repayment plan is allowed in the case of justifiable cases.

REPAYMENT PLANS

For term loans which are characterised by partially liquidating nature, the loan repayment plan is not as similar, as that of short term loans. These loans are recovered through a given number of instalments depending upon the nature of asset and the amount advanced for the asset in question. Various repayment plans, in vogue are listed and briefly explained here.

   (1)   Straight-end payment plan or single repayment plan or lumpsum repayment plan;
   (2)   Partial repayment plan;
   (3)   Amortised repayment plan;
          (a) Amortised decreasing repayment plan;
          (b) Amortised even repayment plan;
   (4)   Variable repayment plan;
   (5)   Optional repayment plan; and
   (6)   Reserve repayment plan.

1. Straight-end Payment Plan or Single Repayment Plan or Lumpsum Repayment Plan

The entire loan amount is to be cleared off after the expiry of loan period stipulated. More clearly in this method, the principal component is repaid by the farmer at a time in lumpsum when the loan matures, while the interest component is paid each year.

2. Partial Repayment Plan or Balloon Repayment Plan

The farmer is expected to settle the entire loan amount in quarterly, half-yearly or annual instalments (principal + interest). It implies that repayment of loan will be done partially over the years. Usually, the instalment amount will be decreasing as the years pass by except in the maturity year (final year) during which the investment generates sufficient revenue for liquidation. Table 4.6 illustrates this.

   Example: Loan amount   Rs 10,000
              Time period   6 years
              Rate of interest   12%

This is also known as balloon repayment plan, as the large final payment is made at the end of the loan period following a series of smaller partial payments.

3. Amortised Repayment Plan

It is an extended version of partial repayment plan. Amortisation means the repayment of the entire loan amount in a series of

TABLE 4.6

Partial Repayment Plan

Year	Principal (in Rs)	Interest (in Rs)	Instalment (in Rs)	Balance amount (in Rs)
1	1,000	1,200	2,200	9,000
2	1,000	1,080	2,080	8,000
3	1,000	960	1,960	7,000
4	1,000	840	1,840	6,000
5	1,000	720	1,720	5,000
6	5,000	600	5,600	—
Total	10,000	5,400	15,400	—

instalments. Here we have two types of amortisation plans, viz., amortised decreasing repayment plan and amortised even repayment plan.

(a) *Amortised Decreasing Repayment Plan:* In this repayment plan, the principal component remains constant over the entire repayment period, while the interest part decreases continuously. With the principal amount remaining fixed and interest amount decreasing, the annual instalment amount decreases over the years. The advance made for the purchase of machinery is one of the suitable examples under this category, for the machinery does not demand much repairs in the initial years of loan payments enabling the farmer to repay a large amount of instalments in the initial years. The diagrammatic representation of the repayment schedule is shown in Figure 4.1.

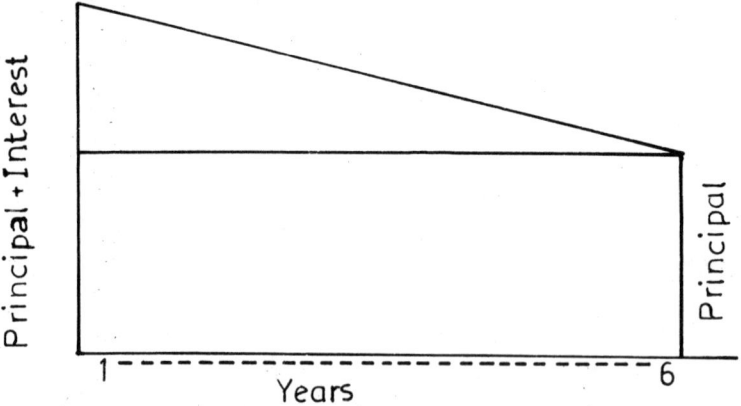

Fig 4.1: Amortised Decreasing Repayment Plan

The arithmetic calculation of the plan is embodied in Table 4.7.

Example: Loan amount   Rs 10,000
           Time period   6 Years
           Rate of interest   12%

TABLE 4.7

Amortised Decreasing Repayment Plan

Year	Principal (in Rs)	Interest (in Rs)	Instalment (in Rs)	Balance amount (in Rs)
1	1,666.67	1,200.00	2,866.67	8,333.33
2	1,666.67	999.99	2,666.66	6,666.67
3	1,666.67	799.99	2,466.66	5,000.00
4	1,666.67	600.00	2,266.67	3,333.33
5	1,666.67	399.99	2,066.66	1,666.67
6	1,666.67	199.99	1,866.67	–
Total	10,000.00	4,199.96	14,199.96	–

(b) *Amortised Even Repayment Plan:* This is called equated annual instalment method. The annual instalment over the entire loan period remains the same in this method. The principal portion of the instalment increases continuously, while the interest part declines gradually. This method is mostly adopted for term loans . Loans granted for farm development, digging of wells, deepening of old wells, construction of godowns, dairy, poultry, etc., are the examples. This is depicted diagrammatically in Figure 4.2.

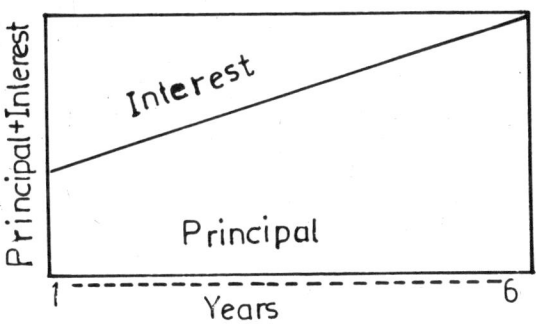

Fig 4.2: Amortised Even Repayment Plan

The annual instalment is arrived at through the formula given below:

$$I = B \frac{i}{1 - (1+i)^{n}}$$

Where,

I = Annual instalment in Rs
B = Principal amount borrowed in Rs
n = Loan period in years
i = Annual interest rate in fraction

or

$$I = B\frac{1}{a \; \overline{n}| \; i}$$

where,

a = Annuity in Rs
n = Loan period in years
i = Annual interest rate in fraction

The plan is shown in Table 4.8.

Example: Loan amount   Rs 10,000
          Time period   6 years
          Rate of interest 12%

$$I = B \; \frac{i}{1-(1+i)^{-n}}$$

$$= 10,000 \times \frac{0.12}{1-(1+0.12)^{-6}}$$

$$= 10,000 \times \frac{0.12}{1-(\frac{1}{(1.12)^6})}$$

$$= 10,000 \times 0.243225$$

$$= Rs \; 2,432.25$$

TABLE 4.8

Amortised Even Repayment Plan

Years	Instalment (in Rs)	Principal (in Rs)	Interest (in Rs)	Balance amount (in Rs)
1	2,432.25	1,232.25	1,200.00	8,767.75
2	2,432.25	1,380.12	1,052.13	7,387.63
3	2,432.25	1,545.73	886.52	5,841.90
4	2,432.25	1,731.22	701.03	4,110.68
5	2,432.25	1,938.97	493.28	2,171.71
6	2,432.25	2,171.64	260.61	—
Total	14,593.50	9,999.93	4,593.57	

4. Variable Repayment Plan

As the very name indicates, various levels of instalments are paid by the borrower over the loan period. In times of good harvest a higher instalment is paid, while in periods of low yields lesser amount is credited towards instalment to the lender. According to the convenience, the borrower effects the repayment. This method is not found with institutional borrowings.

5. Optional Repayment Plan

In this method provision is made for the borrower to make payment towards the principal amount in addition to the regular interest annually.

6. Reserve Repayment Plan or Future Payments

This type of repayment is made by the borrowers in areas which are subject to high income variability of farms. The impending problem here is that the farmers are haunted by the fear that they may not be able to keep up their promise of repaying crop loans or instalments towards term loans at scheduled time. To overcome such situations, the farmers make advance payments of the loan realised from the savings of the previous year. The farmer is not a looser in this transaction by any means since he is paid interest at the rate charged on the loans for the advance amount credited. This type of repayment is advantageous to the banker as the institutional agency need not worry regarding loan collection during the periods of crop failure. The farmer too gains here as he can keep up his integrity in credit transactions.

REFERENCES

1. Kahlon, A.S. and Singh, Karam, *Economics of Farm Management in India, Theory and Practice,* Allied Publishers Private Limited, New Delhi, 1980.
2. Kahlon, A.S. and Singh, Karam, *Managing Agricultural Finance, Theory and Practice,* Allied Publishers Private Limited, New Delhi 1984.
3. Singh, I.J. *Elements of Farm Management Economics,* Affiliated East-West Press Pvt Ltd., New Delhi, 1977.

CHAPTER 5

TOOLS OF FINANCIAL ANALYSIS

Every farm financial manager has to assess the performance of his business, in order to act suitably. Various tools of financial analysis, viz., farm planning and budgeting, the balance sheet, income statement, cash flow statement, break-even-analysis etc., are available to him in this regard. These tools in brief are presented in this Chapter.

FARM PLANNING AND BUDGETING

Farm planning and budgeting are the most important tools of farm business analysis. The most profitable alternative enterprises are selected in the planning process by organising the available land, labour and capital resources into proper combinations. Any scheme of action prepared in advance to attain the set objectives is a plan. A farm plan is a scheme for operation and organisation of farm business to get maximum net returns. Planning refers to the process of formulating a plan. In planning, we specify as to how land is to be allotted among alternative profitable enterprises and how limited capital and fixed family labour are most profitably combined in different periods of time to produce desired crop and livestock products. Economic principles provide the guidelines and rules and simplify the complex decision problems of what to produce, how to produce and how much to produce from crops and livestock enterprises, under the given set of resources. Plans give a systematic and organised procedures by exactly specifying the enterprises and their resource requirements. In fact, a farm manager must formulate sound alternative farm plans and budgets in order to be a successful farm manager. In plans we specify the enterprises along with their resource requirements in physical units but in budgeting we account for their monetary value for judging their profitability.

The need for farm plans stems from the desire of the farmer to attain his set goals and objectives. New ideas and information on technology of farms must be gathered and put into plan for execution, if the farmer aims at achieving higher returns from his given resources. Careful examination of the resources and their efficiencies must be ensured along with minimization in wastages. Judicious use and combination of resources for producing existing and new enterprises, which have potential for furthering income and employment of family labour on a continuous time basis, must be allowed in plans. Sources of procuring the requisite credit along with other essential inputs, marketing arrangements for sale of output, risk and uncertainties in production and marketing, prevention of unnecessary stresses and strains in the use of resources etc., must be considered in making good plans. A good plan must be useful in seeing the future requirements. It must be flexible to suit the changes in the weather, market and farm environment. It should provide food, cash and fodder requirements in combining the crop and livestock enterprises. There should be provision in plans for crop rotation to maintain and improve soil fertility. It should satisfy the stated objectives of the farmer and consider inventory of the scarce resources and financial constraints. Technical coefficients along with techniques of organising the scarce resources and enterprises must be given due consideration in formulating the plans.

Planning Techniques

Some techniques are simple, while others are more complex. Budgeting is the most informal method, whereas Linear Programming and non-Linear Programming are the most sophisticated techniques for providing appropriate solutions under certainty, risk and constrained situations.

Budgeting

In budgeting process, we estimate costs, returns and net profit of a farmer or a particular enterprise and, hence, it helps in advance estimation of expenses and income of a farm business. Budgets are usually prepared for a year, considering the revenue and expenditure. When budgeting is done for a single enterprise or two enterprises, then it is called partial budgeting. If budgeting is done for all the enterprises in terms of costs, revenues and net profits for the whole farm, then it is termed as complete budgeting or total budgeting or whole farm budgeting. In this process, the best combination of enterprises is judged based on the productivity of the resources and the ability of the farm operator to maximise the returns. Budgeting has several implications in farm financial management. Farm budgets assist the farmer in exercising economic control over his farm business. They also help the lending institutions in decisions like justifying the sanction of loan or rejection of the same. Credit needs of the farmer in different time periods of the year are vividly shown by the budgets. Budgets also help in fixing the repayment schedules and sanction of loans at appropriate time. Thus, budgets form a basis to determine the quantum of credit to be given to a particular farm. The following advantages of budgets are also conspicuous.

(1) Estimation of economic viability of agricultural development projects, (2) judging the repayment capacity of the farmer, (3) reorganising the resources and enterprises for amortising the loans, (4) preparation of cash-flow statements, (5) assessment of credit requirements of the farmers in different seasons of a year, and (6) maximisation of net returns from the farm as a whole.

The two types of budgets, i.e., partial and complete distinctly differ from each other in the following ways. In partial budgeting we try to introduce minor changes like, use of high yielding variety of seeds, different doses of fertiliser use, etc., and their corresponding costs and returns in terms of added costs and added returns and bring forth the impact of these minor changes on returns of the enterprise (presented in Chapter 4). In complete budgeting we contemplate complete transformation in enterprises bringing about desired changes in methods of production, techniques of adoption, etc. By doing so, sometimes new potential enterprises are selected replacing the traditional ones. In partial budgeting, only a few alternatives with a good range of profit are considered, while in complete budgeting all the possible alternatives without omission are tried, and the best one is selected in terms of profits. Partial budgeting is done for a part of the farm business only, while in complete budgeting entire farm is considered and the best profitable alternatives are chosen.

Enterprise Budgeting

This is a kind of partial budgeting, but, strictly refers to one enterprise in terms of its importance and frequent use in farm planning. It is a pre-requisite for the preparation of partial budgeting, complete budgeting and programming models.

An enterprise budget considers the expected or average requirement of inputs and their corresponding average output, which are called technical coefficients. These technical coefficients are expressed both in physical units and value terms for a unit of particular activity. Such enterprise budgets, are prepared for production activities on farms which indicate returns over variable costs per unit of activity.

Thus, physical input-output data along with price data on inputs and output are essential for preparing enterprise budgets. Crop enterprise budgets relate to individual crop production activities, while livestock enterprise budgets pertain to milk, eggs, wool, mutton, etc. Several budgets are often formulated for the same enterprise or crop activity, if there is change in technical coefficients for the enterprise.

BALANCE SHEET OR NET WORTH STATEMENT

Any farmer, whether small, medium or large, measures financial performance of the farm business during an agricultural year or over a period of time. There is a possibility in the variation of degree of keenness that is shown by the different categories of farmers. In other words, as the size of the farm gets increased, the capital requirement too gets enlarged forcing the farmer to be more vigilant in running the farm business, since the risk element is much higher in the event of any unforeseen eventuality. Management component plays a pivotal role in managing higher financial outlays. Nevertheless, management of finance is equally important even for a small farmer, if not, at the magnitude that is viewed at by a large farmer in the farm business. The balance sheet indicates an account of total assets and total liabilities of the farm business revealing the financial solvency of the business. More specifically it is a statement of the financial position of a farm business at a particular time, showing its assets, liabilities and equity. If the assets are more than liabilities it is called net worth or equity and its converse is known as net deficit. The typical balance sheet (Table 5.1) shows assets on the left side and liabilities and equity on the right side. Both sides are always in balance hence the name balance sheet. Net worth is placed on the right side, along with liabilities, in order to indicate that like any other creditor the farmer has a claim against the farm business equal to the equity amount. The balance sheet can be easily prepared by the farmer in the presence of farm records. It can be prepared at any point of time to know the financial position of the farm business. It can also be prepared to study the performance of a business over years by preparing the same number of balance sheets. If the net worth increases over the different periods, it indicates efficient performance of the business. To prepare a balance sheet the prime requisites are total assets and total liabilities of the farm.

TABLE 5.1

Balance Sheet of a Hypothetical Farm

Assets	Amount (in Rs)	Liabilities	Amount (in Rs)
Current assets		*Current liabilities*	
Cash on hand	10,000	Crop loans to be repaid to institutional agencies	8,000
Savings in bank	8,000		
Value of grains ready for disposal	38,500	Cost of cultivation (excluding loans)	6,000
Livestock products (eggs, birds, etc.)	60,000	Other loans (unsecured loans due for immediate repayment)	5,000
Fruits, Vegetables,		Cost of maintenance of cattle	3,600
fodder and feed ready for sale	8,000	Costs in poultry enterprise	25,000
Value of bonds and shares to be realised in the same year	2,000	Annual instalments	19,000
Sub-total	1,26,500	Sub-total	66,600
Intermediate assets		*Intermediate liabilities*	
Dairy cattle	10,000	Livestock loans	8,000
Bullocks	9,000	Machinery loan	15,000
Poultry birds	15,000	Unsecured loans	10,000
Machinery and equipment	15,000		
Tractor	1,75,000		
Sub-total	2,24,000	Sub-total	33,000
Long-term assets		*Long-term liabilities*	
Land (book value)	6,00,000	Tractor loan	1,20,000
Farm buildings	25,000	Orchard loan	25,000
		Unsecured loans	10,000
Sub-total	6,25,000	Sub-total	1,55,000
Total of assets	9,75,500	Total of liabilities	2,54,600
		New worth or equity ≈	7,20,900

Assets: Assets are those which are owned by the farmer.

Liabilities: These refer to all things which are owed to others by the farmer.

Assets are of three types, viz. current, intermediate or working and long-term or fixed. So also the liabilities. This classification of assets facilitates the analysis of liquidity of the farm business.

Current assets: They are very liquid or short-term assets. They can be converted into cash, within a short time, usually one year. For example, cash on hand, agricultural produce ready for disposal, i.e., stocks of paddy, blackgram, jowar, wheat, etc.

Intermediate or working assets: These assets take two to five years to convert into cash form. Examples: Machinery, equipment, livestock, tractors, trucks, etc.

Long-term assets or fixed assets: An asset that is permanent or will be used continuously for several years is called a long-term asset. It takes longer time to convert into cash due to verification of records, legal transactions, etc. Examples: Land, Farm buildings, etc.

Current liabilities: Debts that must be paid in the short term or in very near future. Examples: Crop loans, other loans, cost of maintenance of cattle, etc.

Intermediate liabilities: These loans are due for the repayment within a period of two to five years. Examples: livestock loans, machinery loans, etc.

Long-term liabilities: The duration of loan repayment is five or more years. Examples: Tractor loan, orchard loan, land development loan, etc.

Precautions in Preparing the Balance Sheet of a Business Farm (Firm)

(1) Accuracy with regard to valuation of assets is difficult in the absence of records, hence approximations to such valuations need to be defined with reference to a given time period. All farm products say, paddy, pulses, oilseeds, jowar, livestock and livestock products, etc., should be valued based on the market price. Land and other non-liquid assets should be valued based on prevailing sale value for similar type of land at the same time period.

(2) While valuing the durable assets, book value method* (valuing at cost) is no doubt a good procedure but subject to criticism. For example, a farmer bought his farm lands in different time periods say, 1960 and 1970, book value of these lands should be determined after giving an allowance for depreciation and improvements made on the land and

(3) In periods of inflation, the values for durable assets rise. Under such situations, it is desirable to make adjustments in the values of the assets, while entering the same in the balance sheet.

---

*Book value refers to the realistic value of an asset giving due allowance for depreciation and improvement. Hence, book value is neither the market price nor purchase price, but value at cost.

Test Ratios

The test ratios, viz. current ratio, intermediate ratio, net capital ratio, quick ratio, current liability ratio, debt-equity ratio and equity-value ratio can be derived from the balance sheet.

1. Current ratio $= \dfrac{\text{Total current assets}}{\text{Total current liabilities}}$

$$= \frac{1,26,500}{66,600} = 1.90$$

This ratio indicates the capacity of the farmer to meet immediate financial obligations (liquidity). If current assets are more than current liabilities and if the borrower fails to repay the loan, his is a case of wilful-default in spite of his position being solvent. This type of wilful-default is more common in respect of large farmer-borrowers of financial institutions. If by chance the ratio falls less than one due to certain unforeseen contingencies, his case for further lendings cannot be ruled out by the institutional agencies, as it is a temporary setback and he may be given a chance to prove his credit-worthiness. A ratio of more than one indicates a favourable run of the farm business. Current ratio reflects liquidity within one year's time.

2. Intermediate ratio or working ratio $= \dfrac{\text{Total current assets} + \text{Total intermediate assets}}{\text{Total current liabilities} + \text{Total intermediate liabilities}}$

$$= \frac{1,26,500 + 2,24,000}{66,600 + 33,000} = \frac{3,50,500}{99,600} = 3.52$$

This indicates the liquidity position of the farm business over an intermediate period of time, ranging from 2 to 5 years. Here certain time is allowed for the farmer to build up the farm business to improve his liquidity position. This ratio should also be more than one to indicate sound running of the farm business. The progressive intermediate ratio observed for giving farm business over time implies, the increase in the value of current and intermediate assets due to minimal physical loss and price decline. The steady growth of this ratio over a period is a healthy sign of the business.

3. Net capital ratio $= \dfrac{\text{Total assets}}{\text{Total liabilities}}$

$$= \frac{9,75,500}{2,54,600}$$

$$= 3.83$$

It indicates the long-term liquidity position of the farmers. If the net capital ratio is more than one, the funds of institutional agencies are safe. A consistently increasing ratio over the years reveals the sound financial growth of farm business. The farmer with this record should be a very prompt repayer of all types of credit obligations. This ratio is also the most important measure of overall solvency position of the farmer-borrowers.

4. Acid test ratio or quick ratio

$$\frac{\text{Cash receipts + accounts receivable + marketable securities}}{\text{(bonds, shares , etc.) available in more than one year}}{\text{Total current liabilities}}$$

This reflects adequacy of cash and income surpluses to cover all current liabilities during the period of one to two years. If there is no difference in income position of a farmer within that period, current ratio and acid test ratio reflect the same position.

5. Current liability ratio $= \dfrac{\text{Current liabilities}}{\text{Owner's equity}}$

$$= \frac{66,600}{7,20,900} = 0.09$$

This ratio indicates the farmer's immediate financial obligations against the net worth. A ratio of less than one indicates a healthy performance of the farm business and over the years the ratio should become smaller and smaller to reflect a consistently good performance.

6. Debt-equity ratio (Leverage ratio) $= \dfrac{\text{Total debts}}{\text{Owner's equity}}$

$$= \frac{2,54,600}{7,20,900} = 0.35$$

This presents the capacity of the farmer to meet the long-term commitments. Also it throws light on the extent of indebtedness in the farm business or conversely the amount of capital raised by the farmer in running the farm business. A consistently falling ratio indicates a very heartening performance of farming and the ability of the farmer to reduce dependence on borrowings.

Equity-value ratio $= \dfrac{\text{Owner's equity}}{\text{Value of assets}}$

$$= \frac{7,20,900}{9,75,500} = 0.74$$

This ratio highlights the productivity gained by the farmer in relation to the assets he has. The improvement in the ratio over the years makes it crystal clear regarding the increased strength in the financial structure of the farm business. This ratio has a direct bearing on the type of assets one has. Managerial competence of the farmer is an essential element in raising the productivity of the assets.

Income Statement or Profit and Loss Statement

This is entirely different from a balance sheet in the sense that in a balance sheet, we considered assets and liabilities and did not consider operational efficiency in terms of receipts and expenses. In income statement the items included are receipts, expenses, gains and losses. It could be defined as a summary of receipts and gains minus expenses and losses during a specified period. It is prepared for the entire farm for one agricultural year. In income statement monetary values are assigned to inputs and output. It is also prepared over time. The advantages of this statement are that it indicates the trend in various cost items and whether there has been any over expenditure on the farm. Thus, it helps to know the success or failure of a business farm over time. Income statement basically constitutes three items, viz., receipts, expenses and net income. Income statement of a hypothetical farm is presented in Table 5.2.

Receipts: They mean the returns obtained from the sale of crop produce and other supplementary products like milk and eggs, wages, gifts, etc. Gain in the form of appreciation in the value of assets is also included in the receipts. However, returns from the sale of capital assets, such as livestock, machinery, farm buildings, etc. are not included because such returns/income are not really obtained during the period.

Expenses: Operating and fixed costs are recorded here. Losses in the form of depreciation on the asset value fall under the expenditure item. However, the amounts incurred on the purchase of capital assets are not considered.

Net income: It constitutes net cash income, net operating income and net farm income.

Net cash income: It gives the position of cash receipts minus cash expenses only during the period for which income statement is prepared.

Net operating income: It is arrived at by deducting operating expenses from the gross income. Fixed costs are not given any consideration. Operating expenses include crop loans.

Net farm income: Net farm income equals net operating income less fixed costs. Compared to net cash income and net operating income, it is relatively a better measure of assessing the performance

TABLE 5.2

Income Statement of a Hypothetical Farm

Particulars	Amount (in Rs)
I. *Receipts*	
A. Returns from the sale of crop output (paddy + pulse)	52,000
B. Revenue from milk and milk products	5,000
Returns from poultry enterprise	12,000
Returns from supplementary enterprises	17,000
C. Gifts	2,000
D. Gross cash income	7,000
E. Appreciation on the value of assets	3,000
F. Gross income	74,000
II. *Expenses*	
Operating expenses or costs	
A. Hired human labour	10,500
B. Bullock labour	900
C. Machine labour	1,500
D. Seeds	1,100
E. Feeds	5,000
F. Manures & fertilisers	3,000
G. Plant protection measures	1,550
H. Veterinary aid	500
I. Irrigation	250
J. Miscellaneous	2,000
K. Interest on working capital	2,100
Total operating expenses	28,400
Fixed expenses or costs	
A. Depreciation	3,000
B. Land revenue	200
C. Interest on fixed capital (includes interest of Rs 1500 paid towards term loan)	3,200
D. Rental value of owned land	10,000
E. Total fixed costs	16,400
III. *Net cash income* 71,000 − 28,400 = 42,600	
IV. *Net operating income* 74,000 − 28,400 = 45,600	
V. *Net farm income* 45,600 − 16,400 = 29,200	

of a farm. It is the return accrued to owned capital and family labour employed.

Income statement prepared for a given farm for a given year may present a very bright picture of the farm. The same position cannot be taken for granted as the actual position of the farm, since the said year might have been a good agricultural year with respect to weather, yields, prices, etc. A realistic position on the performance of a farm can be gauged by preparing income statements over years to show the actual situation, as the parameters influencing farm business are subject to fluctuations.

Financial Test Ratios

The performance of farm business as indicated in Table 5.2 can be assessed through the income analysis by gainfully using two important parameters, viz. costs and returns. Still, some additional information is left untouched if we do not regard financial test ratios, as they supplement new information. These help the farmers themselves as well as lending institutions, and help in developing standard norms. Two sets of income ratios can be developed. One is directly from the income and expenditure pattern, and another by taking one component from income statement i.e., income levels and conparing against capital investment made on the farm business. The former ratios are called expenses-income ratios and the latter, investment–income ratios.

Following are the ratios which can be obtained directly from the income statement.

$$\text{Operating ratio} = \frac{\text{Total operating expenses}}{\text{Gross income}}$$

$$= \frac{28,400}{74,000} = 0.38$$

As the very name reveals, the ratio explains the relationship of operating costs to gross income. This ratio underlines the magnitude of working expenditure incurred for a rupee of gross income. This is a direct ratio which works out to 0.38.

$$\text{Fixed ratio} = \frac{\text{Fixed expenses}}{\text{Gross income}}$$

$$= \frac{16,400}{74,000} = 0.22$$

This ratio indicates the relationship between fixed expenses and gross income. This particular ratio is 0.22. It depicts the amount of fixed expenses incurred to realise a rupee of gross income. This is an indirect ratio, since fixed costs are indirect costs.

$$\text{Gross ratio} = \frac{\text{Total expenses}}{\text{Gross income}}$$

$$= \frac{44,800}{74,000} = 0.61$$

This is the ratio which is obtained when both operating expenses and fixed expenses are totalled up and compared with gross income. This can be called input-output ratio, which amounted to 0.61.

All these ratios should be less than one to indicate the profitable run of the farm business. When these ratios are estimated over a period of time, a healthy trend of farm business is reflected by the descending ratios.

Investment-Income Ratios: Following two are the ratios which fall under this category.

$$\text{Capital turn over ratio} = \frac{\text{Gross income}}{\text{Average capital investment}}$$

$$= \frac{74,000}{3,00,000} = 0.25$$

This is also a self-explanatory ratio as explained earlier. Here, average capital investment is arrived at by adding the value of assets at the beginning of the agricultural year and at the end of the agricultural year and then averaging the two values. Suppose it is Rs 3,00,000, then the capital turnover ratio is 0.25. This ratio gives the gross income obtained for each rupee of capital invested over the year.

$$\text{Rate of return on investment} = \frac{\text{Net return to capital}}{\text{Average capital investment}}$$

$$= \frac{27,800}{3,00,000} = 0.09$$

Net return to capital is obtained by adding bank interest paid (interest on borrowed funds + interest paid on term loans) to the net farm income and then deducting unpaid family labour for farm and livestock operations and management.

Net farm income (in Rs)	=	29,200
Interest paid during the year (in Rs)	=	+3,600
		32,800
Unpaid family labour wages (in Rs)	=	−5,000
Net return to total capital (in Rs)	=	27,800

This ratio (0.09) gives the net return on capital for every rupee of average capital invested. These above two ratios relate to the income generating capacity of the investment and are hence called income-investment ratios.

Management Ratios

These ratios also measure the productivity of farm business. They are derived not from the data available in income statement but from related information. They are, management return, crop yields and value, livestock income, gross income per man and gross income per rupee investment.

(1) *Management return*: It is derived by deducting unpaid family labour wages and interest on owned capital from net farm income.

Net farm income (in Rs)	=	29,200
Unpaid family labour wages (in Rs)	=	–5,000
Interest on owned capital (in Rs)	=	–900
Management return (in Rs)	=	23,300

Better assessment of the performance of the farm can be made by comparing management return for several years.

(2) *Crop yields and value*: This is worked out by comparing the yields obtained by the farmers for different crops with those of average yields of the area. So also value received can be compared. Here too, this data should be available over time for appraising the ability of the farm financial manager.

(3) *Livestock income*: Since livestock income forms part of the income obtained on the business farm, the efficiency of livestock management can be obtained by comparing the feed expenditure against livestock income. These figures should be available over time for knowing the efficiency parameter of the livestock enterprise.

(4) *Gross income per man*: It is simply knowing the labour efficiency by taking into account the number of labourers employed. This depends upon several factors like nature of crops, i.e., cereals, pulses, commercial crops, oilseed crops, etc., and the other complementary and competitive factor to human labour like machinery. However, in a homogeneous area there should be stability in this measure over time.

(5) *Gross income per rupee investment*: This is simply an input-output ratio. A progressively higher ratio over the years reflects a better run of the business.

Cash Flow Statement

This is also known as cash flow summary or cash flow budget or flow of funds statement. Earlier, we have discussed about balance sheet and income statement. These two financial management tools have inherent weaknesses in presenting certain valuable information, hence another tool in the form of cash flow statement bridges these deficiencies. Cash flow statement, is a summary of cash inflows and cash outflows of a business organisation in a particular period, say a season or a year. It is usually prepared for the future, hence the name cash flow budget. The merit of this particular statement is that, it helps to assess the time at which the funds are required for farming and other allied enterprises, sources from which these can be raised, the purpose for which the loan is required, the need of sale and purchase of capital assets, the time and quantum of repayment, etc. Now, let us see why a farmer borrows funds from a particular source or sources; why he resorts to transactions like selling of farm products and livestock products and selling and buying of capital assets. The answers to these questions are that the small and marginal farmers have poor resource base, and therefore, borrowings aid them in continuing the farm business. Large farmers too borrow for farm operations depending upon the need and time during which they cannot properly recycle the funds. Farmers resort to sale of farm assets like milch cattle, machinery, etc., because they might have become worn out, for which replacements are to be made through purchases.

Cash flow statement is prepared at the beginning of the agricultural year and checked every quarterly. For convenience, quarterly checks are made. The statement prepared over the years serves the purpose of studying the pattern of expenditure and cash receipts and cash balance that have been raised. A close scrutiny of the statement throws light on the performance of the business.

The example provided in Table 5.3 is briefed hereunder.

I. Cash Receipts

(1) *Cash balance*: This is the surplus amount of previous year with the farmer which stood at Rs 3,000.

(2) *Total operating sales*: These are the returns obtained from the sale of farm products and livestock products. Lesser amounts are discernible in the first and second quarters, while the returns to be obtained in the third and fourth quarter are on the higher side. The farmer is sure of getting returns from milk for about 250 days in a year which is more or less uniform in the first three quarters. The returns from crop production will be received in the third quarter for kharif and the returns from rabi crops obtained in the last quarter. The total operating sales amount to Rs 40,750 at the end of the year.

(3) *Total capital sales*: The farmer is contemplating to sell the she-buffalo, which he possesses, in the second quarter and the amount to be received will be Rs 5,000.

TABLE 5.3

Cash Flow Statement of a Hypothetical Farm

Sl. No.	Particulars	I quarter (June–Aug)	II quarter (Sept.–Nov.)	III quarter (Dec.–Feb.)	IV quarter (Mar.–May)	Total
I.	*Cash receipts (in Rs)*					
1.	Cash balance (brought forward from previous year)	3,000	—	—	—	3,000
2.	Total operating sales (farm and livestock products)	1,350	1,400	30,200	7,800	40,750
3.	Total capital sales (milch cattle)	—	5,000	—	—	5,000
4.	Non-farm income (family members working elsewhere)	2,000	1,500	2,000	3,200	8,700
5.	Borrowings (ST, MT and LT loans from institutional agencies)	7,500	—	—	—	7,500
6.	Total	13,850	7,900	32,200	11,000	64,950
II.	*Cash expenses (in Rs)*					
1.	Operating expenses	8,500	6,750	6,200	5,300	26,750
2.	Capital investment (purchase of milch cattle)	—	—	6,000	—	6,000
3.	Family living expenses	2,400	2,800	3,200	3,000	11,400
4.	Payment of previous year's debt	500	—	—	—	500
5.	Payment of ST loans and instalments on investment loans	—	—	7,968	—	7,968
	Total	11,400	9,550	23,368	8,300	52,618
III.	Cash balance (in Rs)	2,450	–1,650	8,832	2,700	12,332

(4) *Non-farm income*: It is the income which will be added by the family members by their earnings elsewhere.

(5) *Borrowings*: The farmer wishes to borrow an amount of Rs 7,500 for kharif crop operations.

(6) *Total*: It is the summation of particulars of 1 to 5 rows which presents the total cash receipts to be obtained in the year.

II. *Cash Expenses*

(1) *Operating expenses*: These include the expenditure to be incurred on the kharif as well as rabi crops and the dairy cattle.

(2) *Capital investment:* Since the farmer proposes to dispose the dairy cattle in second quarter, he wants to buy a new one in lactation in the third quarter.

(3) *Family living expenses*: These include expenditure towards food, medical, education and other items.

(4) *Payment of previous year's debts*: A hand-loan of Rs 500 is due to be paid in first quarter.

(5) *Payment of ST loans and instalments on investment loans*: Since the farmer is proposing to take a crop loan, the repayment of same falls due in the third quarter. Along with the interest and instalments, the amount due to be paid would be Rs 7,968.

(6) *Total*: It is the total expenditure to be incurred.

III. Cash Balance

It is the sum of amount to be realised after deducting expenditure from cash receipts. Barring the second quarter, the farmer is expected to have a surplus in the remaining three quarters. The deficit of Rs 1,650 in the second quarter can easily be cleared off from the savings of previous quarter, i.e., first quarter. Overall, the net surplus would be Rs 12,332.

Advantages of Cash Flow Budget

It is a summary of all the financial matters of the farmer in a comprehensive report. This helps (i) to estimate the total credit needs (ST, MT and LT) of the farmer along with time and quantum; (ii) to plan the repayment schedule, (iii) in making purchases and sales at the appropriate time thereby helping to minimise the credit dependence; (iv) to keep ready input requirements well in advance so that last minute rush can be avoided; (v) to know the farm household expenditure pattern, so that the farmers can keep limits to avoid wastage; (vi) the farmer to exercise a check on farm costs, (vii) the farmer in preparing the farm business plans for the ensuing years, (viii) the banker for revising the scales of finance, rescheduling loans, etc., and (ix) finally, as a tool of financial control to the farmer.

Break-Even Analysis

The point at which the two curves, i.e., total cost curve and total revenue curve intersect is called the break-even point (BEP) which indicates the level of production at which the producer neither loses money nor makes a profit. In other words, the quantity at which all costs allocated to a product are equal to all revenues from its sale is known as break-even point. At quantities smaller than the break-even point, there is a loss and at larger quantities there is a profit. There are two approaches in break-even analysis. One is called linear when the selling price of a product remains constant and the other curvilinear, in which we come across changes in revenue owing to the changes in selling price. The second approach has applications in respect of perennial crops.

1. *Linear Approach*

Here the total cost curve as well as total revenue curve are linear. The total revenue curve is a straight line, since the price is supposed to be constant at all quantities of output sales. The point at which the two curves intersect is the break-even point (B) as indicated in Figure 5.1.

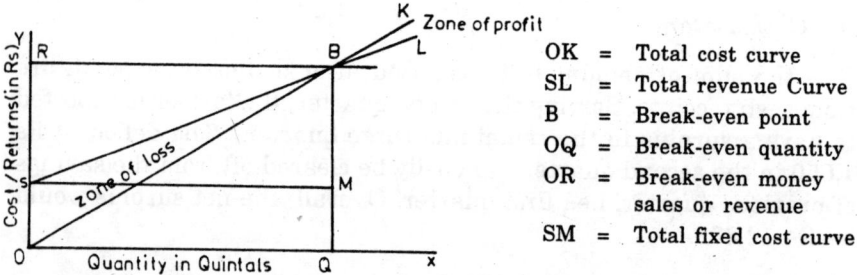

OK	=	Total cost curve
SL	=	Total revenue Curve
B	=	Break-even point
OQ	=	Break-even quantity
OR	=	Break-even money sales or revenue
SM	=	Total fixed cost curve

Fig 5.1: A linear break-even diagram

2. *Curvilinear Approach*

Here, the total cost curve, SL is a straight line and the revenue curve, RK having curvature which is concave downwards, are shown in Figure 5.2. In this situation we notice two break-even points, viz., B_1 and B_2, the former for a relatively high price and the latter for a relatively low price. In this type of analysis it is not the break-even point which the farm financial-manager is interested, but the optimum price (maximum price) which brings in the maximum net profit.

This measure can be identified by the vertical distance at which point the two curves are farthest apart. It is obtained at the point where the two curves are parallel to each other. P is the maximum price which the farmer is interested in, at which point the total quantity sold is OQ and the revenue OR. The break-even output can be calculated with the following algebraic method.

Algebraic method: Computation of *BEP* in units for hypothetical small farms of turmeric crop.

$$BEP = \frac{F}{(P-V)}$$

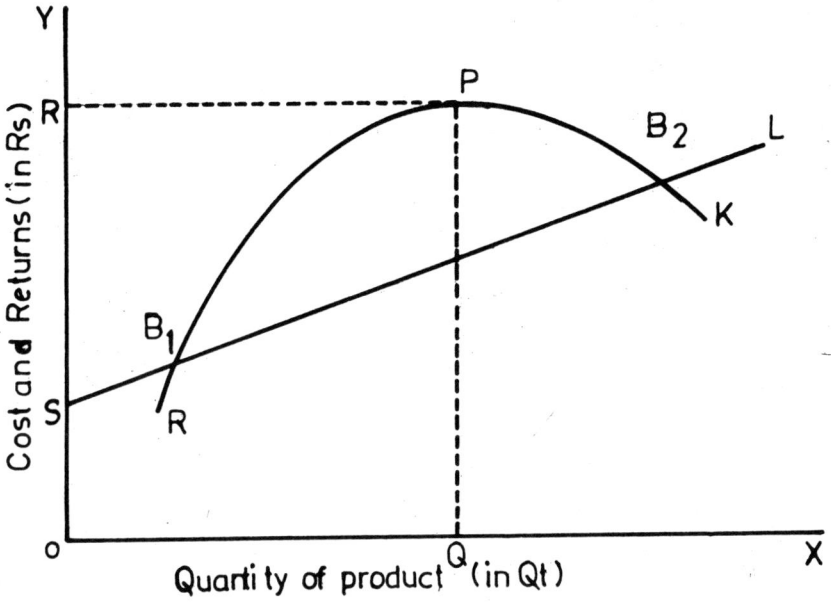

Fig. 5.2: Curvilinear break-even diagram

Where,

F = Fixed costs in Rs per hectare of turmeric crop,

P = Price per quintal of turmeric in rupees,

V = Variable costs per quintal of turmeric in rupees.

$$BEP = \frac{8,000}{(950 - 485)}$$

$$= 17.20 \text{ quintals}$$

For further information see Table 5.4.

Computation of *BEP* in monetary value

$$BEP = \frac{F}{\left(1 - \dfrac{V}{P}\right)}$$

$$= \frac{8,000}{\left(1 - \dfrac{485}{950}\right)}$$

$$= \frac{8,000}{0.49}$$

$$= \text{Rs } 16,326.53$$

The break-even analysis will also facilitate in computation of certain measures, viz., margin of safety and percentage of margin of safety which help in the decision-making.

TABLE 5.4

Break-even Output in Turmeric Cultivation

Size of farm	Fixed costs (in Rs)	Variable costs (in Rs)	Total costs (in Rs)	Price per quintal (in Rs)	Volume of output (qtl)	Total revenue (in Rs)	Variable costs/unit (in Rs)	Break-even output (qtl)	Break-even point in monetary value (in Rs)
Small	8,000	19,400	27,400	950	40	38,000	485.00	17.20	16,326.53
Large	7,700	19,350	27,050	950	37	35,150	522.97	18.03	17,126.33

Margin of Safety

It indicates the difference between total output and output at *BEP* or total revenue obtained from the enterprise and revenue at *BEP*. The positive figure of this indicator reveals the shock-absorbing capacity of the enterprise in the event of fluctuation in returns against anticipation owing to any unforeseen eventuality.

Margin of safety 　 = Total output – output at BEP
(in units)

$$= 40 - 17.20$$
$$= 22.8 \text{ quintals}$$

Margin of safety 　 = Total revenue – Revenue at *BEP*
$$= 38,000 - 16,326.53$$
$$= \text{Rs } 21,673.47$$

Percentage of margin of safety 　 $= \dfrac{\text{BEP output}}{\text{Volume of output}} \times 100$

$$= \frac{17.20}{40} \times 100$$
$$= 43\%$$
OR

$$= \frac{\text{BEP in monetary value}}{\text{Total revenue}} \times 100$$

$$= \frac{16,326.53}{38,000} \times 100$$

$$= 42.96\% = 43\%$$

Similarly, we can also find out *BEP* for large turmeric farms.

REFERENCES

1. Emery, N. Castle and Manning H. Becker, *Farm Business Management*—The *Decision Making Process*, The Macmillan Company, New York, 1965.
2. James C. Van Horne, Fundamentals of Financial Management, Prentice-Hall of India, New Delhi, 1984.
3. Heady, E.O. and H.R. Jensen, *Farm Management Economics*, Prentice-Hall of India, New Delhi, 1964.
4. Milton M. Snodgrass and L.T. Wallace, *Agriculture Economics and Resource Management*, Prentice-Hall of India, 1977.
5. Raymond R. Beneke, *Managing the Farm Business*, John Wiley and Sons, New York. 1966.
6. William G. Murray and Aaron G. Nelson, *Agricultural Finance*, The Iowa State University Press, Ames, Iowa, 1960.

CHAPTER 6

APPLICATION OF REGRESSION MODELS TO FINANCIAL MANAGEMENT

PRODUCTION FUNCTIONS—THEIR IMPORTANCE

Production functions are basically devices for providing information of input-output relationship in the production process. Supply, demand for inputs, income distribution, production determination, etc., are predicted from correctly estimated production functions. Hence, production functions are mostly used to approximate the actual input-output relationship, which depend on the knowledge of these relationships and the type of data available. Production functions in general represent a schedule or mathematical formulations between the inputs and outputs. Production functions indicate the maximum output that could be obtained from the given set of inputs under a given technology. Hence, by definition, production functions encompass technical efficiency.*

PRODUCTION FUNCTION WITH ONE VARIABLE INPUT

$$\text{Here} \quad Y = f(X_1) \tag{6.1}$$
$$Y = f(X_1 \mid X_2, X_3 .... X_n) \tag{6.2}$$

Where,

Y represents output from a particular crop,

X_1 represents capital, i.e. working capital in Rs,

$X_2 ... X_n$ are the fixed inputs.

In equation (6.2) vertical bar represents that X_1 is the variable input, and $X_2...X_n$ are the fixed inputs. In the form of Cobb-Douglas production function equation (6.2) is represented as:

$$Y_i = K\, X_{1i}^{b_1}\, e^{ui} \tag{6.3}$$

---

*A method of production (A) is said to be technically efficient relative to any method of production (B), if A uses less of at least one factor of production compared with B. (Koutsoyiannis A., 1983, *Modern Micro Economics,* Macmillan Press Ltd., Hongkong).

Where,

K represents the combined effects of $X_2, X_3 ...X_n$ on Y when X_1 is zero. It is also called efficiency parameter. b_1 is the elasticity coefficient.

Equation (6.3) is expressed in terms of logarithms as

$$ln\ Y_i \quad = \quad ln\ a + b_1\ ln\ X_1 + U_i \tag{6.4}$$

for i $\quad = \quad$ 1 to n observations

From the production function, several physical and economic concepts such as marginal product, average product, optimum input use level, etc. can be derived.

Average physical product (APP) of working capital, i.e., for example, X_1 is defined as the total yield divided by the amount of X_1 input required to produce that output as in equation (6.5).

$$APP = \frac{Y}{X_1} = f(X_1|X_2, X_3,...X_n) / X_1 \tag{6.5}$$

Marginal physical product (MPP) of X_1 input is the addition to the total output resulting from the use of one more unit of X_1 input, with other inputs held constant at their mean level.

$$MPP \text{ of } X_1 = \frac{dY}{dX_1} \tag{6.6}$$

Mathematically MPP is the first derivative of output with respect to a particular input. For the general production function (6.2) the MPP of X_1 is $\dfrac{dY}{dX_1} = \dfrac{d}{dx_1} f(X_1|X_2, X_3,...X_n)$ (6.7)

DERIVATION OF OPTIMUM INPUT LEVEL

Assume that the farmers' objective is to maximise profit over variable costs in paddy production. In this context additional units of X_1, i.e., working capital, can be profitably used as long as the addition to the total revenue exceeds the addition to the working capital. This idea is embodied in the profit function represented in equation (6.8).

$$\pi = P_y Y - P_1 X_1 = P_y f(X_1|X_2, X_3 ... X_n) - P_1 X_1 \tag{6.8}$$

Where,

π represents profits,

P_Y is the price per unit of output,

P_1 is the price per unit of input, X_1.

When the derivative of profit function with respect to X_1 is set to zero, profits to fixed resources are maximised and are expressed as

$$\frac{d\pi}{dX_1} = P_y \frac{dY}{dX_1} - P_1 = 0 \tag{6.9}$$

By solving equation (6.9) for X_1, we obtain the amount of input X_1 that will maximise the profits.

Returning to the profit maximization condition in equation (6.9), we can simplify the same and express it as in equation (6.10).

$$MP_1 \ \frac{dY}{dX_1} \ = \ P_1 / P_y \qquad\qquad ...(6.10)$$

The above equation states that for profit maximization the inverse price ratio must be equal to marginal physical product of X_1. This criterion is based on assumptions such as the production function is concave to X_1 axis, nature of production function is certain and P_Y and P_1 are constants.

Multi-Variate Production: When two or more variables are considered in the production function, it becomes multivariate production function[*]. In the case of two input variables, the production function is expressed as:

$$Y \ = \ f \ (X_1, X_2 \mid X_3, X_4, \ .... \ X_n) \qquad\qquad (6.11)$$

Vertical bar in the above function separates variable inputs from fixed inputs.

COBB-DOUGLAS PRODUCTION FUNCTION WITH TWO INPUTS

Two Americans, viz., Cobb and Douglas invented in the 1920s this multiplicative production function and it is represented as:

$$Y \ = \ A \ L^a K^b \qquad\qquad (6.12)$$

Where,

L and K are labour and capital inputs respectively and Y, output. A, a and b are the parameters to be estimated. This can be generalized to n inputs

$$Y_i \ = \ AX_{1i}^{a1}, \ X_{2i}^{a2}...X_{ni}^{an} \qquad\qquad (6.13)$$

For $i = 1$ to n observations. Both time series data and cross-section data can be considered as observations. Since the model in equation (6.12) is in multiplicative form, it cannot be estimated by OLS method because multiplicative form is not linear in the parameters. Hence, there is need to convert the function into log-linear form as:

$$ln \ Y_i \ = \ ln \ A + a \ ln \ L_i \ + \ b \ ln \ K_i \qquad\qquad (6.14)$$

Interpretation of A: In the Cobb-Douglas production function, A is the efficiency parameter and it expresses the relative efficiency of

---

[*]It is also known as multiple regression

combining the given inputs. For example, if a and b parameters are the same for any size group of farms but with different levels of A, then higher value of A indicates the relative efficiency of the size of the farm. It displays the relative skill of the manager in combining enterprises. In this context, A sometimes is referred to as management efficiency index.

Interpretation of a and b Parameters

The parameters a and b measure the elasticity of output with respect to a given input. For example, a is the elasticity of output with respect to labour and b is the elasticity of output with respect to capital.

Returns to scale: The sum of the parameters, i.e., $a + b + \ldots$ denotes the degree of returns to scale. It is also called the degree of homogeneity of production function. If $a + b = 1$, it is constant returns to scale, if $a + b < 1$ decreasing returns to scale and if $a + b > 1$ increasing returns to scale. Returns to scale is to be tested for significance.

Factor shares: Under the assumption of perfect competition in both the input and output markets, the parameters a and b give their respective factor shares. But in the case of imperfect competition, factor share for a is given by:

$$\frac{a}{a + b}$$

Similar factor shares can be worked out for other inputs.

Elasticity of Substitution(σ): It is defined mathematically as:

$$\sigma = \frac{d\left(\dfrac{K}{L}\right)}{\dfrac{K}{L}} \div \frac{d(MRS)}{(MRS)} = 1 \qquad \ldots(6.15)$$

The numerator in the above expression is the elasticity of $\dfrac{K}{L}$ (input ratio), and the denominator is the marginal rate of substitution of inputs, and d refers to change.

$$MRS = \frac{b_1}{b_2} \cdot \frac{K}{L}$$

The equation (6.15) after simplication becomes

$$\sigma = \text{elasticity of } \frac{K}{L} \text{ with respect to } \frac{\partial L}{\partial K}$$

The marginal rate of substitution ratio is also equal to marginal rate of technical substitution of factor L for factor K, which is given as

$$MRS_{L,K} = \frac{\partial X / \partial L}{\partial X / \partial K} = \frac{b_1}{b_2} \cdot \frac{K}{L} \tag{6.16}$$

The elasticity of substitution measures how far the MRS increases as we move along an isoquant to a new factor mix.

The marginal product of labour MP (L) is given by:

$$\frac{\partial Y}{\partial L} = \frac{\partial (AL^a K^b)}{\partial L}$$

$$= AaL^{a-1} K^b$$

$$= a \frac{AL^a K^b}{L}$$

$$= a \frac{Y}{L}$$

$$= a \frac{\overline{Y}}{\overline{L}} \tag{6.17a}$$

Where,

$\overline{Y}$ is geometric mean of Y,

$\overline{L}$ is geometric mean of L.

Similarly, the marginal product of capital, MP (K) is $\dfrac{\partial Y}{\partial K}$ for the Cobb-Douglas production function

$$= b \frac{\overline{Y}}{\overline{K}} \tag{6.17b}$$

The profit maximising condition for the farmer is at the level at which the ratio of value of marginal products of inputs is equal to the ratio of marginal input costs. This is expressed by the equation as:

$$\frac{\text{Values of MP}\,(L)}{\text{Value of MP}(K)} = \frac{\text{Marginal cost}\,(MC)\,\text{of}\,L}{\text{Marginal cost}\,(MC)\,\text{of}\,K}$$

$$= \frac{P.a\dfrac{Y}{L}}{P.b\dfrac{Y}{K}} = \frac{w}{r}$$

$$= \frac{a}{b} = \frac{w\overline{L}}{r\overline{K}}$$

where wL is the total wages for labourers, rK is the total payments to capital.

DERIVING DEMAND FOR AN INPUT FROM PRODUCTION FUNCTION

Production function helps in prediction of response of an input on output of crop (measurement of impact of unit input on output of crop). In addition, it allows the derivation of demand function of an input such as capital. Such demand function is called inverse static demand function and it provides marginal value product *(MVP)* of an input. By definition,

$$MVP = P_a . MP$$

Where,

MP is marginal physical product and P_q is price per unit of crop output. Profit maximising condition is implied in the equation (6.18).

$$P_q . MP = P_1 \qquad (6.18)$$

MVP of input = Price of the input

In the case of single input production function the same is expressed as:

$$P_q . \frac{dQ}{dX_1} = P_1 \qquad ...(6.19)$$

In the equation (6.19), profit will be maximised when price of $X_1 (P_1)$, is equated to marginal value product of X_1, $(P_q . dQ/dX_1)$, keeping all other variables fixed.

With P_q and other variables unchanged, MP_1 if increased using less of X_1, the equality between MVP_1 and P_1 is restored. Conversely, if MP_1 is decreased, using more of X_1, the equality is maintained for profit maximisation. Thus, varying levels of P_1 and X_1 are derived keeping P_q constant. These different P_1 and X_1 levels can be used to draw the static demand curve. For this purpose the profit function is to be used for deriving the demand function.

Let the single input production function be:

$$Q = KX_1^{b_1}$$

Let the profit function be represented as:

$$\pi = P_q Q - P_1 X_1 \qquad ....(6.20)$$

Profits will be maximized when the derivative of profit function with respect to the input, X_1, is set equal to zero.

$$\frac{d\pi}{dX_1} = P_q . \frac{dQ}{dX_1} - P_1 = 0 \qquad ....(6.21)$$

$$= P_q K b_1 X_1^{(b_1 - 1)} - P_1 = 0$$

$$= P_q K b_1 = P_1 . \frac{1}{X_1^{(b_1 - 1)}}$$

$$= P_q K b_1 / P_1 = \frac{1}{X_1^{(b_1-1)}}$$

$$= Pq\, K b_1\, P_1^{-1} = X_1^{-(b_1-1)} \ or \ X_1^{(1-b_1)}$$

$$= (P_q K b_1\, P_1^{-1})^{\frac{1}{(1-b)}} = X_1$$

$$X_1 = (P_q\ K b_1\ P_1^{-1})^{\frac{1}{(1-b_1)}} \qquad\qquad ...(6.22)$$

The equation (6.22) is the static inverse demand function of X_1 input. Since the demand of an input relates to a point of time, it is called static demand of the input. The estimated parameters b_1 and K vary directly with X_1 and they define the technical input-output relationship. This means in the presence of new technology the parameters b_1 and K will rise. Hence, if there is rise in b_1, KP_q and other fixed input levels it is profitable to increase the use of X_1 input, otherwise it is not profitable to do so.

Price of input (P_1) varies inversely with the level of input (X_1). Assume different values of P_1 in equation (6.22) and derive X_1 values and plot them on XY plane of the graph and derive the demand curve for the input X_1 (Table 6.1).

Let the estimated Cobb-Douglas production function with single capital input be represented as:

$$\hat{Q} = 1.17\ X_1^{0.4}$$

Where,

X_1 = Capital input in Rs

$\hat{Q}$ = Paddy production in quintals/acre

P_1 = Price of the capital input Rs 1.12

P_q = Price per quintal of paddy Rs 290

$$X_1^* = \left(\frac{P_q K b_1}{P_1}\right)^{\frac{1}{1-b_1}}$$

$$= \frac{(1.17 \times 290 \times 0.4)^{\frac{1}{1-0.4}}}{1.12}$$

$$= \left(\frac{135.72}{1.12}\right)^{\frac{1}{0.6}}$$

$$= (121.18)^{1.67}$$

$$= \text{Rs } 3,015.29\ /\ \text{Acre}$$

Q^* = 1.17 $(3015.29)^{0.4}$

Q^* = 28.83 quintals/acre

Where, X_1^* = Optimal level of capital input

Q^* = Optimal level of output

TABLE 6.1

Derivation of Demand Curve for Capital Input

S. No.	Assumed level of P_1 (in Rs)	Derived level of X_1 (in Rs)
1	1.10	3,060.74
2	1.11	3,107.73
3	1.12	3,015.29
4	1.13	2,970.81
5	1.14	2,927.41
6	1.15	2,885.03

The demand curve for capital input is illustrated in Fig. 6.1.

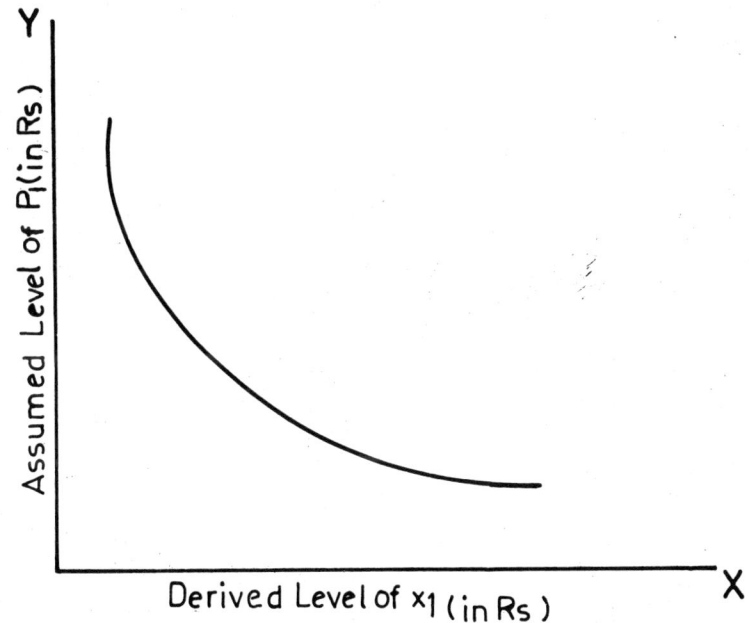

Fig. 6.1: Demand curve for capital input.

PROFIT MAXIMIZATION UNDER CONSTRAINED CONDITIONS

Let the production function with two inputs, viz., labour in days (X_1) and manures and fertilizers in rupees (X_2) be represented as:

$$Y = AX_1^{b_1} X_2^{b_2} \qquad \qquad ....(6.23)$$

with the price per unit of output (P_Y), P_1 the price of X_1 and P_2 price of X_2 inputs. Its profit function is specified as:

$$\pi = P_Y\, Y - P_1 X_1 - P_2 X_2 + \lambda\, (K - P_1 X_1 - P_2 X_2) \qquad ...(6.24)$$

Where,

λ = Lagrangean multiplier, and

K = Capital available with the farmer for investment on crop in Rs.

(6.24) is a constrained profit maximisation equation with Lagrangean multiplier λ.

Setting the first order partial derivatives of equation (6.24) with respect to X_1, X_2 and λ equal to zero, we obtain the optimal input levels for X_1 and X_2 that maximise profits to fixed resources. The following first order set of equations are derived.

$$\frac{\partial \pi}{\partial X_1} = P_y \frac{\partial Y}{\partial X_1} - P_1 - \lambda P_1 = 0$$

$$= P_y b_1 A X_1^{b_1 - 1} X_2^{b_2} - P_1 - \lambda P_1 = 0$$

$$= P_Y b_1 Y X_1^{-1} - P_1 - \lambda P_1 = 0$$

$$= \frac{P_Y b_1\, Y}{X_1} - P_1 - \lambda P_1 = 0$$

$$\frac{b_1 Y}{X_1} = \frac{(1+\lambda) P_1}{P_Y} \qquad ...(6.25)$$

Similarly,

$$\frac{\partial \pi}{\partial X_2} = P_Y \frac{\partial Y}{\partial X_2} - P_2 - \lambda P_2 = 0$$

$$= P_Y b_2 A X_1^{b_1} X_2^{b_2 - 1} - P_2 - \lambda P_2 = 0$$

$$= P_Y b_2 A X_1^{b_1} X_2^{b_2} X_2^{-1} - P_2 - \lambda P_2 = 0$$

$$= \frac{P_Y\, b_2 Y}{X_2} - P_2 - \lambda P_2 = 0$$

$$= \frac{P_Y b_2 Y}{X_2} = (1 + \lambda) P_2$$

$$= \frac{b_2 Y}{X_2} = \frac{(1+\lambda) P_2}{P_Y} \qquad ...(6.26)$$

$$\frac{\partial \pi}{\partial \lambda} = K - P_1 X_1 - P_2 X_2 = 0 \qquad ...(6.27)$$

$$= P_1 X_1 + P_2 X_2 = K \qquad ...(6.28)$$

Dividing equation (6.25) by equation (6.26), we get

$$\frac{b_1 Y}{X_1} \div \frac{b_2 Y}{X_2} = \frac{(1+\lambda)P_1}{P_Y} \div \frac{(1+\lambda)P_2}{P_Y}$$

$$\frac{b_1 Y}{X_1} \cdot \frac{X_2}{b_2 Y} = \frac{-(1+\lambda)P_1}{-P_Y} \cdot \frac{P_Y}{-(1+\lambda)P_2}$$

$$\frac{b_1}{b_2} \cdot \frac{X_2}{X_1} = \frac{P_1}{P_2}$$

$$X_2 = \frac{b_2}{b_1} \cdot \frac{P_1}{P_2} X_1 \qquad \qquad \text{... (6.29)}$$

Substituting equation (6.29) in equation (6.28), we get

$$P_1 X_1 + \left(\frac{b_2}{b_1} \cdot \frac{P_1}{P_2} \right) P_2 X_1 \quad = K$$

$$= P_1 X_1 \left(1 + \frac{b_2}{b_1} \right) \quad = K$$

$$X_1 = \frac{K}{P_1 \left(1 + \frac{b_2}{b_1} \right)}$$

$$X_1^* = \frac{K.b_1}{P_1(b_1 + b_2)} \qquad \qquad \text{... (6.30)}$$

Where,

$X_1^* = $ Optimal level of input X_1

Similarly, $\quad X_2^* = \dfrac{K.b_2}{P_2(b_1 + b_2)} \qquad \qquad$ ... (6.31)

Numerical Example

1. Let the estimated Cobb-Douglas Production function with two inputs, viz., labour in days (X_1) and manures and fertilizers in rupees (X_2). $\hat{Y} = 3 X_1^{0.2} X_2^{0.3}$. Let K represent capital available, i.e., Rs 3,000, P_1 = Rs 10 (price of X_1 input). Using the equation (6.30) we can work out the optimal level of X_1

$$X_1^* = \frac{3,000 \times 0.2}{10(0.2 + 0.3)}$$

$$= \frac{600}{5} = 120 \text{ labour days / ha}$$

TABLE 6.2

Decision Criteria

Input variable	Optimal level	Actual use level	Decision
X_1	120	100	Further use is recommended
X_2	1,800	2,000	Actual use level should be reduced to the optimal level

$$X_2^* = \frac{3000 \times 0.3}{1(0.2 + 0.3)}$$

$$= \frac{900}{0.5} = \text{Rs } 1,800/\text{ha}$$

(2) Let the estimated Cobb-Douglas production function with three inputs, viz., labour in days (X_1), manures and fertilizers in rupees (X_2) and miscellaneous expenditure in rupees (X_3). Let K be capital available with the farmer, i.e., Rs 4,200.

$$\hat{Y} = 4\, X_1^{0.4542}\, X_2^{0.1821}\, X_3^{0.2154}$$

In equation (6.29) X_2 is expressed in terms of X_1 as

$$X_2 = \frac{b_2}{b_1} \cdot \frac{P_1}{P_2} \cdot X_1$$

Similarly, $X_3 = \dfrac{b_3}{b_1} \cdot \dfrac{P_1}{P_3} \cdot X_1$ ...(6.32)

In the case of three input production function

$$\frac{\partial \pi}{\partial \lambda} = P_1 X_1 + P_2 X_2 + P_3 X_3 = K \qquad \text{... (6.33)}$$

Substituting the values of X_2 and X_3 as given in equation (6.29) and (6.32) respectively in the equation (6.33) we get:

$$P_1 X_1 + P_2 \left(\frac{P_1}{P_2} \cdot \frac{b_2}{b_1} \cdot X_1 \right) + P_3 \left(\frac{P_1}{P_3} \cdot \frac{b_3}{b_1} \cdot X_1 \right) = K$$

$$P_1 X_1 \left(1 + \frac{b_2}{b_1} + \frac{b_3}{b_1} \right) = K$$

$$X_1 = \frac{K}{P_1 \left(1 + \dfrac{b_2}{b_1} + \dfrac{b_3}{b_1} \right)}$$

$$X_1^* = \frac{K.b_1}{P_1(b_1 + b_2 + b_3)} \qquad\qquad ....(6.34)$$

$$X_2^* = \frac{K.b_2}{P_2(b_1 + b_2 + b_3)} \qquad\qquad ... (6.35)$$

$$X_3^* = \frac{K.b_3}{P_3(b_1 + b_2 + b_3)} \qquad\qquad ...(6.36)$$

Similarly,

$$\text{for } X_j = \frac{K.b_j}{P_j(b_1 + b_2 + b_3 + ... + b_j)} \qquad\qquad ...(6.37)$$

Applying equation (6.34) we get optimal value(*) of:

$$X_1^* = \frac{4200 \times 0.4542}{10(0.4542 + 0.1821 + 0.2154)}$$

$$= \frac{1907.62}{10(0.8517)} = 162.47 \text{ labour days / ha (optimal level)}$$

Analogously,

$$X_2^* = \text{Rs } 897.99/\text{ha}$$
$$X_3^* = \text{Rs } 1062.21/\text{ha}$$

TABLE 6.3

Decision Criteria

Input variable	Optimal level	Actual use level	Decision
X_1	162.47	152.00	Further use is recommended
X_2	897.99	1,000.00	Actual use level should be reduced to the optimal level
X_3	1,062.21	1680.00	Actual use level should be reduced to the optimal level

OPTIMAL INPUT USE LEVELS FROM GENERAL PRODUCTION FUNCTIONS

Determination of optimal input use level for two variable production functions involving capital (X_1) and labour (X_2) is simply an extension of procedures given previously for single variable production function.

Assuming P_Y, P_1 and P_2 as the prices of output, X_1 and X_2 respectively and FC as fixed cost: profit is defined as

$$\pi = P_Y.Y - P_1X_1 - P_2X_2 - FC \qquad\qquad ...(6.38)$$

Substituting equation (6.11) in (6.38), we get (6.39) which is

$$\pi = P_y f(X_1, X_2 | X_3, X_4) - P_1X_1 - P_2X_2 - FC \qquad\qquad ...(6.39)$$

Setting the first order partial derivatives of equation (6.39) with respect to X_1 and X_2 inputs equal to zero, a system of two equations is obtained:

$$\partial \pi / \partial X_1 = P_y (\partial Y / \partial X_1) - P_1 = 0$$

or $\quad \partial Y / \partial X_1 = P_1 / P_y$

$$\partial \pi / \partial X_2 = P_y (\partial Y / \partial X_2) - P_2 = 0 \text{ or}$$

$$\partial Y / \partial X_2 = P_2 / P_y \qquad \qquad ...(6.40)$$

Solving this system of two equations simultaneously, we obtain the quantity of each of X_1 and X_2 that will maximise profits and substituting the values of X_1 and X_2 in production function, we estimate the crop output which is the profit-maximising output.

In the real farming world working capital is limited. In this case we need to impose capital restriction, such as 'K' so that

$$\text{'k'} \geq P_1 X_1 + P_2 X_2 \qquad \qquad ...(6.41)$$

Equation (6.41) expresses that the mount spent on X_1 and X_2 cannot exceed the available capital K. As a result, the profit maximisation condition of the equation (6.38) is reformulated as in the equation (6.42) with the Lagrangean multiplier λ

$$\pi = P_y Y - P_1 X_1 - P_2 X_2 + \lambda (K - P_1 X_1 - P_2 X_2) - FC \qquad ...(6.42)$$

Obtaining the 1st order partial derivatives of equation (6.40) with respect to X_1, X_2 and λ setting them equal to zero, we determine the levels of input for X_1 and X_2 that maximise profits. Thus we get,

$$\left. \begin{array}{l} \partial \pi / \partial X_1 = P_y \partial Y / \partial X_1 - P_1 - \lambda P_1 = 0 \\ \partial \pi / \partial X_2 = P_y \partial Y / \partial X_2 - P_2 - \lambda P_2 = 0 \\ \partial \pi / \partial \lambda = K - P_1 X_1 - P_2 X_2 = 0 \end{array} \right\} \qquad ...(6.43)$$

The third equation (6.43) shows the capital restriction on the purchase of X_1 and X_2 inputs. The conditions in equation (6.43) must be solved simultaneously.

Here the parameter λ implies increase in profit due to incremental increase in K. i.e., capital available. It is also the opportunity cost of using the last unit of capital in producing crop output, rather than in its most remunerative alternative use.

The interpretation for λ that if an acquired rupee of capital is made available for the farmers for obtaining inputs, the profits would go up by the λ value.

DUMMY VARIABLE TECHNIQUE (STEP FUNCTION)

In this section, the role of qualitative explanatory variables in the regression analysis is first explained, later an attempt is made as to how the dummy variable technique is used to isolate the effects of borrowed capital and available capital in the total capital on the output of the farm.

In the production function analysis the dependent variable, i.e., crop output in quintals or kgs, is expressed as a function of a vector of independent variables which are quantifiable. But, in the real world farm situations, crop output is a function of even qualitative variables also, such as age, education, management, skill, drought, floods, cyclones, etc. Dummy variable technique is in fact aimed at measuring the effect of these qualitative variables on the dependent variable. Since data on these variables are not available for quantification, we assume zero and one values for absence and presence of qualitative variable, respectively which is called dummy variable. Other names of dummy variables are indicator variables, binary variables, categorical variables, qualitative variables, dichotomous variables, etc. In the step function all the explanatory variables are dummies. Such models are called Analysis of Variance Models (AOV Models). There is no quantitative independent variable in the regression.

To cite an example here, let us take the available capital and borrowed capital for a group of farmers over time (say 13 years). The step function can be formulated for hypothetical data presented in Table 6.4.

In the equation (6.44) the mean level of owned capital is given by the intercept term a; b indicates how the borrowed capital increases every year and mean value of borrowed capital is given by $\hat{a}$ plus $\hat{b}$ values. Such information provides the basis for future planning by the institutional agencies with regard to financial allocation to a given set of farmers in a given area. It is an important management tool for the financial institutions in estimation of credit needs for different group or categories of farmers in a village, taluk, district, State and country as a whole.

TABLE 6.4

Hypothetical Data on Available and Borrowed Capital for a Group of Farmers

Years	Sl.No. of observations	Capital (in '000Rs)				
		Borrowed capital		Sl.No.of observations	Owned capital	
		(Y_t)	(D_t)		(Y_t)	(D_t)
1979	1	5	1	14	3.0	0
1980	2	6	1	15	2.5	0
1981	3	4	1	16	1.5	0
1982	4	7	1	17	2.0	0
1983	5	5	1	18	2.5	0
1984	6	6	1	19	3.0	0
1985	7	7	1	20	1.5	0
1986	8	7	1	21	3.0	0
1987	9	8	1	22	4.0	0
1988	10	9	1	23	0.5	0
1989	11	10	1	24	1.0	0
1990	12	5	1	25	2.5	0
1991	13	7	1	26	3.0	0

Let the step estimated function be

$$\hat{Y}_t = \hat{a} + \hat{b} D_t \qquad \qquad ...(6.44)$$

where, $\hat{Y}_t$ = capital in t^{th} year (for t = 1 to 26 observations),

D_t = Dummy variable (independent variable), 1 if it is borrowed capital (for observations 1 to 13)

0, if it is owned capital (for observations 14 to 26).

PIECEWISE LINEAR REGRESSION MODEL

If the regression function includes both qualitative variables (dummy variables) and quantitative variables, such regression models are known as Analysis of Co-Variance Models (ACOV Models).

Let the estimated piecewise regression equation for cross section data of a particular group is represented as:

$$\hat{Y}_i = \hat{a} + \hat{b}_1 X_i + \hat{b}_2 (X_i - X_i^*) D_i \qquad ....(6.45)$$

Where,

$\hat{Y}_i$ = Crop output of the ith farmer in a given category,

X_i = Total capital used by the ith farmer in the production of crop output in Rs,

X_i^* = Owned capital of the ith farmer in Rs,

D = 1 if $X_i > X_i^*$

0 if $X_i < X_i^*$

$X_i - X_i^*$ = Amount of borrowed capital by the ith farmer

$$E(Y_i|D_i = 0) = \hat{a} + \hat{b}_1 X_i \qquad \qquad ...(6.46)$$

$$E(Y_i|D_i = 1) = \hat{a} + (\hat{b}_1 + \hat{b}_2) X_i - \hat{b}_2 X_i^* \qquad ...(6.47)$$

Equation (6.46) gives the mean crop output due to total capital, whereas (6.47) gives the mean crop output due to borrowed capital. $\hat{b}_1$ in equation (6.45) measures the impact of total capital on crop output, $\hat{b}_2$ provides impact of borrowed capital and $\hat{a}$ is the mean crop output due to available capital.

COST FUNCTION

Total cost is determined by many factors, hence it is a multi-variate function and long-run cost is a function of X, T, P_f where X is output, T refers to technology and P_f denotes price of factors. Similarly, short-run cost function is a function of several variables, viz., output (X), technology (T) and price of factors (P_f).

$$C = f(X, T, P_f | K)$$

where, K represents fixed factor.

On the two-dimensional graph, cost is a function of output, $C = f(X)$, *ceteris paribus*, the clause *ceteris paribus*, denotes all other factors which determine cost, remain constant. If there is a change in these costs, they will shift the cost curves, hence called shift factors. The moment along the cost curves is due to changes in output, while, the shift of the cost curves to the right or left is due to changes in other factors, viz., technology, prices of factors and fixed factors. The term, technology refers to the quality and potentiality of the factor inputs, efficiency of entrepreneur, efficiency of the farmers and economic choice of the techniques under the better organisational methods of production. Changes in the technology level, shift the production function and hence bring about shift in the cost curves. In fact, cost curves are derived from the production function and there is one to one correspondence between production function and cost function. The distribution betweeen internal economies and external economies of scale helps in identifying the shapes of the cost curves. The internal economies are built into the long-run cost curves and they get accrued due to the expansion of the level of output. The external economies arise outside the farm, i.e., from improvement of the environment in which farmer operates due to the action of other farmers. Such economies are independent of the actions of farm in question, hence they are external to it and shift in general the cost curves, both in the short run as well as long run. Internal economies of scale relate to the shape of the long-run cost curves, whereas, the external economies affect the position of the cost curves.

STATISTICAL COST FUNCTIONS

Generally cost functions are estimated from two types of data, viz., time-series data and cross-sectional data. Observations on different levels of output, costs and prices of a farm over time are called time-series data, whereas, cross-section data include information on inputs, costs and outputs of different farms at a given point of time. From these types of data, we generally estimate short run and long run cost functions. Short-run cost functions can be estimated from time-series data of a single farm. It has been said that the time-series data are not appropriate for the estimation of long-run cost curves, because there will be problems of changing technology. To overcome such problems, cross-sectional data are more appropriate.

A linear cost function is expressed in the equation (6.48).

$$C = b_1 X_1 + U \qquad \qquad ...(6.48)$$

Where,

C = Total variable cost,

X = Output in physical units, and

U = error term

U represents the influence of all other variables on costs.

In the above linear cost function AVC and MC are constant at all levels of output.

$$MC = \frac{\partial C}{\partial X} = b_1 \qquad \qquad ...(6.49)$$

$$AVC = \frac{C}{X} = b_1 \qquad \qquad ...(6.50)$$

The quadratic cost function is fitted to the data in order to capture the U shape of cost function.

$$C = a + b_1 X - b_2 X^2 + U \qquad \qquad ...(6.51)$$

In this function $MC > AVC$ at all levels of output,

$$so\ MC = \frac{\partial C}{\partial X} = b_1 - 2b_2 X \qquad \qquad ...(6.52)$$

$$AVC = \frac{C}{X} = b_1 - b_2 X \qquad \qquad ...(6.53)$$

Analogously, the cubic cost function is expressed in the equation (6.54).

$$C = b_1 X - b_2 X^2 + b_3 X^3 + U \qquad \qquad ...(6.54)$$

This equation implies a U-shaped AVC and MC curve intersecting the AVC curve at the minimum point from below.

In the cost function if there is no intercept term (b_0), it indicates the absence of fixed costs.

If the long run total cost curve is U-shaped it reflects the law of variable proportions.

$$C = b_0 + b_1 X - b_2 X^2 + b_3 X^3 \qquad \qquad ...(6.55)$$
$$TC = TFC + TVC$$

$$AVC = \frac{TVC}{X} = b_1 - b_2 X + b_3 X^2 \qquad \qquad ... (6.56)$$

$$MC = \frac{\partial C}{\partial X} = b_1 - 2b_2 X + 3b_3 X^2 \qquad \qquad ...(6.57)$$

$$ATC = \frac{C}{X} = \frac{b_0}{X} + b_1 - b_2 X + b_3 X^2 \qquad \qquad ....(6.58)$$

In the long run TC will have a rough shape of S, while AVC, MC and ATC exhibit U-shape. MC curve cuts the minimum points of ATC and AVC from below as shown in Fig. 3.20.

SPECIFICATION OF THE COST FUNCTION

The cost curves drawn from the cost functions assume constant technology and constant prices of inputs used in the production of crops. If the assumption is violated, there will be a shift in the cost curves. For this obvious reason, the cost curves have been criticised by economists many a time in the past. If the short-run cost curves are estimated from the time-series data of a single farm, whose size of land remains constant over the sample period, the assumption of constant techonology is not necessary because the data are drawn from different time periods.

Variations in technology: When using cross-section samples of farms of different sizes for the estimation of long-run cost curves, the assumption of constant technology is not indispensable, because all the available techniques of production are known to all farms existing at a particular point of time. When all the existing farms are included, it means that the differences in technology are considered in the long-run cost curves and technology is randomly distributed among the selected farms. This is because in the adequate sample, representation of efficient as well as inefficient farms in crop production is obtained. If this is true, differences in the technology are absorbed by random variable U and, therefore, do not affect the cost-output relationship. But in sum, both short and long-run cost curves continuously shift due to improvements in the technology and the quality of inputs. Since, these continuous shifts have not been properly accounted for in the estimation of cost curves, we do not often get the theoritical shape of the cost curves from the observed data.

Variations in factor prices: Prices of the inputs of the crops are not independently and adequately treated in the cost functions. The short-run cost curves estimated from the time series data are in fact deflated due to non-consideration of prices. But, according to Johnston (1960), this deflating trends of cost curves do not undermine the cost-output relationship. In general, cost functions estimated from cross-sectional data are thought to be free of problems of price changes because all the farms included in the sample are in the same location and the prices are given at any one time. Hence, there is no need to consider price changes of input factors.

Variations in the quality of crop output: Sometimes criticism has been levelled against cost functions on the grounds that by nature they cannot capture variations in the quality aspects of the crop output. But, it is generally assumed while estimating the cost functions that quality of crop output remains unchanged. If there are significant changes in the quality differences in the output obtained, the cost-output relations become biased. Hence, there is a need for estimating cost functions separately for homogeneous crop output. Given these difficulties in measuring quality differences in crop output over time and among farms, this problem has been, by far, ignored in the statistical cost functions.

SHAPE OF THE COST CURVES VIS-A-VIS DECISION MAKING

Rational economic decisions of the farm sometimes revolve around the shape of the cost curves and the knowledge of the cost functions. Decisions relevant to pricing and output in the short run are drawn from the knowledge of short-run cost curves, while, the long-run cost curves/functions form a basis for the development of the farm and investment decisions. Costs of the farm are one of the main determinants of the price in the markets and provide pertinent information for explanation of the behaviour of the farm. Optimal output of the farm is determined, if the cost curves are U-shaped in pure competition model.

Derivation of Cost Function from Production Function

Consider a Cobb-Douglas Production Function with two inputs and dependent variable.

$$Y = AL_1^{b_1} C_2^{b_2} \qquad ....(6.59)$$

Where,

Y = Crop output,

L_1 = Labour in man days,

C_2 = Fertilizers in rupees,

b_1 and b_2 = Elasticity co-efficients, and

A = Intercept.

Here, if b_1 and $b_2 > 0$, then its corresponding cost function would be

$$C = a^A Y^{1/(b_1 + b_2)}$$

To convert production function into cost function, we need input prices r_1 and r_2. After rearranging the equation, production function is transformed into cost function and represented in equation (6.60).

$$\text{Where, } a = (b_1 + b_2) \left(\frac{r_1^{b_1} r_2^{b_2}}{A b_1^{b_1} b_2^{b_2}} \right)^{1/(b_1 + b_2)}$$

r_1 and r_2 = Input prices

AC and MC are estimated as follows:

$$AC = aY^{(1 - b_1 - b_2)/(b_1 + b_2)} \qquad ...(6.61)$$

$$MC = \frac{a}{(b_1 + b_2)} Y^{(1 - b_1 - b_2)/(b_1 + b_2)} = \frac{1}{(b_1 + b_2)} AC \qquad ...(6.62)$$

If AC and MC are constant and equal, the total cost function is linear.

Similarly, summing the elasticity coefficients of the Cobb-Douglas production function, we can define the shape of the cost function. For example, if $b_1 + b_2 > 1$, then the cost function is concave. If $b_1 + b_2 < 1$, then the cost function is convex.

ISSUES IN THE ESTIMATION OF COST FUNCTIONS

Many a time, researchers confront the problem of correct estimation of cubic function. At times, with the observed data on total costs and corresponding output, the estimated cubic functions will not give expected signs and significant levels. To cite an example, assume that the cubic term in the cost equation turns out to be non-significant for the given data, the researcher opts for quadratic cost function. If the effort of expected signs and significant levels through quadratic function is not fructified, then he looks into the estimation of linear cost function and conclude the shape of the cost curves. As a result, the expected shape of the cost curves will not be obtained from the given data, thereby posing the problem of obtaining optimal output.

The following procedure is adopted to overcome such problems by the researcher:

(1) Estimate the production function with all the variables in their physical quantities.

(2) Substitute the corresponding values of the input levels into the production function and obtain $\hat{Y}$ levels (estimated output levels).

(3) Estimate the total variable cost for each output level by multiplying the input levels with their corresponding prices.

(4) Fixed costs are added to the corresponding variable costs to obtain the total costs.

(5) Generate total variable costs for each output level from the production function parameters.

(6) Cubic cost function is estimated by considering output as independent variable and total cost as the dependent variable, and

(7) It is advocated to go for wide range of output levels based on expansion path to get the theoritical shape of the cost curves.

PROBIT MODEL (NORMIT MODEL)

The behaviour of the dichotomous dependent variable is better explained by the cumulative density function (CDF) variable. In this model, normal CDF is substituted in place of logistic CDF.

TABLE 6.5

Procedure to Estimate Probabilities

Sl. No.	Farm size in acres	Total de-faulters (N_i)	Wilful-defaul-ters(n_i)	Proba-bility $(P_i)= \dfrac{n_i}{N_i}$	U_i (n.e.d.)	Probits $(U_i + 5)$
1	25.0	20	14	0.70	0.52	5.52
2	20.0	30	24	0.80	0.84	5.84
3	16.0	40	30	0.75	0.67	5.67
4	13.0	45	35	0.75	0.77	5.77
5	8.0	50	42	0.84	0.99	5.99
6	5.0	90	54	0.60	0.25	5.25
7	4.0	66	30	0.45	− 0.12	4.08
8	3.5	64	22	0.34	− 0.41	4.59
9	3.0	62	20	0.32	− 0.46	4.54
10	2.0	60	16	0.27	− 0.61	4.39
11	1.5	55	11	0.20	− 0.84	4.16
12	0.5	40	17	0.18	− 0.91	4.09

The probit model is based upon utility theory of rational choice perspective or behaviour of the dependent variable. The probit model is often used in the financial management in order to explain the behaviour of wilful defaulters and non-wilful defaulters. Such behaviour of the borrowers is treated as dichotomous dependent variable and determined by the explanatory variables, such as farm size (X_1), farm expenditure (X_2) non-farm expenses (X_3), etc. Utility index (U_i) is calculated based on the probabilities and then referring to CDF tables. For each P_i the corresponding U_i is obtainied referring to CDF table. If P_i is below 0.5, then the corresponding z value should be indicated with negative sign. If P_i value is 0.5 and above, it should be subtracted from one and then its corresponding z value is treated as positive value. This is how the probabilities of dichotomous dependent variable are converted into utility indices. (Table 6.5).

Steps Involved in the Probit Model

(1) For the grouped data given in the columns 2,3 and 4 in Table 6.5, estimate P_i similar to Logit Model.

(2) Given P_i, obtain normal equivalent deviate (n.e.d.) of simple Normit (U_i) from the standard normal CDF Table.

(3) If any of the U_i is negative, add 5 to all the estimates uniformly in order to convert them into positive probits. These probits are considered as dependent variable and farm size (X_1) and other relevant variables, viz., farm operational expenditure (X_2) family consumption expenditure (X_3), etc., are considered as explanatory variables of the model.

(4) The estimated probit model is specified as:

$$\hat{U}_i = \hat{a} + \hat{b}X_i \qquad \qquad ...(6.63)$$

a and b are parameters to be estimated.

(5) The best functional form of the model should be identified based on R^2, significant levels of the parameters and apriori signs for the parameters.

In Table 6.5 the dependent dichotomous variable, i.e., the probability of wilful-defaulters among total defaulters in the given farm size is worked out and placed in column No. 5. Utility index U_i, is estimated by referring to normal CDF Table for each corresponding P_i. Then this U_i is converted into probit by adding 5 uniformly to all the U_i values in order to avoid negative values.

LOGIT MODEL

For the given P_i in column (5) of Table 6.5, we can estimate the Logit (L_i) from the equation (6.64).

$$L_i = ln \ (P_i/1 - P_i) \qquad \qquad ...(6.64)$$

and this Li value is considered as dependent variable in the logit model. The corresponding farm size X_{1i} is treated as explanatory variable.

Similar to probit model it is specified as:

$$L_i = \alpha + \beta X_i + U_i \qquad \qquad ...(6.65)$$

Where, U_i is stochastic disturbance term, α and β are the intercept and slope coefficients respectively. For this model also different functional forms are to be adopted and the best one among them should be choosen based on *apriori* signs, significant levels of parameters and R^2. There is also need to eliminate heteroscedasticity problem for the model given in equation (6.65).

Linear Probability Model (LPM)

The following simple model is sometimes adopted to measure the relationship between the dichotomous dependent variable and explanatory variable.

$$Y_i = a + bX_i + e_i \qquad \qquad ....(6.66)$$

LINEAR DISCRIMINANT FUNCTION—APPLICATIONS

The method of discriminant function as one of the tools of the multi-variable analyses was first introduced by R.A. Fisher. The discriminant function has wide application to farm financial management aspects. It is popularly used by the researchers and bank officials in order to discriminate between borrowers and non-borrowers, good loans and bad loans, defaulters and non-defaulters, high performance banks and low performance banks, etc. The relevant variables considered in the discrimination of borrowers from non-borrowers are gross income from the farm as a whole, value of assets, working capital, etc. Similarly, for discriminating between good loans and bad loans, many variables, viz., net income, family expenditure, amount diverted for purposes other than farming, size of the holding, literacy, political affiliations, etc., are considered. In the same way, the variables that discriminate between high performance banks and low performance banks are loan recovery percentage, percentage of overdues, profits of the banks, amount advanced, etc. The credit societies can also be discriminated in the same way as high performing ones and low performing ones.

Procedure for Estimation of Discriminant Function

Let X_{ij} variables ($j = 1$ to P variables) in two groups, with N_1 observations in first group and N_2 observations in the second group and total observations ($N_1 + N_2 = N$) be denoted in matrix form.

$\quad X_{ij}$ for $\quad i = 1, 2 \dots N_1$ in the first group

$\qquad\qquad i = N_{1+1}, N_{1+2} \dots N_2$ in the second group

$\qquad\qquad N = N_1 + N_2 \qquad\qquad\qquad\qquad$ ... (6.67)

The mean of the jth variable in the first group is given by:

$\quad \bar{X}_{ij}^1$ for $i = 1$ to N_1 observations

$\qquad\qquad j = 1$ to P variables

$$\bar{X}_{ij}^1 = \sum_{i=1}^{N_1} X_{ij}^1 / N_i \qquad\qquad \text{...(6.68)}$$

The mean of jth variable in the second group is given by:

$$\bar{X}_{ij}^2 = \sum_{i=N_1+1}^{N_2} X_{ij}^2 / N_2 \qquad\qquad \text{...(6.69)}$$

The general or grand mean of jth variable in two groups is given by

$$\bar{\bar{X}}_{ij} = \sum_{i=1}^{N} X_{ij} / N \qquad\qquad \text{...(6.70)}$$

Where,

$\quad N = N_1 + N_2$

The differences of the means of jth variable are given as:

$\quad D_1 = \bar{X}_{i1}^1 - \bar{X}_{i1}^2 \quad j = 1$ to p variables

$\quad D_2 = \bar{X}_{i2}^1 - \bar{X}_{i2}^2 \qquad\qquad\qquad$ ...(6.71)

$\quad D_p = \bar{X}_{iP}^1 - \bar{X}_{iP}^2$

Let the matrix s_{ij} be the sum of squares and cross products of P variables from thir respective arithmetic means be denoted as

$$S_{ij} = \sum_{i=1}^{N} \left(X_{ij} - \bar{X}_j \right)^2 \quad \text{for} \quad j = 1 \text{ to } P \text{ variables}$$

$\qquad\qquad\qquad\qquad\qquad i = 1$ to N observations

$\qquad\qquad\qquad\qquad\qquad$ ...(6.72)

$$\sum_{i=1}^{N} S_{ij} = \text{The sum of square of } j^{\text{th}} \text{ variable if } i = j$$

$$\sum_{i=1}^{N} S_{ij} = \text{The sum of cross products of } j^{\text{th}} \text{ variable}$$

$$\text{if } \quad i \neq j$$

In expanded matrix from the same is denoted as:

$$S = \begin{bmatrix} S_{11} & S_{11} & \dots & S_{1p} \\ S_{21} & S_{22} & \dots & S_{2p} \\ \vdots & \vdots & & \vdots \\ S_{p1} & S_{p2} & \dots & S_{pp} \end{bmatrix} j \times j \qquad \dots (6.73)$$

Let the estimated discriminant function be represented as

$$\hat{Z} = K_1 X_1 + K_2 X_2 \dots + K_p X_p. \qquad \dots(6.74)$$

The required system of equations to solve the unknown parameters $K_1, K_2 \dots K_p$ (discriminant coefficients) are represented as:

$$\begin{bmatrix} K_1 S_{11} + K_2 S_{12} + \dots + K_p S_{1p} \\ K_1 S_{21} + K_2 S_{22} + \dots + K_p S_{2p} \\ \vdots \qquad \vdots \qquad \vdots \\ K_1 S_{p1} + K_2 S_{p2} + \dots + K_p S_{pp} \end{bmatrix} \begin{matrix} = |D_1| \\ = |D_2| \\ \\ = |Dp| \end{matrix}$$

$$\begin{matrix} S & K & \dots & D \\ j \times j & p \times 1 & & \end{matrix} \qquad \dots(6.75)$$

$$K = S^{-1}.D \qquad \dots(6.76)$$

The inverse matrix, S^{-1} is multiplied by D vector to get the discriminant function coefficients vector, $K(K_1, K_2 \dots K_p)$. Substitute the values of K and X_{ij} in equation (6.74) to get the estimated Z value for each observations in the two groups. Based on the value of K, we can judge which variable j is important in discriminating between the two groups.

R^2 is calculated from the formula:

$$R^2 = \frac{N_1 N_2 (K_1 D_1 + K_2 D_2 + \dots + K_p D_p)}{N} \qquad \dots(6.77)$$

R^2 is a measure of goodness of fit of discriminant function to the data.

For testing the significance of the discriminant function, F statistic (variance ratio) is calculated as:

$$F = \frac{R^2 (N - P - 1)}{(1 - R)^2 P} \quad\quad ...(6.78)$$

If the calculated F value is greater than table F value at P and $(N\text{-}P\text{-}1)$ d.f., the discriminant function is said to be significant, otherwise it is non-significant.

. In order to find out the contribution of each factor to total discrimination, the following steps are necessary.

(1) Compute Mahalanobis D^2 value using the formula given in the eqution (6.78A).

$$D^2 = K_1 D_1 + K_2 D_2 + K_3 D_3 \quad\quad ...(6.78A)$$

Where, K = Discriminant coefficient

D = Difference in the means of variables between borrowers and non-borrowers

(2) Contribution of X_1 variable (gross income) is worked out by multplying $D_1 K_1$ by 100 and dividing by D^2 value. The contribution of gross income in our example problem is 83.53% (see Table 6.7). Similar procedure is adopted to work out the percentage contribution of X_2 and X_3 variables.

(3) To know the significant level of D^2 value, F value is calculated using the formula:

$$F = \frac{N_1 N_2 (N_1 + N_2 - P - 1)}{P (N_1 + N_2)(N_1 + N_2 - 2)} \cdot D^2 \quad\quad ...(6.79)$$

$$= 0.16$$

F value follows the d.f. P and $(N_1 + N_2 - P - 1)$

If calculated F value is greater than table F value, then D^2 is said to be significant, otherwise it is non-significant.

Criteria for Inclusion of jth Variable in the Discriminant Function

The following steps are necessary in order to identify relevant variables to be included in the discriminant function.

(1) Work out D_j for each jth variable to be included in the function from the equation (6.80).

TABLE 6.6

Illustration of Discriminant Function

S1. No.	Gross Income (in Rs'000)	Value of Assets (in (in Rs '0000)	working capital (in Rs '000)	Z
		Borrowers		
1	62	60	132	0.2092
2	96	48	15	0.1722
3	92	36	18	0.1708
4	94	62	21	0.1702
5	73	48	16	0.1319
6	75	56	17	0.1343
7	46	50	22	0.0883
8	140	48	23	0.2579
9	78	62	12	0.1338
10	99	33	18	0.1841
11	86	45	16	0.1560
12	68	60	15	0.1190
13	39	32	11	0.0710
Mean	80.62	49.23	25.85	$\overline{Z}^2 = 0.155431$
		Non-borrowers		
1	66	45	6	0.1116
2	61	42	13	0.1094
3	50	54	12	0.0858
4	39	54	14	0.0678
5	42	50	15	0.0751
6	31	46	17	0.0582
7	30	46	6	0.0469
8	22	49	9	0.0344
9	66	50	5	0.1094
10	50	52	11	0.0854
11	43	46	8	0.0719
12	42	47	10	0.0716
13	26	30	8	0.0456
14	47	49	10	0.0799
	$\overline{X}_1^1 = 43.93$	$\overline{X}_2^1 = 47.14$	$\overline{X}_3^1 = 10.29$	$\overline{Z}^1 = 0.076829$
	$\overline{\overline{X}}_1 = 61.59$	$\overline{\overline{X}}_2 = 48.15$	$\overline{\overline{X}}_3 = 17.78$	$\overline{\overline{Z}} = 0.1146625$
d_j	36.69	2.09	15.56	0.0444549

TABLE 6.7

Contribution of Variables to Total Discimination between Borrowers and Non-borrowers

Name of variable	D_j vector	Discriminant coefficients (K)	$D_j.K$	Contribution of factors (in %)
Gross income (X_1)	36.69	0.001789	0.065653	83.53
Value of assets (X_2)	2.09	− 0.000226	− 0.00047234	− 0.60
Working capital (X_3)	15.56	0.0008625	0.0134205	17.07
			$D^2 = 0.0786601$	100.00

$$D_j = \frac{\overline{X}_j^1 - \overline{X}_j^2}{\sqrt{MSW_j}} \qquad \qquad ...(6.80)$$

Where,

$\overline{X}_j^1$ = The mean of the jth variable in the first-group

$\overline{X}_j^2$ = The mean of the jth variable in second-group

$$MSW_j = \frac{\sum_{K=1}^{2} (N^k - 1).S_j^{2k}}{N_1 + N_2 - 2} \qquad \qquad ...(6.81)$$

Where,

N^k = Total no. of observations of jth variable in K^{th} group

S_j^{2k} = Variance of jth variable in K^{th} group,

MSW_j = Mean squae statistic of jth variable, and

k = Two groups (first and second groups),

When k = 1, it refers to first group,

When k = 2, it refers to second group.

Criterion for Selection of Variables

The included j^{th} variable in discriminant function should have the largest absolute D value. When the question of including a particular set of variables arises say, four out of six variables, then the decision should be based on the magnitude of absolute value of D in descending order.

The particular j^{th} variable in the discriminant function is assigned highest importance in the discrimination of two groups based on the magnitude of K value ($K = K_1, K_2 ... K_p$ which are called discriminant coefficients). For the example problem, variable X_1 has highest discriminating power followed by variable X_3. The negative coefficient indicates the zero discriminating power.

GROWTH MODELS

Linear Growth Rates

Linear growth rate is estimated from the linear trend equation.

$$Y_t = a + bt \qquad \qquad ....(6.82)$$

Let us denote the time rate of change of Y variable, i.e., agricultural credit advanced by institutional agencies by

$$\dot{Y} = \frac{dy}{dt} = b$$

'b' gives us unit increase in Y per year, if 't' is considered in discrete years.

The per cent rate of growth (r) is given by

$$r = \frac{\dot{Y}}{Y} = \frac{dy}{dt}$$

The linear trend equation gives us an absolute increase per unit time. The per cent rate of growth (r) is obtained when 'b' obtained from equation (6.82) is divided by harmonic mean, H_Y of Y. In other words:

$$r = b.\frac{1}{H_Y}$$

Where,

$$\frac{1}{H_Y} = \frac{1}{t} \sum_{t=1}^{t} \frac{1}{Y_t}$$

Compound Growth Rates

The compound growth rate of any time series variable, Y is worked out from the well known compound interest rate formula which is represented as:

$$Y_t = Y_o (1 + r')^t \qquad \qquad ...(6.83)$$

Where,

Y_o and Y_t are the values of the time-series variable, Y in the initial and t^{th} year respectively and r' is the compound growth rate of the time-series variable in percentage. This percentage represents increased percentage over that of the previous year (Y_0) Putting $B = 1 + r$, equation (6.83) is written as:

$$Y_t = Y_o \, \beta^t \qquad \qquad ...(6.84)$$

Taking logarithms of the equation (6.84) to base 10 gives

$$\text{Log } Y_t = \log Y_0 + \left[\log (1 + r')\right] t \qquad \qquad ....(6.85)$$

$$= \log Y_0 + t \log \beta \qquad \qquad ...(6.86)$$

In the equation (6.85) and (6.86), t represents data in discrete years $(t = 1, 2, 3...n)$ and r' denotes a constant rate of growth in time series variable, Y per year. The equation (6.86) with constant growth rate in exponential form is represented as:

$$Y_t = e^{(\alpha + \beta t)} \qquad \qquad ...(6.87)$$

$$\ln Y_t = \alpha + \beta t \qquad \qquad ...(6.88)$$

$$Y_t = Y_0 e^{\beta t} \qquad \qquad ...(6.89)$$

Equation (6.88) is used to estimate the compound growth rate of time series variable Y_t.

Taking the logarithm of equation (6.89) to the base 10 gives:

$$\log Y = (\beta \log e)\, t + \log Y_0 \qquad \qquad ...(6.90)$$

Comparing equations (6.85) and (6.90) we can show that

$$(\beta \ \log e)t \ = \ \log \ [(1 + r')]\, t \qquad \qquad ...(6.91)$$
$$= \ \beta \log e = \log (1 + r')$$
$$\beta = \ \ln (1 + r') \qquad \qquad ...(6.92)$$

In terms of annual compound growth rate,

$$r' = (e^{\beta} - 1) \times 100 \qquad \qquad ...(6.93)$$

Where,

$$\beta = \text{Continuous compounding}$$

We generally first use equation (6.88) and then find out β and from β, we work out annual compound growth rate which is constant over time from the equation (6.93).

REFERENCES

1. Dennis J., Aigner, *Basic Econometrics*, Prentice-Hall, Inc., Englewood Chiffs, New Jersey, 1971.
2. Johnston, J. *Statistical Cost Analysis*, McGraw-Hill Company, 1960.
3. Johnston, J., *Econometric Methods*, McGraw-Hill, International Editions, 1984.
4. Julia Hebden, *Applications of Econometrics*. Heritage Publishers, New Delhi, 1988.
5. Lawrence R. Klein, *A Text Book of Econometrics*. Prentice-Hall of India, New Delhi, 1975.
6. Maddala, G.S., *Econometrics*. McGraw-Hill Kogakusha Ltd., Tokyo, 1977.
7. Heady, E.O. and J.L. Dillon, *Agricultural Production Functions*, Kalyani Publishers, New Delhi, 1960.

CHAPTER 7

APPLICATION OF OPERATIONS RESEARCH METHODS TO FINANCIAL MANAGEMENT

Of late, allocative and decision problems of agriculture are being given crucial importance in the literature and research related to agricultural economics. To such problems operations research methods are the apt devices for taking up appropriate actions. For instance, the decision problems like what to produce, how much to produce, in what combinations and with what financial activities involved in profit maximisation of the business farms, are solved in the quantitative sense through operations research methods. Operations research methods are used for the attainment of set goals, ends or objectives under a given set of resource endowment base represented by technology, prices and resource restrictions. Operations research methods provide numercial solutions for the decision variables, and hence, they have very high potential use in scientific planning and budgeting. Many operations research techniques facilitate analyses of different farm goals, i.e., from optimisation of farm income to the specific optimisation of local problems. For example, dynamic programming is best suited to find out the optimal solution over a period of time, with two or more years interlinked in the investment activity. A simple linear programming model is applied to find out optimal solutions for a single year or a point of time with specific objectives of profit maximisation or cost minimisation. With respect to time, the solution is only local optimum which means optimal plan is drawn for a particular period of time, say kharif or rabi season in an year. Waiting line models or queueing models provide answers for questions that may arise with regard to number of repairs, milching problems in livestock, loading and unloading problems in marketing, etc.

LINEAR PROGRAMMING (LP)

In linear programming methods, the objective of the typical farm*

---

* The farm that occurs most frequently in the sample.

i.e., maximisation of net profit, or cost minimisation is achieved through optimal plan generated from its solution. Hence, it is the method of determining the best or optimal plan of the given farm under the given linear constraints. The objective function specified, i.e., profit maximisation or cost minimisation, is linear in form and constraints or resource restrictions also specified in linear form. In non-linear programming, objective function is specified in non-linear form, i.e., power form. LP has been used in agriculture since 1950s. It provides solutions to whole farm planning problems. In this context the works of Heady and Love (1952), Heady and Candler (1958), Samuel (1961), Steven (1961), etc., are worth citing. The LP model provides prudent solutions, particularly to problems of farm financial management at micro level, such as how much capital to be allocated for what enterprise. Its application at macro level for solving the problems of marketing and spatial allocation are also remarkable. Transportation models are indeed the simple form of LP models in agriculture. As a normative tool,* it always aims at combining the efficient enterprises giving weightage to constraints and profit maximisation.

COMPONENTS OF LP PROBLEM

There are three quantitative components in LP model. They are: (1) an objective function; (2) resource requirements; and (3) resource availability.

Algebraically it is stated in compact form as:

Maximize $\Pi = C'X$;

subject to   ... (7.1)

$\quad AX \gtrless B, X \geq 0$

$\quad$ where,

$\quad A$ is an $m \times n$ matrix of technical coefficients

$\quad C$ is an $n \times 1$ vector of prices or other weights for the objective function

$\quad X$ is an $n \times 1$ vector of activities (crops and livestock to be produced which are unknown decision variables)

$\quad B$ is an $m \times 1$ vector of resources or other constraints, availabilities in physical units, such as labour, credit, land etc., and

$\quad C'X = \Pi$, the objective function.

$\quad$ In expanded form it is written as:

$\quad$ Maximize $\pi = c_1 x_1 + c_2 x_2 + \quad\quad \cdots \quad + c_n x_n$ ...(7.2)

---

* This tool indicates 'what should be'.

Subject to $a_{11} x_1 + a_{12} x_2 + \quad\quad \dots \quad + \quad a_{1n} x_n \leq b_1$

$$a_{21} x_1 + a_{22} x_2 + \quad\quad \dots \quad + \quad a_{2n} x_n \leq b_2$$

$$a_{m1} x_1 + a_{m2} x_2 + \quad\quad \dots \quad + \quad a_{mn} x_n \leq b_m$$

and x_j (columns 1 to n) all should be specified in positive values starting from zero or any positive value $(X_j \geq 0)$ $a_{ij} = i^{th}$ resource required to produce one unit of jth crop or livestock activity. With Σ notation it is written as:

Maximize $\pi = \sum\limits_{j=1}^{n} C'_j \, X_j$ ... (7.3)

subject to

$$\sum\limits_{J=1}^{n} a_{ij} X_j \leq B_i$$

$$X_j \geq 0$$

$B_i = i^{th}$ resource available with farm for use in the production of crops and livestock.

i ranging from 1 to m denoting the number of rows (constraints) in the problem.

j ranging from 1 to n indicating number of columns (crop and livestock activities) in the problem.

ASSUMPTIONS OF LP PROBLEM

There are seven basic assumptions, viz., (1) additivity of the resources and activities, (2) linearity of the objective function, (3) non-negativity of the decision variables, (4) divisibility of the activities as well as resources, (5) finiteness of the activities and resource restrictions, (6) proportionality of activities to resources, and (7) single value expectation.

(1) Additivity of the Resources and Activities: This assumption implies that the total sum of the used resources must be equal to the total quantity of resources used by each activity for all resources individually and collectively. If the resource is used up fully, it should equal the sum of the same resources used by all the activities appearing in the optimal solution. This condition holds good for all the resources specified in the model.

(2) Linearity of the Objective Function: All the decision variables in the objective function, i.e., crop and livestock activities are in

linear form (without power form) and the objective function is specified for example, as $\pi = 250\,X_1 + 350\,X_2 + 500\,X_3 + \ldots + 400\,X_n$. The coefficients of X_1 are the net returns/prices of the crops and livestock. The non-linear objective function is specified with decision variables with power form such as $X_1{}^2, X_2{}^2, X_3{}^3$ etc. For such type of non-linear programming problem, a separate algorithm is to be used such as quadratic programming, separable programming, etc. LP problems should be specified invariably in linear form both in objective function and constraints.

(3) Non-Negativity of the Decision Variables: All the crops and livestock activities should have positive value in their magnitude. Negative value for such decision variables cannot make any sense. Hence, this assumption is imperative.

(4) Divisibility of the Activities as well as Resources: Continuity of resources and output is implied in this assumption. This means fractional quantities such as 0.2 ha of land and 3.5 qtl of paddy, etc. are allowed. But divisibility for livestock activities and labour resources appears to be unrealistic. To get integer values for such livestock activities an integer programming is being used.

(5) Finiteness of the Activities and Resource Restrictions: With the advent of computers and availability of flexible programmes, a large number of activities and constraints are now being specified in the model. But, there should be a limit for such number, because infinite number of activities and resource restrictions cannot be accommodated in the model. Hence, this assumption is important in the LP model. In general, it is desirable to have more number of activities than the constraints in LP model.

(6) Proportionality of Activities to Resources: According to this assumption, linear relationship is held between activities and resources. This means resource requirement to produce one unit of crop or livestock activity varies directly with the level of output of crops and livestock.

(7) Single Value Expectation: This assumption connotes certainty assumption and imparts to the LP model, the name of deterministic model. According to this assumption, input-output coefficients (a_{ij}), resource availabilities (B_i) and prices of activities (C_j) are all specified correctly with the known quantities in the model and they all relate to a particular period of time. In the risk programming models this assumption is relaxed.

BASIC CONCEPTS IN LP

(1) *Activity or Process*

The word activity is used to refer to crop and livestock enterprises being undertaken. A typical method of production with specific resource requirements in crops and livestock is referred to as a process or activity. Based on this concept, crops or livestock activities are delineated into separate or individual activities in the model, for example, local paddy crop requiring different levels of inputs for obtaining various output levels are treated as separate activities. Similarly, if two cows of the same breed are reared on different rations, they can be taken as separate activities in the model. The crop activities of the model are based on the varietal response, resistance to pests and diseases, drought resistance, etc. A process concept is based on input-output coefficient, to put it in another way, a process is a method of converting a resource into a product with specified input-output relationship. This is also often referred to as technical coefficient. In the literature we find these two terms being used synonymously.

Types of Activities: These are: (i) real activities, (ii) intermediate activities; (iii) disposal activities; and (iv) artificial activities.

Real Activities include both purchasing and producing activities. Purchasing activities mean the inputs like fertilizers and pesticides which are purchased from the market and used in the production process. Paddy, sugarcane, poultry eggs, milch cattle, etc., are real activities because they are produced on the farm for sale in the market. Fodder, though produced on the farm and if not sold in the market, it cannot become real activity, so it is intermediate activity. Disposal activities are included in the model in solving the problems to allow non-use of resources. Their magnitude indicates the amount of unused resource. Artificial activities also facilitate the obtaining of solutions of the LP model.

(2) *Decision Variables*

These are also called real activities which are specified in the objective function of the LP problem. Their magnitude in the optimal solution affect the decisions of the manager, and are hence called decision variables. Suppose the optimal solution obtained from the LP problem is quite different from the actual practice of the typical farm, particularly in respect of crop areas and livestock number, then the decisions of manager are to be altered according to the solution in order to get the maximum profit.

In addition to the production activities, activities such as buying and/or selling inputs and products are also considered in the objective · function of the model. Production activities such as crop and livestock activities can be divided into numerous activities based on the information available from research and experiences of efficient farmers in a given locality. Crop activities can be defined in terms of unit products (quintal basis) or unit area (hectare basis). Similarly, livestock activities can be defined in terms of heads of cattle or their products per unit of cattle.

(3) *Product Prices and Input Prices:* Prices for products are to be ascertained with certainty. Too high or too low prices for products will distort the income estimates or net prices, often leading to results of unrealistic magnitude. In general, the average prices, pooled over three to five years are considered for LP model.

(4) *Restraints:* These are also called limitations, constraints, etc. Land, labour and capital are generally considered as restraints. In the development of models for obtaining realistic results, sometimes 150 to 200 restraints are also considered by researchers in economic studies. In general, macro level studies will have more constraints than micro level studies, because of the complexities involved in macro level situations. At micro level the farmers may have restrictions regarding number of livestock animals, crop acreages, etc. Amount of labour availability during peak seasons of the crop growth is generally considered as the most common restriction seen in the LP model. Likewise, a farmer may have access to limited quantities of many resources. If any resource is unlimited, then there is no need for such resource to be considered as a constraint. The availability, and requirements in respect of machine labour, bullock labour, hired human labour, family labour, skilled labour, unskilled labour, etc., in different time periods, i.e., a week, a month, a season and a year may be considered in the programming model as separate restrictions or constraints. All these restrictions can be specified in the model in three types, i.e., greater than equal to constraints ($\geq$) or less than equal to constraints ($\leq$) or equal to or equality constraints (=). The equality constraints are called balance rows. Management constraints inhibiting the desired size of the farm can be included in LP model at times.

Goals of the Programming Model: Programming model guides the farmer to specify the farm plans which will give him maximum income under the given constraints, prices, yields and resource requirements. LP models with certainty assumption are not applicable under risk and uncertainty problems. Risk programming models are developed as the best devices to provide solutions under such situations. Quadratic Risk Programming (QRP) model, Minimisation of Total Absolute Deviation (MOTAD) model, etc., are the examples here.

Cost minimisation in the cattle feeding problems, poultry feeding problems and transportation models, is considered in the objective function of LP model.

Procedure: In the following sections an attempt is made to provide a better understanding of the format of the LP model and explanation of the computation procedures involved in solving the LP model. Finally, the interpretation of the optimal solution is presented.

Statement of the Problem: Crop production problem to maximise net returns from crop enterprises is shown below subject to the following restraints for a typical farmer in Chittoor district of Andhra Pradesh.

Land   5 acres

Family labour availability in kharif season   180 days

Owned capital (in hundred Rs)   50

Crop activities are: Paddy, groundnut and bajra. Crop activities are defined in units of 1 acre. Net prices are the net returns after subtracting the variable costs from gross income. These are the X_j values in the objective function.

Net prices for the given problem are

Paddy (HYV) (in hundreds)   Rs 30
Paddy (improved) (in hundreds)   Rs 28
Groundnut (in hundreds)   Rs 26

Resource requirements are specified in terms of crop unit areas, i.e., per acre basis for land, labour and capital resources. These are specified in the matrix format of the LP problem as a_{ij} coefficients, i.e., i^{th} resource per one acre of jth crop. The net prices are given in the objective function of the problem, i.e., c_j values are given in the bottom row of the matrix Tabel (7.1).

TABLE 7.1

Crop Production Problem Arranged in Matrix Format (Initial Table)

Net price	Restriction	Restriction level (b)	Production Activities			Disposal activities		
			Paddy (1 ac)	Paddy (1 ac)	G.nut (1 ac)	Land	Labour	Capital
0	Land	5	1	1	1	1	0	0
0	Labour	180	90	80	70	0	1	0
0	Capital	50	20	18	25	0	0	1
	Net price	(C)	30	28	26	0	0	0
	Opportunity cost	(Z)	0	0	0	0	0	0
	Z–C (Shadow price or net evaluation row)		–30	–28	–26	0	0	0

Algebraic formulation

The crop production problem is stated algebraically as follows.
Let,

X_1 = units of paddy (HYV) cultivated in acres.
X_2 = units of paddy (improved) cultivated in acres.
X_3 = units of groundunt cultivated in acres.

These are the unknowns in the initial table of the LP problem.

SIMPLEX METHOD

It is an algorithm adopted to solve LP problem which allows us to choose an initial basic feasible solution with all the real activities at zero level, and disposal activities at the largest positive level to arrive at the optimal solution through iterations.

Steps Involved in Solving the LP Problem

The LP problem is algebraically stated as

Maximise π =	$30x_1 + 28x_2 + 26\ x_3$	...(7.4)
Subject to	$1x_1 + 1x_2 + 1x_3 \le 5$	...(7.5)
	$90x_1 + 80x_2 + 70\ x_3 \le 180$	...(7.6)
	$20x_1 + 18\ x_2 + 25\ x_3 \le 50$	...(7.7)
	$x_1 \ge 0,\ \ x_2 \ge 0$ and $x_3 \ge 0$	...(7.8)

Step 1: All the three inequality constraints should first be reduced to equality constraints by introducing disposal activities in order to facilitate non-use of resources. In adding disposal activities, we must consider a number of resource constraints in the problem. If there are 'm' constraints to the given problem, then 'm' number of disposal activities should be added. In our example, there is need to add three disposal activities and they are x_4 = land disposal activity, x_5 = labour disposal activity and x_6 = capital disposal activity. According to this, the given problem of the equation (7.4) is restated as shown in the equation (7.9A) through (7.9D)

Maximise $\pi = 30\ x_1 + 28\ x_2 + 26\ x_3 + 0\ x_4 + 0\ x_5 + 0\ x_6$ ...(7.9A)
  Subject to

$1\ x_1 + 1\ x_2 + 1\ x_3 + 1\ x_4 + 0\ x_5 + 0\ x_6 = 5$	...(7.9B)
$90\ x_1 + 80\ x_2 + 70\ x_3 + 0\ x_4 + 1\ x_5 + 0\ x_6 = 180$	...(7.9C)
$20\ x_1 + 18\ x_2 + 25\ x_3 + 0\ x_4 + 0\ x_5 + 1\ x_6 = 50$	...(7.9D)

$x_1 \ge 0,\ x_2 \ge 0,\ x_3 \ge 0,\ x_4 \ge 0,\ x_5 \ge 0$ and $x_6 \ge 0$

Equation (7.9B) states that land requirement of the plan including the land disposal activity (x_4) must equal to 5 acres of land (i.e., the available land for allocation to different crops).

Equation (7.9C) reveals that labour requirement for three crops in the plan including labour disposal activity (x_5) must equal to 180 labour days which is labour availability for allocating to different crops. Similar implication holds good for equation (7.9D).

Profit level specified in equation (7.9A) assumes zero profit and non-use of resources. This problem is modified in the matrix form in the following manner.

Maximise $\pi = \begin{bmatrix} 30 & 28 & 26 & 0 & 0 & 0 \end{bmatrix} \begin{bmatrix} x_1 \\ x_2 \\ x_3 \\ x_4 \\ x_5 \\ x_6 \end{bmatrix}$

Subject to

$$\underset{A}{\begin{bmatrix} 1 & 1 & 1 & 1 & 0 & 0 \\ 90 & 80 & 70 & 0 & 1 & 0 \\ 20 & 18 & 25 & 0 & 0 & 1 \end{bmatrix}} \underset{Im}{\begin{bmatrix} x_1 \\ x_2 \\ x_3 \\ x_4 \\ x_5 \\ x_6 \end{bmatrix}} = \begin{bmatrix} 5 \\ 180 \\ 50 \end{bmatrix}$$

$$\begin{bmatrix} x_1 \\ x_2 \\ x_3 \\ x_4 \\ x_5 \\ x_6 \end{bmatrix} \geq 0 \qquad\qquad ...(7.10)$$

Step 2: Here we will have to define the initial feasible solution. A feasible solution is one that satisfies all the constraints including non-negativity constraints. In such a solution all real activities (x_1, x_2, x_3) are at zero level. Such a solution is called an initial basic feasible solution.

Hence, $\pi = 0$
$X_4 = 5$
$X_5 = 180$
$X_6 = 50$

General structure of the initial table of the simplex method is shown in Section 1 of the Table 7.2. This table contains 10 columns. First column contains net price, second column name of the restrictions, third column restriction level, fourth, fifth and sixth columns production activities, seventh, eighth and ninth columns disposal activities and finally the tenth column contains ratios. The 'C' row (Net price) shows the net profits for each activity unit. The 'Z' row (opportunity cost row) shows for each activity the value of other activity which must be sacrificed to produce one more unit of output. All values in 'Z' row are zero because all resources are unused in the I Section.

Step 3: In this step, we should attempt to increase the profits from the initial basic feasible plan. Here we begin a routine substituting of real activities (x_1, x_2 and x_3) for disposal activities (x_4, x_5 and x_6) in the plan. This procedure leads quickly to optimal plan.

Procedure for Computation of Iterations

(1) The column with the larger Z–C value in the shadow price row is the outgoing column from Section I and it is the incoming row in Section II.

(2) To compute the ratio column, i.e., column 10 in Section I, divide resource available quantities in the B column (column 3) of the I Section by the coefficients in the outgoing column (4th). To determine the level at which the new activity, i.e., incoming row the smallest positive value in the ratio column should be considered and this key row is encircled similar to outgoing column. The smallest coefficient in the ratio column indicates the level to which the incoming activity (Paddy I) could be increased in Section II.

(3) The row with the smallest ratio value in Section I is the outgoing row. This is called key row. In selecting the smallest ratio value, we should ignore the negative value.

(4) This step is concerned with the computation of rows for Section II. Identification of key number in the outgoing column and row is the first step here. Key number or pivot element lies at the intersection of the outgoing column and outgoing row. It is 90 in our problem and is designated with asterisk mark, and

(5) Compute the incoming row in Section II by dividing the entries in each column of the key row of Section I by key number, 90. This entire row thus obtained in Section II is now designated as transformed key row.

TABLE 7.2
Simplex Table

Net price (I)	Name of the restriction (II)	Resource level (B) (III)	PRODUCTION I REAL ACTIVITIES			DISPOSAL ACTIVITIES			Ratio (X)
			Paddy I (X_1) (IV)	Paddy II (X_2) (V)	Groundnut (X_3) (VI)	Land (X_4) (VII)	Labour (X_5) (VIII)	Capital (X_6) (IX)	
SECTION I									
0	Land (X_4) (acres)	5	1	1	1	1	0	0	5/1 = 5
0	Labour (X_5) (days)	180	90*	80	70	0	1	0	180/90 = 2
0	Capital (X_6) (in '00 Rs)	50	20	18	25	0	0	1	50/20 = 2.5
	Net price (C)		30	28	26	0	0	0	
	Opportunity cost (Z)		0	0	0	0	0	0	
	Shadow Price (Z–C)		–30	–28	–26	0	0	0	
SECTION II									
0	Land (X_4)	3	0	1/9	2/9	1	–1/90	0	$13\frac{1}{2}$
30	Paddy (X_1)	2	1	8/9	7/9	0	1/90	0	$2\frac{4}{7}$
0	Capital (X_6)	10	0	2/9	85/9*	0	–2/9	1	$1\frac{1}{17}$
	Net price (C)		30	28	26	0	0	0	
	Opportunity cost (Z)		30	80/3	70/3	0	1/3	0	
	Shadow Price (Z–C)		0	–4/3	–8/3	0	1/3	0	

SECTION III

c									
0	Land	$2\frac{13}{17}$	0	$\frac{9}{85}$	0	1	$-\frac{1}{170}$	$-\frac{2}{85}$	$26\frac{1}{9}$
30	Paddy I	$1\frac{3}{17}$	1	$\frac{74}{85}$*	0	0	$\frac{1}{34}$	$-\frac{7}{85}$	$1\frac{13}{17}$
26	Groundnut	$1\frac{1}{17}$	0	$\frac{2}{85}$	1	0	$-\frac{2}{85}$	$\frac{9}{85}$	45
	Net price (C)		30	28	26	0	0	0	
	Opportunity Cost (Z)		30	$26\frac{62}{85}$	26	0	$\frac{23}{85}$	$\frac{24}{85}$	
	Shadow price ($Z-C$)		0	$-1\frac{23}{85}$	0	0	$\frac{23}{85}$	$\frac{24}{85}$	

SECTION IV

c								
0	Land (X_4)	$2\frac{23}{37}$	$-\frac{9}{74}$	0	0	1	-0.00946	0
28	Paddy II (X_2)	$1\frac{13}{37}$	$\frac{85}{74}$	1	0	0	$\frac{5}{148}$	0
26	Groundnut (X_3)	$1\frac{1}{37}$	$-\frac{1}{37}$	0	1	0	-0.0243	$\frac{9}{85}$
	Net price (C)		30	28	26	0	0	0
	Opportunity cost (Z)	$64\frac{20}{37}$	$31\frac{17}{37}$	28	26	0	0.3141	$2\frac{64}{85}$
	Shadow price ($Z-C$)	$64\frac{20}{37}$	$1\frac{17}{37}$	0	0	0	0.3141	$2\frac{64}{85}$

*Key number or Pivot number

Computation of Other Rows in Section II

To compute any new row in this section or of the subsequent sections, the following formula is to be followed:

$$N = 0 - (I \times P) \qquad \qquad ...(7.11)$$

Where,

N = Co-efficients for new row of the new Section (succeeding section)

O = Co-efficients in the corresponding row of old Section (preceding section)

I = Co-efficients of the transformed key row in the new Section, and

P = Co-efficients of the intersection of outgoing column and outgoing row in old Section.

For the example problem all the rows of Section II are computed using the equation (7.11).

Computation of 'Z' Row for Section II

The co-efficients in column I are multiplied by the corresponding coefficients in column IV to get the co-efficients in the 'Z' row (30) under column IV.

$0 \times 0 + 30 \times 1 + 0 \times 0 = 30$

Similarly, the other coefficients of the 'Z' row are obtained using the above procedure. Highest negative coefficient in the $Z–C$ row (shadow price row) is identified and its corresponding column is designated as outgoing column. The smallest positive coefficient in the ratio column helps to identify key row and key number. Outgoing column and key row are encircled and key number is star marked.

Following the same procedure adopted for computation of rows in Section II, the rows of Section III and Section IV are computed.

Criterion for Stopping Computation of Sections

To arrive at the optimal solution all coefficients in $Z–C$ row should change to positive values. This is an indication that we should stop at that section without further iterating the procedure. The values in the B column of the last section (in our example IV section) show the normative acreages under different crops. In our example, out of 5 acres of available land, 1.35 acres should be allotted to paddy (improved) and 1.03 acres to groundnut crop and remaining 2.62 acres should be kept fallow. The maximum net income derived from such plan would be Rs 6,454.

The foregone model which we have formulated is much too limited in the restraints like capital and labour. As a result, the available land is not fully utilised and fallow to an extent of 2.62 acres is observed. Even with a limited number of enterprise activities and resource constraints, the requisite computations are substantial. If all the realistic constraints and the activities are introduced in the model, computation further becomes cumbersome and complicated. A realistic application of the farm planning, model with 30 to 40 cropping and livestock activities and 20 to 30 resource constraints definitely require computer facilities for solving the problem.

DUAL SOLUTION

The maximisation problem, i.e., maximisation of net income from crop and livestock enterprises given the resource requirements (a_{ij} coefficients) and resource levels (b_i values) is generally called primal problem. A very different approach is also possible to obtain the same solution as from the primal problem. This approach is called dual solution. It emphasises the relationship between price of the products (production activities) and marginal value products (MVPs) of the resources.*

This sum of the marginal value products of resources used to produce crop or livestock product must equal the price of the crop and live stock products. A marginal value product of any particular resource > 0, implies that the resource is in short supply relative to its demand. Hence, further use of that resource is having potentiality in the production of a particular product. If MVP of a resource = 0, this means the resource is in excess supply. Hence, its further use is not recommended for production of crops and livestock, in question. The manager can divert that particular resource to other uses.

Steps in the construction of dual problem:

Primal Problem	Dual Problem
Maximise $\pi = 30x_1 + 28x_2 + 26x_3$	Minimise cost (C)
subject to	$= 5y_1 + 180y_2 + 50y_3$
$1x_1 + 1x_2 + 1x_3 \leq 5$	subject to
$90x_1 + 80x_2 + 70x_3 \leq 180$	$1y_1 + 90y_2 + 20y_3 \geq 30$
$20x_1 + 18x_2 + 25\ x_3 \leq 50$	$1y_2 + 80y_2 + 18y_3 \geq 28$
and	$1y_1 + 70y_2 + 25y_3 \geq 26$ and
$x_1 \geq 0,\ x_2 \geq 0$ and $x_3 \geq 0$	$y_1,\ y_2$ and $y_3 \geq 0$

*MVPs are seen in the optimal section IV in our example in the Z–C rows under the columns of disposal activities in Table 7.2.

TABLE 7.3
Dual Formulation for the Example Problem

Activity	B (Net price)	Resources			Disposals			Artificials		
		Land	Labour	Capital	Paddy I	Paddy II	Groundnut	Paddy I	Paddy II	Groundnut
Paddy I	30	1	90	20	-1	0	0	1	0	0
Paddy II	28	1	80	18	0	-1	0	0	1	0
Groundnut	26	1	70	25	0	0	-1	0	0	1
C (resources)	—	5	180	50	0	0	0	M	M	M
Z (opportunity cost)	—	0	0	0	0	0	0	0	0	0
Z–C (shadow price)	—	-5	-180	-50	0	0	0	-M	-M	-M

Here we compare the dual model with the primal model.

(1) B_i column entries (resource levels) are entered as objective function coefficients. These are the prices of the crops in the dual problem, but not the resource quantities as in the primal problem.

(2) The resources used in the production are the activities

(3) a_{ij} coefficients in the primal problem are now transposed (rows becomes columns) in the dual problem.

(4) Less than inequalities in the primal problems are converted into greater than inequalities in dual problem.

(5) Crop activities, i.e., x_1, x_2 and x_3 in primal solutions are now designated as y_1, y_2 and y_3 resource activities in dual problem. The objective function in the primal problem is maximisation of net income from the combination of crop activities. In the dual problem the objective is to minimise the total values of resources, used in the production. Dual problem can be solved with the same simplex routine, by adding additional artificial activities equal to the number of the disposal activities. In the objective function of the dual problem, the largest penality cost $(+M)$ is indicated for each artificial activity.

In solving dual problem as specified in Table 7.3 first proceed by selecting the highest positive Z–C value (as against highest negative Z–C value in primal) as the outgoing column and incoming row in the subsequent section. With regard to ratio column, the same positive minimum values for selecting the key row are to be considered similar to primal problem. The procedure for computation of transformed key rows and other rows in the subsequent sections is the same. But, the iteration should be stopped at the section when all the values in Z–C row turn into negative. That is an indication of obtaining the optimal solution for a dual problem. The marginal value product of primal problem will now appear in optimal solution of dual problem under 'b' column. The optimal solution to the dual problem indicates the imputed value to each resource. The total 'C' value is the total value of the resources used.

The objective function value = $64\dfrac{20}{37}$

= Marginal value product of land x land available + Marginal value product of labour x available labour + marginal value product of capital x available capital

= $0 \times 5 + 0.3141 \times 180 + 0.1619 \times 50$

= $64\dfrac{20}{37}$

Development of the Linear Programming Model

Restraints

Maximum restraints: In the LP maximisation problem, most of the constraints are defined with $\leq$ sign and these are called maximum restraints. These restraints specify that activities included in the model can utilise the given available resources to the extent mentioned. For example, $1\,x_1 + 1\,x_2 + 1\,x_3 \leq 5$, where, x_1, x_2 and x_3 represent activity levels and their unit coefficients indicate the quantity of land required per unit of crop activity. This maximum restraint does not show that all the available (5 acres) land must be utilized. By adding a disposal activity x_4, we get the following equation, i.e., $1x_1 + 1x_2 + 1x_3 + 1x_4 = 5$ (7.12). Here the disposal activity in equation (7.12) has a positive sign. This indicates some quantity of land may go unused in x_4 activity and permits under-use of land.

Minimum restraints: Farmers sometimes require minimum area under crops in order to meet their consumption requirements. This requirement can be introduced in the model with minimum restraint specifications. For the example problem, we can specify the minimum restraint as follows:

$$1x_1 + 1x_2 + 1\,x_3 \geq 1 \qquad\qquad ...(7.13)$$

This means minimum area under paddy crops x_1, x_2 and x_3 should be one acre. Note in the equation (7.13) the $\geq$ symbol is for minimum restraints. To solve such constraints, the disposal activity should be specified with negative sign. This is specified in equation (7.14).

$$1x_1 + 1x_2 + 1x_3 - 1\,x_4 = 1 \qquad\qquad ...(7.14)$$

Such minimum restraints permit overuse of land and x_4 indicates the extent of overuse.

Equality Constraints

Thus far, we have known about the maximum restraints (in the case of minimisation problem) and minimum restraints (in the case of maximisation problem). These equality constraints permit neither, under-utilisation nor over-utilisation of resources. Hence, no disposal activity is attached to the equality constraints in the LP model. Such restraints are useful in specifying balanced rows and crop rotation constraints which will be discussed later.

Here $1\,x_1 + 1\,x_2 + 1\,x_3 = 3 \qquad\qquad ... (7.15)$

The above equation reveals that the area under crops should be exactly equal to 3 acres.

Activities: Three major categories of activities are noticed in the foregone problems. They are real activities, disposal activities and artificial activities. In the maximisation problem, we have real activities and disposal activities. But in the minimisation problem, we have all the three types of activities.

Real Activities: These are divided into the following forms:

(1) Crop-producing/crop-growing activities,
(2) Livestock rearing/raising/feeding activities,
(3) Transferring activities,
(4) Sale activities of crops and livestock products,
(5) Buying/purchasing/borrowing activities of inputs/credit and services,
(6) Harvesting activities, and
(7) Fixed cost activity/activities of family living expenses.

These several forms of activities can sometimes be clubbed into a single activity. For example, growing, harvesting and marketing activities can be clubbed into a single crop activity. But, combining several activities often leads to confusion and complexities in interpretation. The activities can be defined on the basis of unit of crop or livestock. Unit may be a quintal of crop and livestock products or sometimes activities are defined on area basis, say per acre or per ha. The units of activities should be clearly defined before building a model. The choice is left to the researcher to select the unit of activities in the model. It is generally more convenient to define the crop activities on area basis and livestock activities on unit basis, i.e. number of milch cattle.

MINIMISATION PROBLEM

Preparing the feed mixtures and fertiliser mixtures involve least cost problems. Minimising the marketing cost per unit of the product shown is another form of cost minimisation problem. Solutions to such problems save large amounts of scarce capital. It is from this point that minimisation problems in agriculture assume vital importance. The minimisation problem is specified in the matrix notation as:

Minimise $C'X$ ...(7.16)

Subject to $A\,X \geq B$

$X \geq 0$

The same is converted into maximisation problem as

Maximise $C'X$ subject to

$A\,X \leq B, \quad X \geq 0$

In the minimisation problem the objective function coefficients (C_j) indicate the costs per unit of the jth ingredient used in the preparation of feed mixtures (Rs/tonne). A_{ij} matrix in the minimisation problem denotes i^{th} nutrient say proteins, fats, etc., available in one unit of jth ingredient, and B vector reveals the equality of feed mix required by the farm. The required level of different feed mixtures with varying nutrients levels are specified in B vector. The solution of the minimisation problem will provide different levels of nutrients to prepare the required levels of feed mixtures. The value of the objective function is the total cost required (in Rs) to prepare different feed mixtures of known quantities which are specified in the B vector. The skeleton of the minimisation problem is furnished in Table 7.4.

TABLE 7.4

Simplex Method of Cost Minimisation Problem

C_s	Resources or activities	Supply of activity level	Real activities (Ingredients)			Disposal activities			Artificial activities			Ratio column
			X_1	X_2	X_3	X_4	X_5	X_6	q_1	q_2	q_3	
0	A	B	1	2	3	4	5	6	7	8	9	10
Initial Plan												
m	q_1	20	10	15	20	-1	0	0	1	0	0	1
m	q_2	2	2	5	4	0	-1	0	0	1	0	0.5
m	q_3	2	2	3	5*	0	0	-1	0	0	1	0.4
C_j (Net price)		0	80	100	120	0	0	0	+m	+m	+m	
Z (Opportunity cost row)		24m	14m	23m	29m	-m	-m	-m	m	m	m	
$Z-C$ (Shadow price)		24m	-14m 80	-23m 100	-29m 120	-m	-m	-m	0	0	0	

*Key number

To compute the subsequent sections, the same simplex procedure as adapted in the maximisation problem is followed. In the minimisation problem to select the outgoing column and row the highest positive value in $Z-C$ row and the lowest negative value in the ratio column (10th column) should be identified. Further, iterations of the sections should be stopped when all the coeffiecients in $Z-C$ row of the section become either zero or negative.

SENSITIVITY ANALYSIS OR PARAMETRIC PROGRAMMING

The solutions that emanate from LP models will apply to a given farm situation, i.e., with definite input-output coefficients (matrix A) prices of resources (C vector) and resource availabilities (B vector).

But, all these values which are specified in the model are subject to change over time. Resource supplies (coefficients of B vector) may change by 10 to 50 per cent for the given farms over time. Similarly, the C vector coefficients are subject to fluctuations owing to risk and uncertainty components in agriculture. A sudden spurt in technology adaption changes the coefficients of A matrix. At this juncture, it may be of interest to examine how the optimal solutions of Table 7.2 in maximisation problem and Table 7.4 in minimisation problem will change, if the objective function coefficients will change by a certain percentage, say 10 to 50 per cent. A certain percentage in the jth C coefficients (objective function coefficients) is assumed and its impact on the optimal solution is obtained. Similarly, a fixed simultaneous change (10 to 20 per cent) in all the objective function coefficients is assumed and corresponding optimal solution is obtained. This process is termed as sensitivity analysis which is also known as parametric programming. Such analyses aim at determining the effects of changes in matrix A, Vector B and C on the optimal solutions. The following assumptions should be relaxed to the advantage of sensitivity analysis.

(1) The coefficients of A matrix B and C vectors undergo change over time, and

(2) In some cases the assumption of divisibility of resources and activities is not realistic. For example, optimal solutions such as keeping 3.1 cows and 3.2 tractors on the farm are unrealistic and meaningless. To avoid such optimal solutions from LP models an integer programming can be used for providing optimal solutions in whole numbers. Integer programming is a sort of sensitivity analysis because it is done after obtaining optimum solution. If researcher is interested to find out the effects of changes in the C vector in the optimal solution, he has to adopt the procedure of variable price programming. Similarly, variable resource programming is to be opted for determining effects of changes in the coefficients of B vector.

Suppose, a farmer wants to increase the area under a given crop from the existing situation. The desire of the farmer to do so will have several implications on input requirement for the proposed change, say additional capital required, human labour requirement, fertiliser requirement, water requirement, etc. Changes in land allocation under different crops will lead to altogether different levels of income. This will have several implications for the financial management decisions. Similarly, changes in labour supplies and credit availability will bring about far reaching implications for financial management. Changes in objective function coefficients will alter crop acreage, livestock units, credit requirement, labour and other input requirements. Then, the farm manager has to make altogether different observations with regard to financial outlay. Hence, sensitivity analysis of LP models will have far reaching implications and greater bearing on the financial management decisions. So it is relevant to study the concepts of sensitivity analysis.

VARIABLE PRICE PROGRAMMING

Step I: Changes in the net price of the maximisation problem given in Table 7.2 are assumed. Generally 10 to 50 per cent change in all the coefficients of the observations are assumed and these are mentioned in the *C* row of the final section of the Table 7.2.[*]

Step II: Compute the '*Z*' row and *Z–C* rows for the final selection.

Step III: Check if all the elements in the *Z–C* row are positive or not. If positive, stop the iterations and the same optimal solution holds good for changes in the objective function.

Step IV: If any element is negative, then its corresponding column in the outgoing column is encircled for easy identification.

Step V: Entries in the ratio column should be worked out for the optimal section dividing the *B* column coefficients by corresponding outgoing coefficients. Key row is encircled corresponding to lowest positive value of the ratio column. Transformed key row is obtained by following the Simplex Method mentioned earlier, as in the case of maximisation problem, and subsequent sections are computed. This procedure is to be continued till we get all positive coefficients in *Z–C* row and note down the corresponding optimal values in B column and shadow prices in *Z–C* row.

VARIABLE RESOURCE PROGRAMMING

Step I: We take the help of inverse matrix in the optimal solution and B vector in the initial table (section I) and then compute the corresponding optimal vector. For our example problem, B^{-1} matrix of Table 7.2 in section IV is given under disposal activities. The corresponding inverse matrix is furnished below:

$$B^{-1} = \begin{bmatrix} 1 & -0.00946 & -0.0135 \\ 0 & 5/148 & -7/74 \\ 0 & -0.0243 & 0.1081 \end{bmatrix}$$

---

[*]Changes in one of the C_j coefficients or simultaneous change in all the C_j coefficients can be opted as per the discretion of the researcher.

The B vector in the section I of the Table 7.2 is as follows:

$$B = \begin{bmatrix} 5 \\ 130 \\ 50 \end{bmatrix}$$

Optimal B vector is designated as $\overline{X}_B$ and this is given below:

$$\overline{X}_B = \begin{bmatrix} 2\frac{23}{37} \\ 1\frac{13}{37} \\ 1\frac{1}{37} \end{bmatrix}$$

As per the definition $\overline{X}_B = B^{-1} . B$

In variable price programming, we assume the new values for B vector and derive $\overline{X}_B$ vector by multiplying with B^{-1} matrix. In this process if we get positive values for all the elements of $\overline{X}_B$ vector, no further computation is required.

Step II: In case any element in $\overline{X}_B$ vector exhibits negative sign then the following procedure is to be followed:

(1) Multiply the row having negative values by –1.
(2) Introduce artificial activity with –m in the objective function row and +1 in the corresponding row where – sign appears.
(3) In the first column of the optimal section, –m should be placed replacing the earlier coefficient.
(4) We will have to proceed for further computation to get highest negative value in the Z–C row and lowest positive value in the ratio column.
(5) Computation of further iterations should be stopped when all the elements in Z–C row turned into positive value, and
(6) Note down the corresponding values in $\overline{X}_B$ vector and shadow prices in the Z–C row in order to assess the impact due to changed B vector.

NORMATIVE CROP PLANNING UNDER CHANGING SITUATIONS OF CREDIT SUPPLY

The need for credit has picked up greater momentum with the advent of new technology in agriculture. The supply of credit to agricultural sector to purchase requisite potential inputs has increased manifold, particularly after nationalisation of the banks. It is alleged that the present use of credit is not keeping pace with the requirement of credit due to availability of limited funds at macro as well as micro level. To tide over the problem of scarcity of finance, the judicious use of limited available funds is the need of the hour. This calls for proper planning and its effective implementation by the people at macro as well as micro level. Many a programming model are being formulated to meet this requirement. LP technique is generally employed to determine the optimal crop plans both at macro and micro levels in order to maximise the income from the given resources. The solutions for such models emphasise the need for crop adjustment under changing supply situations of credit, so that the reduction in net farm income could be avoided. Variable resource programming would be of great help to situations of above nature. Such solutions, inter alia, indicate the scope for increasing net farm income under existing credit supply vis-a-vis changing credit supply situations. Further, they also highlight the need for increased supply situation of credit for maximising the net income from the given resources.

PLANNING UNDER RISK

Need for Planning the Whole Farm

Farmers in general are endowed with limited supplies of land, labour, machinery and capital. Hence, alternative crop and livestock enterprises or activities compete for limited resources. Most of the enterprises are also interdependent for obtaining expected income on a continuous basis. Here arises the need for whole farm planning process which give solutions to problems such as, which enterprise to adopt and what method of production to employ and with how much of capital and other resources to be allocated to the different enterprises.

QUADRATIC RISK PROGRAMMING MODEL

In LP we generally assume that a_{ij}, b_i and C_j are all known planning constants. This assumption is fully justified when the known constants are incorporated in the model with certainty. But in reality, most of the planning coefficients (a_{ij}, b_i and C_j of the model) are not known exactly. Variances and co-variances of C_j coefficients are represented in the objective function of non-linear programming as a proxy for risk and uncertainty situations of income from crops and livestock activities over time. In non-linear programming such as Quadratic Risk Programming (QRP), the objective function is in the non-linear form. The non-linear programming models provide acceptable farm plans to risk averse farmers. The non-linear form is represented by variance and co-variance matrix of gross margins of different crops and livestock activities derived from time-series data. This matrix in the objective function of quadratic risk programming explicitly accounts for risk in gross margins of the different crop and livestock activities. The constraints of QRP are analogous to the constraints of linear programming model and in a matrix notation it is specified as:

$$\text{Max } U = C'X - \phi/2X\ QX \qquad \qquad \text{... (7.17)}$$

$$\text{Subject to} \quad AX \leq B$$

$$X \geq 0$$

Where,

$U =$ Utility function of the farmer for gross margins (maximisation of farm income from the activities of crop and livestock).

$C =$ An $n \times 1$ vector of expected crop gross margins.

$X =$ An $n \times 1$ vector of crop activity levels.

$\phi =$ A scalar (constraint) denoting the Pratt's constant, (risk aversion coefficient).

$Q =$ An $n \times m$ variance covariance matrix associated with the gross margins of crop activities.

$A =$ An $m \times n$ matrix of technical coefficients.

$B =$ An $m \times 1$ vector resource availabilities.

The QRP model requires complicated algorithm for finiding out the solution. For further details please refer Branson, Richard (1986).

MOTAD (MINIMISATION OF TOTAL ABSOLUTE DEVIATION) MODEL

Hazell (1971) developed MOTAD model as a linear alternative to quadratic and semi-variance programming for farm planning under uncertainty. This model uses linear decision criterion with expected return and mean absolute deviation. Hazell using the same data for MOTAD and QRP concluded that the optimal plans generated by these two models were nearly the same. Further, he observed that the MOTAD model could be solved with conventional linear programming packages. Risk is incorporated in the model as mean absolute deviation of farm profit. In matrix notation the MOTAD model is specified as:

$$M = s^{-1} \sum_{t=1}^{s} \left| \sum_{j=1}^{n} \left(C_{tj} - \overline{C}_j \right) X_j \right| \qquad \qquad \text{... (7.18)}$$

$M =$ Mean absolute deviation that can be minimised for a given level of expected profit

$S =$ Number of years

$C_{tj} =$ Gross margin per unit of jth crop or livestock activity in the tth year (unit here is one hectare)

$\overline{C}_j$ = Sample mean gross margin per unit of jth crop or livestock activity

X_j = Level of jth crop or livestock activity to be obtained from the solution of the model

t = Refers to t^{th} year

n = Number of activities

$| \ |$ = Denotes absolute value of the figures (modulus) ignoring the signs within the two vertical bars.

In this model, a measure of risk of gross margins which is given in the modulus, is incorporated into LP model of a whole farm planning problem. The mean absolute deviation, M is minimised for a given level of expected gross margin [E(Z)], varies parametrically over zero to some desired range.

Another simple and tidy approach is also suggested by Hazell, considering the negative deviations about the mean gross margin as mean absolute value. The objective function of the LP model is specified as:

$$D = M/2 = S^{-1} \sum_{t=1}^{s} \left| \min\left[\sum_{J=1}^{n} \left(C_{tj} - \overline{C}_j\right) X_j, 0\right]\right| \qquad ...(7.19)$$

min = minimise

The negative deviations of gross margin from their mean income in the tth year of sample data is defined by a new variable, Y_t and it is defined as:

$$Y_t = -\sum_{J=1}^{n} \left(C_{tj} - \overline{C}_j\right) X_j \qquad ...(7.20)$$

j = 1 to n crop or livestock activities,

C_{tj} = Gross margin from j^{th} crop or livestock activity in the tth year,

$\overline{C}_j$ = Mean gross margin of jth crop or livestock activity. The LP problem is formulated as minimisation of Y_t in the objective function subject to usual technical constraints and parametric constraints on expected total gross margin from crops and livestock. The MOTAD model is formulated as:

Minimise Y_t

subject to

$$\sum_{J=1}^{n} a_{ij} X_j \left(\geq = \leq\right) b_i \quad \text{for } i = 1 \text{ to } m \qquad ...(7.21)$$

$$\sum_{j=1}^{n} \left(c_{tj} - \overline{C}_j\right) X_j + Y_t \geq 0 \qquad ...(7.22)$$

$$\sum_{j=1}^{s} Y_t \le \lambda \qquad \qquad ...(7.23)$$

$$x_j \ge 0,\ Y_t \ge 0 \text{ for } j = 1 \text{ to } n,\ t = 1 \text{ to } s \qquad ...(7.24)$$

Equation (7.21) is technical constraint,

Equation (7.22) is deviation constraint,

Equation (7.23) is parametric constraint, and

Equation (7.24) is non-negativity constraint.

In the equation (7.22) the variable Y_t is to measure the negative deviation of total gross margin from mean of crop or livestock for each year, i.e., $t = 1$ to s years. The total deviation for each year is computed in the summation term of equation (7.22). If the sum is positive, the corresponding Y_t variable will be zero and this is assured by non-negativity restrictions. The total value of the objective function is limited through parametric constraint on the sum of the Y_t variable in the equation (7.23). Suppose, if the sum of the gross margin deviations in any year is negative, the corresponding variable Y_t will be forced to be a positive value, hence the λ in equation (7.23) will measure the sum of the total negative deviations over s years. Changing the values for λ in the parametric constraint in equation (7.23) the efficient E–A plans are generated. The formulation of MOTAD model for the hypothetical Indian farm is presented in Table 7.5.

Illustration of MOTAD Model for a Hypothetical Indian Farm

To formulate the model, we require information on the gross margin of different crop and livestock enterprises over time along with resource requirements and resource availabilities. The data for a hypothetical farm are assumed and furnished in Table 7.5.

TABLE 7.5

Particulars of Gross Margin from Crops and Livestock

Year	Gross margin/ha from crop and livestock enterprises of the farm (in '000 Rs)					
	Groundnut (Impoved)	Groundnut (HYV)	Paddy IR-20	Paddy IET-1444	Jersi cow per head	Buffalow per head
	X_1	X_2	X_3	X_4	X_5	X_6
1985	60.3	70.3	45.20	50.90	35.4	30.3
1986	64.2	68.3	42.80	48.50	37.1	32.1
1987	70.1	70.2	43.60	44.20	36.5	28.4
1988	66.8	74.5	45.10	51.30	38.5	25.6
1989	69.5	72.0	49.90	52.20	39.6	34.5
1990	68.3	76.0	52.80	57.40	38.8	33.1
1991	66.6	75.1	54.10	59.00	40.9	35.2
Mean	66.54	72.34	47.64	52.64	38.11	31.31

The above MOTAD model presented in Table 7.6 is solved by using simplex algorithm by changing the λ values. Through this different optimal crop plans are derived. The MOTAD model is very useful to provide acceptable farm plans to risk averse farmers starting from zero income levels up to infinity.

Derivation of Demand for Capital

Capital Constraints: Capital is a scarce resource on most of the Indian farms. Enough care should be taken to formulate meaningful capital constraints in the LP model. In fact, all the facets of the LP model must be familiar to the model builder to incorporate capital constraints and capital coefficients into the model. We often see models with no capital constraints in literature on the subject. Such a model implies that the farmer is able to invest required capital in the farm business without any problem. Models of this nature do not provide any estimate of required capital to carry on the farm business. But, in reality, without capital, executing the farm business is difficult. Hence, it is desirable to include capital constraints in all models.

Models with Capital Constraints: These provide solutions on the requisite capital for executing the optimal plan. But, they do not provide information on the optimal use of scarce capital. In our example problem, capital constraint is specified as $20\,x_1 + 18\,x_2 + 25\,x_3 \le 50$ (equation 7.7). Hence, the capital coefficients of the three crops are 20, 18 and 25 and they indicate the required capital to produce one acre of x_1, x_2 and x_3 crops. The available capital with the farmer is Rs 50 (in hundreds). Capital coefficient is maximum restraint and is specified with $\le$ sign. The farmers will have some working capital with them from their own savings. This working capital is added to the borrowed capital to finance purchase of seeds, fertilisers, feeds and labour. This situation is depicted in the LP model as follows:

	Real crop activities			Borrowing credit (Rs)	Sign	RHS
	x_1	x_2	x_3.....	x_j		
Objective function (rupees)	c_1	c_2	c_3	$-i$		
Credit row (Rs)	k_1	k_2	k_3	-1	$\le$	b

Where,

b = Available funds with the farmer for investment on the farm,

x_j = Borrowing credit activity,

TABLE 7.6

Initial Table of MOTAD for a Hypothetical Indian Farm

| Rows | Crop Activity (Rs/ha) | | | | Livestock (per head) (Rs) | | $\bar{Y}_1$ | $\bar{Y}_2$ | $\bar{Y}_3$ | $\bar{Y}_4$ | $\bar{Y}_5$ | $\bar{Y}_6$ | $\bar{Y}_7$ | RSH |
	X_1	X_2	X_3	X_4	X_5	X_6								
Objective function							1	1	1	1	1	1	1	Min $=\lambda$
Mean gross margin ('000 Rs)	66.54	72.34	47.64	52.64	38.1	31.31								
Land (ha)	1	1	1	1										≤ 5
Labour (days)	150	165	240	260	220	210								≤ 400
Capital (in '000 Rs)	50.23	48.38	55.42	60.32	18.54	19.20								$\leq 10,000$
Rotational constraint	–1	–1	1	1	–1	1								≤ 0
Risk rows														
1985	–6.24	–2.04	–2.44	–1.74	–2.71	–1.01	1							≥ 0
1986	–2.34	–4.04	–4.84	–4.14	–1.01	0.79		1						≥ 0
1987	3.56	–2.14	–4.02	–3.44	–1.61	–2.91			1					≥ 0
1988	0.26	2.16	–2.54	–1.34	0.39	–5.71				1				≥ 0
1989	2.96	–0.34	2.26	–0.44	1.49	3.19					1			≥ 0
1990	1.76	3.66	5.16	4.76	0.69	1.79						1		≥ 0
1991	0.06	2.76	6.46	6.36	2.79	3.89							1	≥ 0

i = Interest rate in fraction charged by commercial banks. For instance 12% interest rate is shown as -0.12.

c_1, c_2 & c_3 = Objective function coefficients of crops x_1, x_2 and x_3 (gross margins in Rs/ha)

k_1, k_2 & k_3 = Working capital required per unit of x_1, x_2 and x_3 crops (Rs/ha)

Here, interest is indicated as a cost in the objective function of the model with $-$ sign and correspondingly in the credit row -1 is shown in the a_{ij} matrix under borrowing credit activity. -1, when it is transferred to RHS becomes positive and adds to available funds.

The borrowing activity of any input, say borrowing (purchasing) fertilisers, borrowing hired labour, borrowing pesticides, etc., can be specified in the model directly in a similar way. Separate activities to specify different sources of credit, for example money-lenders, co-operatives, commercial banks, etc., can be considered in the formulation of LP model. The interest rates charged by the different agencies and their limit on the amount of credit lent to the farmer can also be included in the formulation of the model. This is shown in the following way.

	Real crop activities			Borrowing credit (Rs)	Sign	RHS
	x_1	x_2	x_3.....	(x_j)		
Objective function (Rs)	c_1	c_2	c_3	$-i$		
Credit row (Rs)	k_1	k_2	k_3	-1	$\leq$	b
Credit limit (Rs)				1	$\leq$	λb

Here,

λb = Maximum amount of loan that could be given to the farmer as per the norms of the bank.

The borrowing activity for credit constraints denotes demand for credit for executing the optimal plan. The demand for credit denotes the additional requirement of the capital over and above the available capital on the farm. The total demand for credit is the available capital plus required capital. Similarly, the demand for labour, fertilisers, pesticides, machine labour, bullock labour etc., can be obtained by introducing borrowing activity in the LP Model.

LINEAR PROGRAMMING VIS-A-VIS BUDGETING

Budgeting is a non-mathematical tool, whereas LP is a sophisticated mathematical tool of analysis. Simplex procedure is the most popular method of solving the objective function of LP problems subject to linear inequality equations. LP provides solutions to the profit-maximisation problems as well as cost-minimisation problems by allocating resources most efficiently, but in the budgeting technique, resource allocation does not necessarily lead to profit maximisation or cost minimisation. When there are many alternative enterprises, selection of the most efficient enterprise becomes complicated with budgeting technique. LP, if properly formulated finds no limit to the size and number of enterprises. The optimal mix of enterprises regardless of the number of enterprises is almost certain, provided LP problem is formulated cautiously. In fact it is the only tool available to the manager when there are numerous complexities in resource requirements and resource restrictions for finding out the profit maximisation/cost minimisation solutions. The additional information provided from LP is the marginal value products of limiting resources, which are also known as shadow prices. Finding out such information is not possible through budgeting technique. The superiority of the individual enterprise which is reflected in higher net income per unit area with lower resource requirements is being searched in LP technique for providing optimal solutions. This is similar to budgeting and partial budgeting techniques. These give importance to the costs and returns, aspects of individual enterprises and compare them for selecting the best one. The optimal solution obtained through LP is unique, while it is not so in the case of budgeting. The optimal solutions generated from LP algorithm are normative (what they should be) in nature, in the sense, that they indicate the desirable optimal combination of enterprises under given resource restrictions and resource availability. Budgeting solutions are in fact taken from the experiences of proven research or farmers in homogeneous areas elsewhere or nearest to the farmer. In this sense, the solutions are positive (what they are). Thus, in sum, budgeting is an approximation tool, while LP as already said is a sophisticated tool.

LINEAR PROGRAMMING VIS-A-VIS PRODUCTION FUNCTION

Profit maximisation or cost minimisation problems are solved by both LP algorithms and production function analyses. But, there lies a vast difference in obtaining the solution to such problems from these techniques. Production function analysis which is a technical relationship between output and input vectors defines the cause and effect relationship. Profit from the production of a particular output is maximised when the MVPs (marginal value products) of the inputs are equal to their respective marginal costs of the inputs. When this condition prevails for all the inputs in production of a particular product then maximum profits in the production of that product will be obtained. In other words, when the ratio of MVPs and the MICs are equal for all the inputs used in the production of products, profits are maximised which is an utopian concept. In real farm situations, the resources are underutilised or overutilised through the production function analysis. In the production function analysis profit maximisation or cost minimisation is stated as continuous function of independent variables specified in the function. But in LP, maximisation of profit or minimisation of cost is a linear function of linear constraints and inequality of resource supplies. Optimisation process in production functions or cost functions is called marginal analysis and takes the help of differentiation techniques such as first order partial derivative condition and second order partial derivative condition as necessary* and sufficient conditions**. In LP algorithm, simplex method has a built-in mechanism for solving the profit maximisation problem or cost minimisation problem through iterations. In this process at every subsequent iteration the objective function value is increased and in the optimal section (final section) the objective function value is maximised. The special feature of LP is profit maximisation, subject to resource constraints and inequalities of resource supplies, but in production function this is not given importance. In LP, output is limited due to input restrictions, but in production function technique, there is no such restriction.

There is also another gross difference in the MVPs of resources obtained through these two techniques. The MVPs of resources in LP are called shadow prices. They indicate returns per unit of resource or increased value in the objective function due to additional use of a resource under perfect competition. The MVPs in production function reflect the returns from a unit of resource under imperfect competition (real world situation). In LP when MVP of a resource is positive, it means that the resource is completely used up and it has greater potentiality for further use in crop and livestock enterprises. When the same is zero, it implies that the resource is in surplus position. The decision rule in LP is that the resource use is to be continued whose MVP is positive. Such type of information cannot be obtained from the production function results. If MVP of an input in production function is positive, it indicates that there is a scope of further use of the respective input. Decisions like up to what unit the input is to be used depend

---

*The farm is said to be earning maximum profit, when it equates the marginal productivities of factors with their prices.
**This condition means that marginal product curves of the factors must have a negative slope.

upon ratio of MVP and factor price and its optimum point lies at the equality of the MVP of input and its price. Information on elasticities and returns to scale is possible from the estimates of the production function, while the same cannot be obtained through LP.

REFERENCES

1. Branson, Richard, *Theory and Problems of Operations Research, Schaum's outline series*, Mc-Graw Hill Book Company, 1986.
2. Hazell, P.B.R. (1971), "A Linear alternative to quadratic and semi-variance programming for farm planning under uncertainty," *American Journal of Agricultural Economics*, 53 (1): 53-62.
3. Norbert Lloyd Enrick, *Management Operations Research*, Amerind Publishing Co., New Delhi, 1979.
4. William J. Baumol, *Economic theory and operations analysis*, Prentice-Hall of India, New Delhi, 1987.

CHAPTER 8

AGRICULTURAL PROJECTS—EVALUATION

The technique of evaluation of projects, be it in industry or agriculture, throws light on the capacity of the different projects to offer returns on investments. In order to evaluate the projects, one has to be kept informed about the various concepts and techniques of capital investment among alternative prospects. These aspects are presented in this Chapter.

AGRICULTURAL PROJECTS—MEANING, DEFINITION AND CONCEPTS

Projects are the cutting edges of development. They are meant for increasing the output from the given resources. Evaluation of projects needs projecting the future trend of output, sales, expected costs, returns, flow of funds, etc. The World Bank has recognised six important aspects in the project preparation. They are technical, administrative, organisational, commercial, financial and economic aspects. All the technological aspects of the project must be thoroughly studied under techincal analysis. Goods and services required for the project execution need a detailed assessment. The awareness of the lending agency regarding the technology to be used, i.e., captial-intensive technology, labour-intensive technology, latest technology or the existing technology, is to be assessed. Another important factor is the technical feasibility which determines the size of the project based on capital requirement, future and present demand for product, cost-benefit aspects, etc. The selected area for the project must be adequate in the resource endowment base and infrastructural facilities. The need for a particular project picks up the priority in the project implementation. Under administrative coverage, managerial aspects, project staff, extension personnel, credit agencies and farmers (beneficiaries) will be studied. Organisational aspects deal with relationship of project administration and the Government, training arrangements, disbursement of wages etc. Regarding commercial aspects of the projects, arrangements for the supply of input materials, services needed for the project, marketing of output, etc., are to be assessed. Regarding the financial aspects, the items which fall under this category are sources of funds, cost of funds, repayment, etc. The estimated costs based on tecnical aspects, estimated sales based on commercial analysis and probable profits from the operation of the project are to be properly evaluated. Financial gains accrued as well as incentives offered to the farmers (participants) in the project should also be viewed. On the other hand economic analysis concentrates, in determining project's contribution to the development of the economy as a whole and justifying the use of scarce resources. Proper identification of costs and benefits is an important aspect in the economic analysis of projects.

Project

Project is an investment activity where we spend capital resources to create a productive asset for realising benefits over time. Generally "Project is an activity on which we spend money in expectation of returns, which lends itself to planning, financing and implementation as a unit. It also refers to specific activity, with specific starting point and specific end point to achieve a specific objective. It should be measurable in costs and returns. It must have priorities for area development and reach specific clientele group."

In sum, the meaning of project may be comprehended as follows. "It is an investment activity meant for providing the returns for specific clientele group for specific activity, specific objective and specific area development. It should facilitate analysis in planning, financing, implementation, monitoring, controlling and evaluation."

TYPES OF AGRICULTURAL PROJECTS

Water Resource Development Projects

These projects include irrigation projects, ground water projects, projects for land reclamation, drainage projects, salinity prevention and flood control. These projects are aimed at bringing about overall agricultural development, by bringing water to the project area, providing drainage and reclaiming soil salinity. Suitability of soil to sustain production over time under irrigation must be carefully examined.

Agricultural Credit Projects

These are called "on-lending projects". These projects provide credit to the farmers for farm investment for increasing agricultural production, raising their standard of living and the economy as a whole. These projects need to be defined in terms of farm investment and investment on agro-industries and ancillary industries, such as investment programmes on livestock, mechinery, etc. The end use of the credit on these investment programmes need to be evaluated to assess the benefits that accrue to the beneficiaries. All the financial institutions, i.e., commercial banks, co-operatives and regional rural banks should act as the "credit houses" in the implementation of all these investment activities.

Agricultural Development Projects

These are the projects aimed at improving farm economy of individuals and regional development. Here, diversified cropping systems approach as well as farming systems approach are followed for bringing about the development of agriculture.

Agro-Industries and Commercial Development Projects

Projects of input supply, services to farming, projects concerned with processing, storage, market development, projects for fisheries development, and projects for development of co-operative farms are cited under this category.

Having known the meaning and types of projects and their uses, now it is relevant to understand the different constituents of projects, and how different phases or stages in a project begin and complete.

PHASES IN PROJECT CYCLE

The important phases in project cycle are:

1) Conception or Identification,
2) Formulation or Preparation of the project,
3) Appraisal or Analysis,
4) Implementation,
5) Monitoring, and
6) Evaluation.

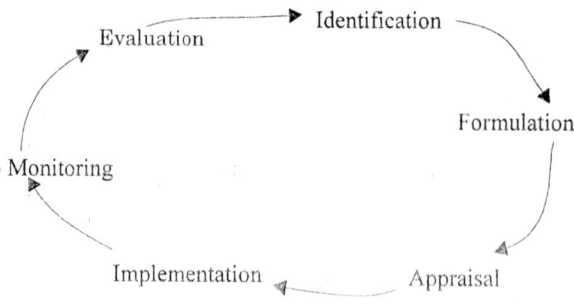

Fig. 8.1:   Project cycle

Project is considered as a cycle (Fig. 8.1) because, each phase not only grows out of the preceding one, but leads into the subsequent phase and it is a self-renewing cycle, so that new projects come out of the old ones in a continuous manner.

Conception or Identification of the Project

In agricultural projects, costs are easier to identify than benefits because the expenditure pattern is easily visualized. The various types of costs involved in the project are:

i) Project Costs: These include the value of the resources in maintaining and operating the projects.

ii) Associated Costs: Costs that are incurred to produce immediate products and services of the projects for use or sale.

iii) Primary costs or Direct costs: These include costs incurred in construction, maintenance and execution of the projects.

iv) Indirect costs or Secondary costs: Value of goods and services incurred in providing indirect benefits from the projects such as houses, schools, hospitals, etc.

v) Real costs and nominal costs: Costs at current market prices are nominal costs, whereas if costs are deflated by general price index, these are termed as real costs.

vi) Social costs: These are technological externalities and technological spill-over accrued to the society due to presence of projects, i.e., pollution problems, health hazards, salinity conditions, etc.

Next to identifying the costs, the estimation of benefits is imperative to ascertain the impact of the project. This is generally done by taking into account two situations, i.e., 'with' and 'without' the projects. The difference is the net additional benefit arising out of the project. Benefits are split into two: tangible and intangible benefits.

Tangible benefits: Incremental income due to the existence of projects is obtained from the following changes.

i) Improvement in cropping pattern involving high value crops.

ii) An increase in the productivity of crops.

iii) Adoption of recommended package of practices.

iv) Increase in the intensity of cropping.

v) Reduction in the cost of cultivation of crops, and

vi) Large scale economies due to specialisation.

Intangible Benefits: These include better income distribution, national integration, better standard of living, etc.

In identification phase, it is also important to see whether the project is implemented in high priority areas, and whether on *prima-facie* grounds the project is economically feasible. It is also imperative to identify problems and objectives of the projects and whether the Government gives sanction for the project implementation or not.

The important stages in the process of identification are:
  i)   Preliminary study,
  ii) Pre-feasibility study, and
  iii) Project report.

In these stages we assess whether the project proposed on the grounds of *prima-facie* is feasible and the objectives of the project are achieved. On this ground, the preliminary study should embody the investment proposals, benefits extended from the projects and method of implementation. Assessment of the demand for the project's products, technical feasibility of the project, import and export requirements, marketing aspects, investment prospects, etc., should be exhaustively covered by the feasibility studies, including the analysis of sensitivity.

Some of the sources through which the projects are identified are:
  i)   Agricultural and allied programmes proposed in the plans of the country as well as States;
  ii) Areas identified as potential of further development through Governmental surveys;
  iii) Special developmental programmes like IRDP;
  iv) Irrigation projects which offer scope for development through forward and backward linkages; and
  v)   New projects emerging out of existing projects, etc.

Formulation or Preparation

The following points are considered while formulating the projects. The location of the project and project site must be based on techincal analysis and technical feasibility of the project. The location of the project depends upon available physical resources, market conditions, marketing facilities, alternative investment prospects, administrative experience, farmers' objectives, technical skill, motivations, demand for products, etc. Technical analysis must take into consideration all aspects of technology to be used in the project, and account for all inputs of goods and services. Assessment of suitability and adequacy of natural resources in advance based on the scientific investigations is also essential. Alternatives to the resource use are to be considered in formulation of the project. Due consideration is to be given to all the aspects such as technical, financial, commercial, managerial, organisational, social, economic, etc., in the formulation of the projects. Identification of the missing links in the infrastructure system, particularly in relation to adequacy of communication systems, markets and storage facilities is important.

The above aspects of the project are briefly outlined hereunder.

Technical Aspects: The issues which need technical examination are thoroughly analysed here. For example, in the case of agricultural projects, the issues include the aspects relating to the pre-production, production and post-production aspects. To begin with, we have to examine the soil types, problems associated with different types of soils, potentiality which the soils offer for development, irrigation supply and availability, crops to be grown, availability of desired variety of seeds in required quantities, availability of other complementary inputs as per choice, credit facilities, pests and disease problems, possibility of mechanization, expected yields, storage, processing, marketing facilities, etc. for confirming technical feasibility.

Financial Aspects: Here, we have to find out the sources of raising financial assistance and terms and conditions of obtaining finance from the credit agencies. The implementing agency should be in a position to estimate financial requirements and anticipated returns, through farm planning and budgeting. Once the incremental income is arrived at, the repayment capacity duly giving allowance for risk and uncertainty can be worked out. Cash flow chart can be profitably used here.

Commercial Aspects: These aspects focus on the estimation of effective demand, availability of input supplies and arrangements for the output marketing. Market potentiality for the products needs a careful scrutiny.

Managerial Aspects: If we want successful implementation of the project, effective managerial issues are very crucial. The need to identify the beneficiary is the foremost item. Once identification process is over, we have to find out the managerial competence of the beneficiaries. The managerial skills can be sharpened, if necessary; technical skills are imparted by the extension agencies who have the onerous responsibility of technology transfer. Ability of the implementing agency needs a closer scrutiny.

Organisational Aspects: Organisation refers to the process of putting the priorities in an orderly form. Prepare the organisational hierarchy of the implementing agency. The availability of staff at various cadres, demarcation of authority and linking of authority and responsibility, etc., are expected to be dealt with, under this aspect. For proper administration of the projects, efficient personnel and other requirements are indispensable.

Social Aspects: Here customs, culture, traditions and habits, etc., of the beneficiaries are considered. The other relevant implications like the probable changes in the living standards, material welfare, consumption habits, income distribution effects, etc., fall under this coverage.

Economic Aspects: Here we have to examine the benefits, which the project is going to contribute in terms of the utilization of scarce resources of the nation. The point of merit is to whom the project is going to benefit i.e., to one section of the society or the entire area of the project. The indirect effect like, the income distribution, needs to be assessed. Under income distribution, we are interested to know whether income imbalances are going to be narrowed down or accentuated as a result of proposed projects. Overall, what one expects of a project is that it should bring in the greatest contribution to the national economy.

Appraisal or Analysis

Appraisal should take place before the implementation of the project. It is done independently by specialists. In the appraisal stage, it is important to know whether the project is technically feasible according to the data available. The technical data for assessing the feasibility of the project should be consistent with the information available in the office of the sanctioning authority or elsewhere. Managerial aspects play a key role in the project appraisal. Projects become abortive due to the failure to consider managerial aspects, i.e., such as new skills and information gained by the farmers in the project area, including adoption of new technology. The managerial capabilities and capacity of administrative personnel must also be assessed in project appraisal.

Implementation

This is the most crucial phase of the project cycle. The secret of successful implementation depends upon the extent of realism put into the plans drawn before hand. It is often not uncommon, to notice our plans getting deviated from the reality. Here the role of prudent decisions by the personnel incharge of implementation to tackle the situation comes into play. Project implementation can be divided into three different periods, viz., investment period, development period, and full-production period. Investment period may range from few months to few years depending upon the nature of assets to be acquired. Assets proposed should be of superior quality. Development period too consumes time. Implementing agency should make all efforts to reduce the gestation period as per the plan envisaged in the beginning. Full production period is the time during which the beneficiaries start. reaping the benefits of the project. Implementing agency should ensure that the beneficiaries do continue to receive benefits during the entire life span of the project.

Monitoring

Monitoring is the timely collection and analysis of data on the progress of a project, with the objective of identifying constraints which impede successful implementation. This is highly desirable, particularly when projects fail, to be completed as per time schedule or in the process of attaining the set goals. It is imperative to get the feedback on the problems faced so that effective measures can be taken up to plug the deficiencies, which hamper the speedy implementation. Monitoring has to be done continuously to offset various shortcomings that crop up from time to time with regard to various aspects of implementation.

Evaluation

This is the last phase of the project cycle. It is not confined to the completed project. Evaluation can be done several times during the life of a project. In the evaluation process, it is important to see, how far the objectives set out in the project are achieved. Deficiencies, snags or failures to achieve the objectives may be analysed and appropriate solutions to such failures answered. Evaluation process is to be completed in three phases. They are mid-course evaluation, concurrent evaluation and ex-post evaluation. In the first phase, evaluation is attempted before any change occurs in the existing situation. This is primarily meant to assess economic feasibility of the projects, since it is done at the very beginning. This type of analysis is otherwise called pre-project evaluation. Sometimes it is also important to take up evaluation when the project is in execution, and such evaluation is called concurrent evaluation. This type of evaluation is basically meant for identifying and analysing the pitfalls in the execution of the project. Evaluation is also resorted to particularly when the project is completed in all its phases, in order to assess the achievement of ends or objectives set out by the projects. Such evaluation is called ex-post evaluation or end-evaluation. Evaluation is done by the agency other than the implementing one, like financing bank or sponsoring agency or Government.

CRITERIA FOR SELECTION OF AGRICULTURAL PROJECTS

The following criteria are indispensable for evaluating agricultural projects

i)   Work selection criterion: This relates to immediate needs of the project area and has a direct or indirect relation to increasing prospects of agricultural production, income and employment.

ii) Priority criterion: Here it deals with whether the project implemented falls under priority area or not.

iii) Social criterion: It considers the direct employment prospects, ecological balances, externalities, pollution, etc.

iv) Financial criterion: According to this criterion it is determined whether the required amount of capital is supplied or not for the implementation of the project. In case the execution is delayed, additional capital requirements are to be assessed.

v)   Supply criterion: This is concerned with available resources, like physical inputs, labour availability and other resource endowment. Supply of skilled labourers and un-skilled labourers and technical personnel are to be evaluated for the completion of the project on time.

vi) Implementation criterion: This is based on organisational capabilities and managerial abilities of technical personnel.

vii) Project benefits criterion: Both tangible and intangible benefits must be correctly assessed and evaluated. In this process the benefits accrued due to forward linkages and backward linkages* need to be given specific weightage.

METHODOLOGICAL ISSUES IN FINANCIAL AND ECONOMIC EVALUATION OF AGRICULTURAL PROJECTS

It is a general practice that the benefit-cost analysis of the projects is worked out considering the market prices at the time the project is proposed to be taken up. But, such procedure will not be sufficient for economic analysis of agricultural projects, because the project is not going to be operated in perfect marketing situations, wherein, prices reflect the relative scarcity value of various goods and services. But, in

---

*Secondary benefits: These are of two types. One is forward linkage (stemming linkage) and the other is backward linkage (induced linkage). New values would arise consequent to the increased production of crops and livestock from the new proposed project, i.e., irrigation project.

The direct benefit is the increase in the output of crops and livestock, and smaller increase in the farmers' costs. The increased output will facilitate increased activities in marketing, transportation, processing and add to the profits of the persons involved in these activities. This is forward linkage. The extra profits accrued to the input suppliers as a result of project implementation reflect the backward linkage.

developing countries a market is protected through various Governmental measures and there will be scarcity of foreign exchange and hence, market price of goods and services often do not provide a reliable guide to the costs and returns of the projects. So, it is appropriate to consider the costs and values of the inputs and outputs of the projects at the international exchange rates, i.e., border rates excluding the effects of domestic tariff, subsidies, excise and other taxes in the economic analysis of the projects.

Cost Aspects: Annual capital costs of the project at current prices must be ascertained and then they should be weighted by the price index in order to get the costs at constant prices. Afterwards the same is multiplied by the Construction Conversion Factor (CCF) to get the economic costs of the project.

The CCF also plays a crucial role in giving weightage to the different commodities and inputs of the projects, such as traded commodities, non-traded commodities and services and unskilled labourers. The traded commodities include capital-intensive works which require imported machinery and material. In this case the Conversion Factor (CCF) is taken as one. The non-traded commodities (goods) and services include works, which require skilled labourers and locally manufactured material. In this case, a conversion factor of 0.8 is used to get the economic value of these goods and services. The conversion factor of unskilled labourer employed in the project work is around 0.75. This is based on the rationale of considering the extent of employment and unemployment and migration of labourers from agriculture to other sectors.

Farm Level Input Costs: These costs are to be valued at the projected world market prices. In doing so, it is also necessary to make allowance for duties, subsidies, taxes, marketing costs, etc., for which again conversion factor is used. Economic shadow wage rate for farm labourer, fodder values and miscellaneous expenditure are generally weighted by the Standard Conversion Factor (SCF) to convert the same into economic prices. The *SCF* is calculated using the following formula:

$$SCF = \frac{X + M}{X + Sx + M + Tm} \qquad (8.1)$$

where,

X = F.O.B. (free on board) value of exports at the official exchange rate(OER)

M = C.I.F. (cost insurance and freight) value of imports at OER

Sx = Export subsidies, and

Tm = Import duties

Generally SCF is taken as 0.80 in the economic analysis of irrigation projects in India. The following coversion factors have been used to derive the economic costs of four input factors.

Seeds	=	1.0
Bullocks	=	1.0
Fodder	=	0.8
Farm implements	=	0.88

Benefit Estimation

Agricultural commodities produced under project area need to be valued based on the border prices at the Official Exchange Rate (OER) in the economic analysis of the projects. The economic prices for non-traded foodgrains, vegetables, pulses, etc. have been derived applying Food-grain Conversion Factor (FCF) to the market prices (financial prices). The following formula is employed to arrive at the FCF.

$$FCF = \frac{(Q \text{ rice} \times PE \text{ rice}) + (Q \text{ wheat} \times PE \text{ wheat})}{(Q \text{ rice} \times PF \text{ rice}) + (Q \text{ wheat} \times PF \text{ wheat})} \qquad \ldots (8.2)$$

Where,

Q = Production in the project region,
PE = Economic price, and
PF = Financial price.

Methodology for Social Benefit-Cost

In ranking agricultural projects and assessing the socio-economic objectives of the projects, a realistic attempt is necessary through adoption of appropriate methodology. UNIDO Method (1978) suggests that all the items, i.e., costs and benefits involved in the projects are to be valued in terms of present aggregate consumption. Considering the market prices, which are inadequate in reflecting the real social costs and benefits of the projects, the goods and services are to be valued in terms of shadow prices, which indeed, reflect social costs and benefits.

The various parameters involved in the agricultural projects are as follows:

1) Social rate of discount;
2) Shadow price of investment;
3) Shadow prices of labour;
4) Shadow prices of foreign exchange; and
5) Income distribution: Weights which are proxies for regional income differentials.

The estimates of these parameters are specified by the National Planning Agencies and the concerned project authorities.

Social Rate of Discount (SRD)

There is a time lag between the investment and the returns from the agricultural projects, which is termed as "Gestation period". As a result, different values are to be attached in the economic analysis of the projects, particularly to costs and benefits. The present value of the future benefits/costs (called discounting) depends on the magnitude of social rate of discount and this considerably brings about change in the values of costs and benefits. For instance, a higher social discount rate will reduce the net present value of the benefits or costs and vice-versa. Hence, the choice of appropriate Social Rate of Discount (SRD) is of vital importance, especially in agricultural projects where there is a long gestation period.

SRD is used in computing the Benefit-Cost Ratio (BCR), Net Present Worth (NPW) of the project, Internal Rate of Return (IRR), etc. It is the opportunity cost of the capital which just reflects, the choice made by the society as a whole, between the present and future returns and hence, it represents the approximate amount of total income, the society as a whole is willing to save over time. Finding out the correct discount rate entails many problems. In practice, by the rule of thumb an approximate and agreeable social discount rate is adopted in the economic analysis of the projects. The popular choice is 12 per cent discount rate and in some countries, in the evaluation of agricultural projects it varies from 8 to 15 per cent. The factors that determine the social rate of discount are:

1) Society's present level of consumption,
2) Expected growth of consumption,
3) Expected growth of population,
4) The marginal utility of consumption, and
5) Pure time preference.

SRD values can be estimated by using the following expression:

$$SRD = (1 + \bar{g})^{-e} - 1 + PTP \qquad \ldots (8.3)$$

where,

g = Growth rate of percapita consumption,

e = Elasticity of diminishing marginal utility of consumption, and

PTP = Pure time preference.

Shadow Prices: If any country faces the problem of balance of payments (BOP) foreign exchange becomes scarce for that country. Under such situation the official exchange rate does not reflect true value of foreign exchange earned or spent. In order to get real foreign exchange impact on EXIM policies[*], it is important to make adjustment by using shadow foreign exchange rate. Shadow foreign exchange rate is calculated by using the following formula (UNIDO, 1978).

$$SER = OER \frac{(M + Ti) + (X + Sx)}{(M + X)} \qquad \ldots (8.4)$$

Where,

- SER = Shadow exchange rate
- OER = Official exchange rate
- M = c.i.f. values of imports
- Ti = Import tax revenues
- X = F.O.B. values of exports, and
- Sx = Export subsidies (export subsidies treated as negative subsidies).

World bank uses Standard Conversion Factor (*SCF*) using the following formula:

$$SCF = \frac{(X + M)}{(X + Sx + M + Tm)} \qquad \ldots (8.5)$$

where,

- X = F.O.B. values of exports at the official exchange rate (OER)
- M = c.i.f. values of imports at OER
- Sx = Export subsidies, and
- Tm = Import duties.

Shadow prices are otherwise known as accounting prices. These are subject to criticism and controversy. In the financial analysis of the projects usually market prices are considered, but, in the economic analysis, true value of the prices is needed. This is due to imperfect market situations in the economy. If the economy is operating in a perfect marketing situation, the market prices are considered to be true values, if not, there will be bias in the prices of goods and services and the economic analysis of the projects becomes erroneous. For example, if the price of foreign exchange is low compared to the market prices of the economy, there will be an error tending to favour the projects with high import content. If the wages are high in the market, capital-intensive projects are favoured over labour-intensive projects.

---

[*]Export and Import Policies.

To avoid such errors in the economic analysis of projects, we generally use shadow prices, in place of market prices to reflect the true values of commodities. Hence, in the project analysis there is need to compute shadow prices for foreign exchange, labour, capital, etc.

If the capital is scarce in an economy, where the projects are proposed to be implemented, a general practice of including borrowing rate of capital, in the project analysis does not appear to be realistic and rational because, the borrowed capital must reflect the opportunity cost of capital. To do so, shadow prices of the capital are to be considered in the economic analysis of the projects.

Shadow Prices of Investment (Savings)

Shadow price of investment (savings) is defined as the present value of additional consumption generated by additional unit of investment in a project.

Shadow prices are worked out by the following formula:

$$I = \frac{(1-a)r}{(i-ar)} \qquad \qquad \dots (8.6)$$

Where,

I = Shadow price of investment,
i = Social rate of discount,
r = Opportunity cost of the capital, and
a = Rate of reinvestment.

Shadow Price of Labour: It is also called shadow wage rate. Agricultural projects require large number of skilled, semi-skilled and unskilled labourers during their implementation. Assessment of employment of labourers is one of the objectives of the projects. In order to assess the employment levels, shadow wage rates are considered against the market wage rates of labourers. In labour surplus economies, the wage rates are not equal to social opportunity cost of labour. The following factors are to be considered in working out the social opportunity cost of labour.

1) The output foregone elsewhere in the economy as a result of employing labourers in the project.
2) Cost of migration, training and additional consumption, when a labourer is moved from rural area to project site.
3) The potential difficulty encountered by the labourer in finding out a new job in the new area, and
4) The cost in terms of increased aggregate consumption due to increased employment in the project.

Using all these factors the shadow price is worked out employing the following formula.

$$SWR = m + s\,(I - 1)\,W\ (or)\ \frac{SWR}{W} = \frac{m}{W} + S\,(I - 1) \qquad \ldots (8.7)$$

Where,

SWR = Shadow wage rate,

m = Marginal product in present employment (or in the alternative employment when viewed in the context of the project),

W = The market wage paid to a labourer in a new job (Agricultural operations or construction),

S = The rate of savings from profits, and

I = The accounting price of investment.

If the commodities produced in the project area are tradable, their values are to be worked out using shadow prices, which are in turn based on the CIF and FOB prices of the imported and exported commodities respectively.

INVESTMENT ANALYSIS (CAPITAL BUDGETING)

Investment in agriculture is of two types. The first type involves operating investment such as seed, feed, fertilizers, etc., and the second one is concerned with capital assets such as land, machines, projects, etc. Analysis of investment is different for these categories of investment, owing to differences in timing of expenses and their associated returns. Investment on operating inputs occurs within one production cycle of a year or sometimes less, but investment on capital assets entails a longer time period.

In the profit maximisation principle, time is not brought into consideration because both expenses and returns are assumed to fall in the same production cycle. But, capital investments made in agricultural projects are made in different time periods and the returns are also spread over time. In order to assess the returns from investments, available alternatives must be weighted for different lengths of time in respect of costs and returns i.e., recognition of time value of money, profitability and economic viability of capital investment.

Time Value of Money

Future value of present money: A rupee today is worth more than a rupee in future. This is primarily due to its opportunity cost, i.e., interest. Interest will be added to the principal over time and hence its value increases. Future value of present sum is an important concept in financial analysis and this is called compounding. In the compounding process, the interest is added to the principal at the end of each time period which, in turn, earns interest. The future value of present investment in the project is calculated by using the well-known formula of compound interest:

$$A = P (1 + i)^t \qquad \qquad \dots (8.8)$$

Where,

A = Future value of the present sum invested in the project,
P = Principal amount invested in the project,
i = Interest rate in per cent, and
t = Number of years.

Let us assume that investment made in an agricultural project is Rs 10 crore and that the expected rate of return from the project is 80 per cent. We are interested to know what would be the value of investment made after 40 years. This could be readily found using the equation.

Annuity: By definition annuity means a stream of payments or returns over time. The future value of annuity can be estimated using the following equation.

$$A = P \frac{(1+i)^t - 1}{i} \qquad \qquad \dots (8.9)$$

Where

A = Future value,
P = Annual investment,
t = Time period, and
i = Rate of interest.

Present Value of Future Money: The present value of future sum is the current value of investment to be received in the future. This present value is worked out through discounting process in which the future sum is discounted back to the present time to find out its current or present value. The rationale behind this process is that a sum to be received in future is somewhat less now, because of time difference assuming a positive interest rate. Discounting is the inverse procedure of compounding. A present sum is compounded to know the future value and future sum is discounted to know the present value of future amount.

$$PW = \frac{P}{(1+i)^t} \ \text{ or } \ P \frac{1}{(1+i)^t} \qquad \qquad \dots (8.10)$$

Where,

PW = Present worth of future money,
P = Money value in future
i = Rate of interest,
t = Project life period in years.

The present value of annuity or stream of constant annual payment is found out using the following formula

$$PW = P\frac{1-(1+i)^{-t}}{i}$$
...(8.11)

Where,

PW = Present worth of future money,

P = Money value in future

i = Rate of interest, and

t = Project life period in years.

Investment analysis is also called capital budgeting. The profitability of two or more alternative investment projects are determined through capital-budgeting technique. Four components are required for the analysis of investment. They are: (1) net cash revenues from different projects, (2) their costs, (3) termial or salvage value of investment, and (4) interest or discount rate to be used.

Cash receipts less cash expenses give net cash revenue resulting from the alternative proposed projects.

The cost of investment is the actual total expenditure for its implementation. The terminal value of the project will also be estimated and it is set equal to the junk value for depreciable assets of the project. For simplicity junk value is assumed to be zero. The land values of the projects should be estimated at the market rate, at the time at which the project is terminated.

Another problem in economic analysis is with the estimation of discount rate. This discount rate is the opportunity cost of capital, which represents the minimum rate of return for justifying the investment. If the proposed investment in the project fails to earn this minimum rate of interest, then the capital should not be invested in the said project and alternative projects must be chosen as worthy of investment.

If capital is to be borrowed for investment on the project, then the discount rate chosen for the economic analysis should be higher than the cost of borrowed capital. Under risk situations, the discount rate is to be equalled to the expected rate of return from alternative projects of equal risk. Many problems are involved in deciding upon the actual rate of discount in project evaluation particularly, when the discount rate is to be adjusted to the risk. The methodology on the exact rate of discount to be used in the economic analysis is already discussed.

Broadly there are two methods of project appraisal, viz., undiscounted measures and discounted measures. In the undiscounted measures, payback period, ranking by inspection, proceeds per rupee of outlay, average annual proceeds of rupee outlay, etc., are important.

Under discounted measures Net Present Worth (NPW), Benefit-Cost Ratio (B-C ratio), Internal Rate of Return (IRR), and Profitability Index are prominent.

UNDISCOUNTED MEASURES

The undiscounted measures are the naive methods of choosing among the alternative projects. The methods listed under these measures often mislead in ranking of the projects and hence, choices go wrong.

Ranking by Inspection: It is based on the size of costs and length of cash-flow stream. Suppose if the two projects are with the same investment and the same net value of production, but with difference in the length of the period, then the project with longer duration is preferred to the one with shorter time period. This leads to bias in the choice obviously due to the absence of more elaborate and appropriate analysis.

Payback Period

Another simple method of ranking a project is the length of time required to get back the investment on the project.

The payback period of the project is estimated by using the straight forward formula:

$$P = \frac{I}{E} \qquad \qquad \ldots (8.12)$$

Where,

P = Payback period of the project in years,

I = Investment of the project in rupees, and

E = Annual net cash revenue in rupees.

The preference of a particular project is based on the lesser payback period. This is shown in Table 8.1

TABLE 8.1

Calculation of Payback Period

Initial investment = Rs 20,000

Year	Cash Flow (in Rs)	
	Project 'A'	Project 'B'
0	−20,000	−20,000
1	5,000	4,000
2	5,000	4,000
3	5,000	4,000
4	5,000	4,000
5	5,000	4,000
6	5,000	4,000

$$\text{Project 'A'} = \frac{\text{Rs } 20,000}{\text{Rs } 5,000} = 4 \text{ years}$$

$$\text{Project 'B'} = \frac{\text{Rs } 20,000}{\text{Rs } 4,000} = 5 \text{ years}$$

It is inadequate to exercise the option among the alternatives, because it fails to consider very important points like, consistency of running, timing of the proceeds, returns after the payback period and whether the cash-flows would be positive or negative in future.

Proceeds Per Rupee of Outlay

This is worked out by dividing the total proceeds with the total amount of investment, and a given project is ranked based on the highest magnitude of the parameter.

Average Annual Proceeds of Rupee Outlay

This is another simple choice criterion and in this procedure, total receipts are first divided by the project life span and the average proceeds obtained per year are divided by the initial investment on the project. Here too, ranking is given to the projects, based on the highest magnitude of the estimate.

The major drawback with undiscounted measures is that for the same data of the project, we get different rankings, hence, choice process becomes useless. Rankings by these methods are inconsistent and incompatible.

Discounted Measures

Cash flows are yearly net benefits accrued from the project. It they are weighted by discount rate, they become discounted cash flows. These discounted cash flows are the best estimates to decide on the worth of the project. This approach will give the Net Present Worth of the project. The present worth of the costs is subtracted from the present worth of the benefits in order to arrive at the Net Present Worth of the project every year.

Measurement of the Cash Flows of the Project: From the annual stream of gross benefits of the project, the capital invested and the other input costs like labour, machinery, fertilisers, pesticides, management, etc., are deducted. From the residual, the return of capital and return on capital or return to capital, i.e., recovering investment made in the project (depreciation) and compensation for the use of money (interest) are computed. This residual is called cash flow of the project. In financial analysis the cash flow is the net incremental benefit of the project. But, in accounting, the term implies the sum of cash flows of projects plus depreciation allowance. The concept of cash flow in the financial analysis includes, both return of capital and return to capital. We generally do not resort to deduction of depreciation, i.e., allowance of return of capital or interest in the economic analysis, because our analytical technique automatically takes care of return of capital in determining the worth of the project. In economic analysis, income taxes, sale staxes, custom duties are only transfer payments, but not payments used in the production process. Hence, from the gross returns these are not deducted. But, in financial analysis, taxes are a cost, which the individual must pay before arriving at the recovered capital, and compensating it for the use of capital.

By far, financial analysis aims at estimation of returns to all resources employed in the project. Hence, borrowed capital is considered as a benefit received, while, its interest is considered as a cost and it is deducted from the gross returns. In economic analysis, this consideration is ruled out because of the assumption, that all the resources employed in the project belong to someone or the other, within the society. In the economic analysis, it is important that the prices of some of the inputs must be shadow prices. In financial analysis all prices are market prices and they must include taxes and subsidies. For vivid distinction between cash flows in the economic analysis vis-a-vis financial analysis (Gittinger, 1976) may be referred.

Net Present Worth (NPW)

This is simply the present worth of the cash flow stream. Sometimes, it is referred to as Net Present Value (NPV). The choice of discount rate to be used in the measurement of Net Present Worth (NPW) poses many problems as discussed earlier. NPW is helpful in working out benefit-cost ratio of the project. The selection criterion of the projects depends upon the positive value of the net present worth, when discounted at the opportunity cost of the capital. This could be satisfactorily done, provided there is a correct estimate of opportunity cost of capital. NPW is an absolute measure, but not relative.

NPW of the project is estimated using the following equation:

$$NPW = \frac{P_1}{(1+i)^{t_1}} + \frac{P_2}{(1+i)^{t_2}} + \dots + \frac{P_n}{(1+i)^{t_n}} - C \qquad \dots (8.13)$$

Where,

P_1 = Net cash flow in first year,

TABLE 8.2

Estimation of NPW for Two Projects (Hypothetical)

Sericulture (one ha)

Year	Cost (in Rs)	Returns (in Rs)	Net income (in Rs.)	Discount factor at 12%	NPW (in Rs)
1	38,900	—	-38,900	0.8929	-34,733.81
2	9,239	28,475	19,236	0.7972	15,334.94
3	10,575	32,550	21,975	0.7118	15,641.81
4	11,952	35,610	23,658	0.6355	15,034.66
5	12,858	39,802	26,944	0.5674	15,288.03
				NPW	26,565.63

Mango Orchard (one ha)

Year	Cost (in Rs)	Returns (in Rs)	Net income (in Rs)	Discount factor at 12%	NPW (in Rs)
At the end of 6th year	25,000	—	-25,000	0.507	-12,675
" 7th year	4,250	10,260	6,010	0.452	2,716.52
" 8th year	4,792	12,550	7,758	0.404	3,134.23
" 9th year	5,368	14,530	9,162	0.361	3,307.48
" 10th year	5,975	16,275	10,300	0.322	3,316.60
" 11th year	6,456	19,396	12,940	0.287	3,713.78
" 12th year	7,187	21,470	14,283	0.257	3,670.73
				NPW	7,184.34

i = Discount rate,

t = Time period, and

C = Initial cost of the investment.

Projects with positive NPW are given weightage in the selection compared to those with negative present values, while zero NPW makes the investor indifferent. Table 8.2 presents the particulars of NPV calculations for two projects.

Benefit-Cost Ratio (B-C Ratio)

Here, we compare the present worth of costs with present worth of benefits. Absolute value of the benefit-cost ratio will change based on the interest rate choosen. While ranking the projects depending upon the B-C ratio, the most common procedure of selecting projects is, to choose the projects, having B-C ratio of more than one, when discounted at opportunity cost of capital. Finally, the given project is opted for implementation, among alternatives based on the highest B-C ratio. Following formula depicts the estimation of B-C ratio.

$$B\text{-}C \text{ Ratio} = \frac{\sum_{t=1}^{n} \dfrac{B_t}{(1 + r)^n}}{\sum_{t=1}^{n} \dfrac{C_t}{(1 + r)^n}} \qquad \qquad ...(8.14)$$

The estimation procedure of B-C ratio is embodied in Table 8.3.

Internal Rate of Return (IRR)

In the computation of Internal Rate of Return (IRR), the time value of money is accounted. The method of working IRR provides the knowledge of actual rate of return from the different projects. Thus IRR is known as 'marginal efficiency of capital or yield on the investment'. It is the discount rate at which the present values of the net cash flows are just equal to zero, i.e., NPW = zero. When NPW is set equal to zero, the equation (8.15) is solved for 'i'. This is the internal rate of return. The IRR must be found out by trial and error with some approximation. The procedure is elucidated for the projects on sericulture and mango in Tables 8.4 and 8.5 respectively.

In the working procedure, an arbitrary discount rate is assumed and its corresponding NPW is arrived at. The positive NPW value of the project indicates that IRR is still higher and the next assumed arbitrary IRR value must be comparatively higher than the initial level. This process is continued until NPW becomes negative. Then by interpolation method the exact IRR is found out using the following formula:

TABLE 8.3

Benefit-cost Ratio Calculation for 2 Projects (Hypothetical)

Sericulture (One ha)

Year	Costs (in Rs)	Gross returns (in Rs)	Discount factor (12%)	Present worth of costs (in Rs)	Present worth of gross returns (in Rs)
1	38,900	—	0.8929	34,733.81	—
2	9,239	28,475	0.7972	7,365.33	22,700.27
3	10,575	32,550	0.7118	7,527.29	23,169.09
4	11,952	35,610	0.6355	7,595.50	22,630.16
5	12,858	39,802	0.5674	7,295.63	22,583.65
				64,517.56	91,083.17

$$\text{Benefit-Cost Ratio} = \frac{\text{Present worth of gross returns}}{\text{Present worth of costs}} = \frac{91,083.17}{64,517.56}$$

$$= 1.41$$

Mango Orchard (one ha)

Year	Costs (in Rs)	Gross returns (in Rs)	Discount factor (12%)	Present worth of costs (in Rs)	Present worth of gross returns (in Rs)
End of 6th year	25,000	—	0.507	12,675.00	—
" 7th year	4,250	10,260	0.452	1,921.00	4,637.52
" 8th year	4,792	12,550	0.404	1,935.97	5,070.20
" 9th year	5,368	14,530	0.361	1,937.85	5,245.33
" 10th year	5,975	16,275	0.322	1,923.95	5,240.55
" 11th year	6,456	19,396	0.287	1,852.87	5,566.55
" 12th year	7,187	21,470	0.257	1,847.06	5,517.79
				24,093.70	31,278.04

$$\text{Benefit - Cost Ratio} = \frac{31,278.04}{24,093.70}$$

$$= 1.30$$

TABLE 8.4

Estimation of IRR for Sericulture (One Hectare) (Hypothetical)

Year	Costs (in Rs)	Gross income (in Rs)	Net income (in Rs)	Discount factor (40%)	Net present worth (in Rs)	Discount factor (43%)	Net present worth (in Rs)
1	38,900	—	-38,900	0.7143	-27,786.27	0.6993	-27,202.77
2	9,239	28,475	19,236	0.5102	9,814.21	0.48902	9,406.4
3	10,575	32,550	21,975	0.3644	8,007.69	0.3419	7,513.25
4	11,952	35,610	23,658	0.2603	6,158.17	0.2391	5,656.62
5	-12,858	39,802	26,944	0.1859	5,008.89	0.1672	4,505.04
			52,913		1,202.69		-121.46

$$\text{IRR} = 40 + 3\left(\frac{1202.69}{1,202.69 + 121.46}\right)$$

$$= 40 + 3\ (0.9083)$$

$$= 40 + 2.7249$$

$$= 42.7249$$

TABLE 8.5

Estimation of IRR for Mango Orchard (One Hectare) (Hypothetical)

Year	Costs (in Rs)	Gross income (in Rs)	Net income (in Rs)	Discount factor (25%)	Net present worth (in Rs)	Discount factor (30%)	Net present worth (in Rs)
End of 6th year	25,000	—	-25,000	0.262	-6,550	0.207	-5,175
" 7th year	4,250	10,260	6,010	0.21	1,262.01	0.159	955.59
" 8th year	4,792	12,550	7,758	0.168	1,303.30	0.123	954.23
" 9th year	5,368	14,530	9,162	0.134	1,227.71	0.094	861.23
" 10th year	5,975	16,275	10,300	0.107	1,102.10	0.073	751.90
" 11th year	6,456	19,396	12,940	0.086	1,112.84	0.056	724.64
" 12th year	7,187	21,470	14,283	0.069	985.53	0.043	614.17
			35,453		443.49		-313.24

$$IRR = 25 + 5 \left(\frac{443.49}{443.49 + 313.24} \right)$$

$$= 25 \times 5 \ (0.586)$$

$$= 25 + 2.93$$

$$= 27.93$$

$$
\begin{pmatrix} \text{Internal} \\ \text{rate of} \\ \text{return} \end{pmatrix} = \begin{pmatrix} \text{Lower} \\ \text{discount} \\ \text{rate} \end{pmatrix} + \begin{pmatrix} \text{Difference bet -} \\ \text{ween the two} \\ \text{discount rates} \end{pmatrix} \left(\frac{\begin{array}{c} \text{Present worth of} \\ \text{the cash flow at the} \\ \text{lower discount rate} \end{array}}{\begin{array}{c} \text{Absolute difference between the} \\ \text{present worths of the cash flow} \\ \text{at the two discount rates} \end{array}} \right) \quad ..(8.15)
$$

Profitability Index

Here we relate the NPV of the cash flows of the project to the total capital required (cr) for a project through "profitability index". It is defined as the ratio of net present values of the cash flows to the initial capital expenditure (co). Assuming that all the capital expenditure is incurred in year zero, the profitability index (PI) is as follows:

$$
PI = \frac{NPV}{co} = \frac{1}{co} \sum_{1=0}^{n} \frac{cr}{(1+i)^n} \qquad \ldots (8.16)
$$

Table 8.6 deals with this measure.

TABLE 8.6

Estimation of Profitability Index

Orginal amount invested in a Project = Rs 60,000

Year	Cash flow (in Rs)	Discounting factor (15%)	Net Present Worth (in Rs)
1	14,500	0.8929	12,947
2	14,900	0.7972	11,878
3	16,600	0.7118	11,816
4	18,700	0.6355	11,884
5	19,000	0.5674	10,781
6	20,000	0.5066	10,132
	1,03,700		69,438

$$
\begin{aligned}
PI &= \frac{\text{Net present value of cash flows}}{\text{Original amount invested}} \\
&= \frac{69,438}{60,000} \\
&= 1.1573
\end{aligned}
$$

APPROPRIATE SELECTION OF CHOICE INDICATOR

As regards discounted measures, the problem lies with the choice of an appropriate discount rate. Many a time, opportunity cost of capital is substituted for the borrowing rate. In the view of Gittinger, appropriate social discount rate is used in the project analysis, which in fact poses a problem. Ranking of acceptable alternative projects is not possible with NPW because it is an absolute measure, but not relative. A small but highly attractive project will have a small NPW than a large but less acceptable project. B-C ratio is mostly used to evaluate social projects but not private projects (Gittinger). In General IRR method is preferred for the following obvious reasons.

(1) It is an unambiguous estimate; (2) it is consistent with intuition; (3) its estimate is unique and it accounts for all cash flows associated with the projects and time value of money; and (4) it has got wider applicability.

The only limitation is that a precise IRR is obtained with narrow difference in the two discount rates assumed. Complications are involved in the computation process.

SENSITIVITY ANALYSIS

Project appraisal techniques above, provide us certain measure of project's worth and this is related to a certain period of time and we will be forming this measure of the project under the assumption that the data used in the project evaluation remain unchanged over a length of time. But, in reality this is not a valid assumption because our estimates of costs and returns go awry over time, as prices of agricultural produce as well as the costs of inputs are subject to change. Under these conditions our estimates of economic analysis will be misleading. Hence, there is a need for considering the probable changes in the data required for the project appraisal. It is also sometimes necessary to know, how far our estimates of project appraisal remain constant under the changing situation of costs, prices and yields. If any analysis is able to provide clues to all these questions, we call such analysis as 'sensitivity analysis'. If a thought is given to the forecasting behaviour of costs and prices in the sensitivity analysis, indeed, it becomes very much useful to the policy makers and planners of development. Since forecasting process is a difficult proposition, our project appraisal tends to go wrong. But, a simplified procedure of sensitivity analysis, which is not subject to criticism is always welcome. The sensitivity analysis of the project appraisal includes the following points:

(1) Consideration of the length of the period over the existing one;
(2) Changes (increase or decrease) in the prices of goods and services by certain proportions of the project say by 10 per

cent, 20 per cent, 30 per cent, 40 per cent, 50 per cent, etc.,
(3) Changes (increase or decrease) in the levels of costs say by 10 per cent, 20 per cent, 30 per cent, 40 per cent, etc.;
(4) Changes (increase or decrease) in the yield levels of crops and livestock; and
(5) Delays in the implementation, i.e., varying gestation periods.

Assuming the changed values for the above parameters, by a definite proportion, the project worth is calculated time and again. This procedure deals with the question of risk and uncertainty to a certain extent in the project analysis. But, in fact, this is not adequate. Elaborate risk analysis using probability analysis and simulation models employing the randomization, are the most appropriate tools to indicate the real worth of the project under the conditions of risk and uncertainty.

REFERENCES

1. Dwivedi, D.N., *Managerial Economics*, Vikas Publishing House, 1980.
2. Gittinger, J.C. Price, *Economic Analysis of Agricultural Projects*, A World Bank Publication, 1976.
3. John J. Hampton, *Financial Decision Making—Concepts, Problems and Cases*, Prentice-Hall of India, New Delhi, 1983.
4. Johnson, D.T., *The Business of Farming, A guide to Farm Business Management in the Tropics*, Macmillan Publishers, London 1982.
5. Puttaswamaiah, K. (Ed.), *Project evaluation criteria and Cost Benefit Analysis*, Oxford & IBH Publishing Co., New Delhi, 1989.

CHAPTER 9

LENDING ASPECTS OF DEVELOPMENT SCHEMES

Identification and selection of technically feasible and economically viable schemes suitable to the given area are crucial from the point of view of bringing about development in agriculture and allied sectors. Keeping this in view an attempt is made in this Chapter to provide a brief outline of certain schemes with regard to their importance in the given areas in generating higher income, scale of finance, mode of repayment, etc.

SCHEME FOR FINANCING MANGO PLANTATION

Fruit farming is gaining wide recognition due to its increased demand in exports and sizeable foreign exchange earnings. Besides, there is a growing internal demand for fruits due to increased population. In this context, mango cultivation has become an important commercial proposition in most parts of the country among fruit crops. The banks are formulating mango plantation schemes, particularly to improve the economic conditions of the farmers and maintaining the ecological balance. Mango cultivation is generally less risky and requires less recurring expenditure. The scheme is implemented in areas where, there is good potential of underground water resources and where, the climate and soil are suitable to its cultivation. The requisite material and inputs such as mango grafts, water and fertilizers should be ensured along with technical support, viz., services of officals of Department of Horticulture. Adequate facilities for packing and transport should also be provided with regard to economic and financial aspects of the scheme. Mango orchard requires nearly Rs 8,300 per acre (40 trees) over a period of six years towards cost of cultivation. This expenditure is met from the income obtained from sale proceeds of inter-crops grown up to the 6th year. From 7th year onwards the annual maintenance cost is Rs 9,600. The total financial outlay for a 10-acre farm is Rs. 2,24,000. The net return after paying the loan instalments range from Rs 10,288 in the 7th year to Rs 1,04,740 in the 12th year. The details of economics of mango cultivation are furnished in Appendix B, Tables 1 to 3.

As per the NABARD guidelines, 25 per cent of the bank loan is fixed as margin money, which is to be contributed by the borrower before obtaining the loan. Repayment period is spread over six yearly instalments commencing from the 7th year. The loan will be terminated at the end of the 12th year. The rate of interest is 15.5 per cent per annum. The mango scheme as evident from the economic aspects is technically feasible, economically viable and hence, it is a bankable proposition to raise the incomes of the farmers.

SCHEME FOR FINANCING INLAND FISH CULTURE

Fish production from inland water has great economic significance in the low lying coastal areas. Fish culture provides lucrative returns to the farmers, employment in rural areas, besides supplying good quality protein diet for the people. This enterprise is taken up in the areas of plentiful water. Total culture period of finerlings varies from 10 to 12 months. The economics per one acre of water spread area is worked out and furnished in Appendix B, Tables 4 to 5. The capital outlay for one acre of fish pond works out to Rs 18,970 and the annual recurring expenditure amounts to Rs 19,880. The total financial component required is Rs 38,850, out of which bank loan stands at Rs 29,100. The rate of interest is 14 per cent per annum. The loan shall be secured primarily by hypothecation of equipment and standing crop of fish and collaterally by the registered mortgage of land d property. Comprehensive insurance cover will be arranged for the fish ponds. The net income expected is Rs 36,000 per year. The loan is to be repaid in six years. The instalment amount varies from Rs 7,375 to Rs 7,750. The annual net surplus varies from Rs 28,250 to Rs 28,625 (Appendix B, Table 6). Since the enterprise pays handsomely, it is bankable.

SCHEME FOR FINANCING SERICULTURE

The crop husbandry is taking a gradual diversification from the age-old cultivation practices of various crops grown, to suit the available natural resources like favourable climate, scarce water potential, and immense manpower for maximising the returns from the investment made. In recent past mulberry cultivation has emerged as an attractive alternative cultivation for the farmers. The proportionate returns on the investment made in mulberry cultivation are much higher than that of traditional crops. The advantages of mulberry cultivation are: (i) It improves the financial conditions of the farmers as mulberry cultivation yields comparatively higher income, (ii) it provides a greater extent of employment opportunities to the rural population, (iii) it improves earnings on foreign exchange and (iv) it commercialises agriculture at a rapid pace.

Sericulture comprises of two major activities, viz. (i) Cultivation of mulberry for raising the leaf to feed the silk worms, and (ii) rearing of silk worms for the production of cocoons, which will be the raw material for silk reeling industry. Sericulture requires equipment like chandrikas, trays, wooden stands, leaf cutters, etc. The areas of mulberry cultivation should have marketing facilities for disposal of cocoons.

The unit includes construction of rearing shed, purchase of rearing equipment, cost of raising mulberry of one acre and cost of rearing silk worms during the 1st year. The unit cost thus worked out to Rs 12,500 per acre (Appendix B, Table 7).

The rate of interest chargeable on loan amount will be as stipulated by NABARD from time to time. The present rate is 10 per cent to small and marginal farmers and 12.5 per cent to others.

Loans for purchase of rearing equipment will be disbursed directly to the suppliers as far as possible. In the case of construction of rearing shed, loan amount will be disbursed to the borrowers in cash in 2 to 3 instalments after conducting the inspection of work in progress. The expenditure and income pattern as presented in Appendix B, Tables 7 to 9 reveal that the sericulture enterprise is highly profitable and bankable.

SCHEME FOR FINANCING DAIRY

Milk has an important place in the predominantly vegetarian diet of our people. In India, average daily per capita milk availability is about 150 grams against standard requirement of 250 grams. There is still about 36 per cent shortage in the availability of milk, when compared to the needs of the population. For many small and marginal farmers, it is an important source to supplement the farm income. To meet the demand of an ever-increasing population, dairying is to be encouraged as a supplementary enterprise.

The dairy enterprise is capable of increasing the standard of living of people, providing gainful employment, providing nutritive diet to the people and supplying cattle manure, which contribute for increased agricultural production.

The climate during winter and rainy seasons is suited for graded murrah buffaloes (G.M.B.). During summer additional precautions are to be taken to provide suitable climate to the G.M.Bs. In selection of quality animals, veterinary doctor should assist the beneficiaries.

The economic aspects are presented in Appendix B, Tables 10 to 12. A farmer having at least 0.5 acres owned/leased-in-land with water facilities to grow green fodder should be selected under the scheme. Loan for 2 animals will be sanctioned. After documentation, loan amount for first animal will be released. After 6 months, another animal will be purchased for continuity in milk production. The bank loan is Rs 9,600. Rate of interest is 12.5 per cent per annum. The animals will be insured against all risks which is 4 per cent of the cost of animal. The loan is repayable in 5 years in monthly instalments with a grace period of 2 months. The economic analysis of the dairy enterprise indicates that it is highly profitable and bankable.

SCHEME FOR FINANCING PIPELINE

The most important activity in the development of farm for increasing agricultural production is enhanced area under irrigation. This can be done by (1) creating new sources of irrigation such as digging new wells, bore wells, etc. (2) improving existing source of irrigation like development of old wells, and (3) bringing water from a far-off place through a pipeline. The laying of a pipeline is necessitated by topo graphical or locational reasons. The main objectives of the scheme are:

(1) to bring more area under irrigation thereby increasing agricultural production;
(2) to increase productivity of land and water;
(3) to increase the standard of living of farmers; and
(4) to provide employment.

The soils in the area should have generally drainage facilities and fairly fertile. The selected area should have electricity. Mostly 3 H.P. and 5 H.P. electric motors are used which lift the water and convey through pipeline. PVC pipelines which will be laid underground should be available. To assess viability of the scheme, a model 5 acre plot is taken and the crops grown under 'with' and 'without' project situations are furnished in Appendix B, Table 13.

Under 'without project' situation the farmer can irrigate only 2.5 acres. Remaining 2.5 acres are kept fallow. After pipeline is provided, the entire area can be brought under irrigation. The eligible farmers whose acreage can be brought under irrigation by providing pipelines need to be identified.

It is evident from Tables 13 to 18 of Appendix B that financing the pipeline scheme in areas where there are abundant water resources is economically viable, technically feasible and bankable because such development schemes will fetch a net surplus of around Rs 14,000 every year and the loan will be liquidated within 5 years.

SCHEME FOR FINANCING SHEEP FARMING

In view of the erratic rainfall, cultivation of crops is becoming very difficult day by day, deteriorating the economic status of the small and marginal peasants in our country. So in order to supplement the low agricultural income, allied agricultural activities play a vital role. Among the allied agricultural activities, sheep rearing is one. The sheep survive by grazing in the forests and waste lands. Agricultural labourers and even big land-lords prefer sheep rearing activity, because sheep neither require much attention while grazing nor do they need special feeding.

The advantages of sheep farming are:

(1)   it improves the economic conditions of the small and marginal farmers and agricultural labourers as sheep rearing yields higher income to the farmers;

(2)   it provides greater extent of employment opportunities to the rural population; and

(3)   it increases the production of meat for human consumption and provides sheep manure.

Pasture lands, grazing lands and waste lands are pre-requisites for operation of the scheme. Adequate water facility should be available to the sheep. The main breeds of sheep are Deccani, Nellore and Bellary. One of the advantages of sheep farming is that it does not require housing. A floor space of 1–2 sq. mts is provided for each sheep in the pens.

No separate grain is required for sheep except concentrated feeds for breeding rams. A mature ram of 2½ years old can breed 50 to 60 ewes during a breeding season. Rams should be culled when they are 7 years old.

Ram lambs and sheep are sold normally at body weight of 15–20 kgs. Adult body weight may vary from 20–40 kgs depending on breed and feeding. The cost of the scheme (20 ewes and one ram) is Rs 8,800. The details of the unit cost and economics of the scheme for one unit are furnished in Table 19 of Appendix B. Fifteen per cent of the unit cost will be borne by the applicant. The loan will be repaid within a period of 5 years in yearly instalments with a gestation period of one year. The rate of interest chargeable on loan amount will be as stipulated by NABARD from time to time. The present rate is 11.5 per cent. Sheep purchased will be insured against diseases. As evident from Table 19 of Appendix B, the scheme is profitable.

REFERENCES

1. Reports of State Bank of India, Regional Office, Tirupati.
2. Reports of State Bank of India (ADB), Chandragiri, Chittoor District, Andhra Pradesh.
3. Reports of Farmers Service Society, Narasingapuram, Chittoor District, Andhra Pradesh.

APPENDICES

APPENDIX A

Derivative: In the function $K = f(m)$, we are interested to know the rate of change of K due to change in m, i.e., Δm and we want to measure the approximate value of $\dfrac{\Delta K}{\Delta m}$. If Δm is infinitesimally small, then we will get a closer approximation of the true value of $\dfrac{\Delta K}{\Delta m}$.

$\lim\limits_{\Delta m \to 0} \dfrac{\Delta K}{\Delta m}$ is called difference quotient

$\lim\limits_{\Delta m \to 0}$ of $\dfrac{\Delta K}{\Delta m}$, it should be read as the limit of $\dfrac{\Delta K}{\Delta m}$ as Δm approaches zero. As $\Delta m \to 0$, then the limit of the difference quotient, i.e., $\dfrac{\Delta K}{\Delta m}$ exists. This limit is identified as the derivative of the function $K = f(m)$. Derivative is the derived function, while the original function $K = f(m)$ is the primitive function. The difference quotient, i.e., $\dfrac{\Delta K}{\Delta m}$ is a function of m_0 and Δm. $m_0 =$ initial level of m and Δm is new level of m. The difference $\Delta m - m_0$ is called as rate of change. The rate measured by the derivative is called instantaneous rate of change.

Given a primitive function of $K = f(m)$, its derivative is represented by the symbol $f'(m)$. The other common notation is $\dfrac{dk}{dm}$. The notation $\dfrac{dk}{dm}$ measures the rate of change.

Using $\dfrac{dk}{dm}$, derivative of primitive function $K = f(m)$ is expressed as

$$\frac{dk}{dm} \equiv f'(m) \equiv \lim\limits_{\Delta m \to 0} \frac{\Delta k}{\Delta m} \qquad \qquad ...(A1.1)$$

dk and dm are called differentials of K and m respectively.

Rules of Differentiation

The following rules of differentiation are applied to a function of one independent variable.

(i) Constant function rule: The derivative of constant function, i.e., $k = f(m)$ is zero for all values of m.

Suppose in the cost function $C = f(Q) = $ Rs. 3,000, which is called fixed cost function, the derivative of the fixed cost function for all the values of Q must be zero.

$$\frac{d}{dQ} \cdot C_F = \frac{d}{dQ} \text{ Rs } 3,000.00 \text{ or } f(Q) = 0 \qquad \text{...(A 1.2)}$$

(ii) Power function rule: The derivative of power function $K = f(m^n)$ is nm^{n-1}. Symbolically, it is represented in equation as:

$$\frac{d}{dm} \cdot m^n = nm^{n-1} \text{ or } f'(m) = nm^{n-1} \qquad \text{... (A 1.3)}$$

Example 1: $\quad K = m^2 = \dfrac{d}{dm} m^2 = 2m^{2-1} = 2m^1 = 2m \qquad \text{... (A 1.4)}$

Example 2: $\quad K = m^{12} = \dfrac{d}{dm} m^{12} = 12m^{12-1} = 12m^{11} \qquad \text{... (A 1.5)}$

Example 3: $\quad K = m^0$, applying power function rule

$$\frac{d}{dm} m^0 = 0 \ (m^{0-1}) = 0 \qquad \text{... (A 1.6)}$$

Example 4: $\quad K = \dfrac{1}{m^3} = K = m^{-3}$, applying power function rule

$$\frac{d}{dm} m^{-3} = -3m^{-3-1} = -3m^{-4} = \frac{-3}{m^4} \qquad \text{... (A 1.7)}$$

Example 5: $\quad K = Cm^n$ its derivative is

$$\frac{d}{dm} \cdot Cm^n = Cnm^{n-1} \text{ or } f'(m) = Cnm^{n-1} \qquad \text{.. (A 1.8)}$$

(iii) Sum difference rule: Give the two functions

$$f(m) = 3m^2$$
$$g(m) = 4m^3$$

To get the derivative of these two functions, we apply the sum difference rule which is stated as the derivative of sum (difference) of two functions in sum (difference) derivatives of the two functions.

$$\frac{d}{dm} [f(m) \pm g(m)] = \frac{d}{dm} f(m) \pm \frac{d}{dm} g(m)$$
$$= f'(m) \pm g'(m) \qquad \text{... (A 1.9)}$$

$$K = 3m^2$$
$$K = 4m^3$$
$$\frac{dk}{dm} = \frac{d}{dm}\left(3m^2 + 4m^3\right) = \frac{d}{dm}3m^2 + \frac{d}{dm}4m^3$$
$$= 6m + 12m^2 \qquad \qquad \text{... (A 1.10)}$$

(iv) Product rule

Let $f(m) = 5m + 6$
$$g(m) = 4m^2$$

We have to find out the derivative of these two functions using the product rule.

$$\frac{d}{dm}[f(m)g(m)] = f(m)\frac{d}{dm}g(m) = g(m)\frac{d}{dm}f(m)$$
$$= f(m)g'(m) + g(m)f'(m) \qquad \qquad \text{... (A 1.11)}$$

Following the product rule the derivative of the function

$$K = 5m + 6$$
$$K = 4m^2$$
$$K = (5m + 6)(4m^2)$$
Let $(5m + 6)$ is $f(m)$
$(4m^2)$ is $g(m)$

Applying product rule of (A1.11)

$$(5m + 6)(8m) + (4m^2)(5 + 0) = 40m^2 + 48m + 20 \, m^2 = 60 \, m^2 + 48 \, m$$

(v) Quotient rule: The derivative of the quotient of two functions, $f(m)/g(m)$ is

$$\frac{d}{dm}\frac{f(m)}{g(m)} = \frac{f(m)g(m) - f(m)g'(m)}{g^2(m)} \qquad \qquad \text{...(A 1.12)}$$

In the function

Let $K = \dfrac{6m - 4}{2m + 2}$

Then its derivative as per the equation (A 1.12) is

$$\frac{6(2m + 2) - (6m - 4)^2}{(2m + 2)^2}$$

$$= \frac{12m + 12 - (12m - 8)}{2m^2 + 2.2.2m + 4}$$

$$= \frac{20}{2m^2 + 8m + 4}$$

vi) Chain rule: If we have a function $K = f(m)$ where m is turn is a function of another variable p. Say, $m = g(p)$. Then the derivative of

K with respect to p is expressed as:

$$\frac{dk}{dp} = \frac{dk}{dm} \cdot \frac{dm}{dp}$$ ... (A 1.13)

$$= f'(m)\,g'(p)$$

Suppose if $K = 4\,m^2$

$m = 3p + 2$, then the derivative could be found by using equation (Al . 13)

$$\frac{dk}{dp} = 8m(3) = 24m$$

$$= 8\,(3p + 2)\,(3)$$
$$= (24p + 16)3$$
$$= 72p + 48$$

(vii) Inverse function rule

Let $K = 3m + 5$

Its derivative is 3

Its inverse function is

$3\,m = k - 5$

$$m = \frac{1}{3}K - \frac{5}{3} = \frac{1}{3}(K - 5)$$

Derivative: $\dfrac{dm}{dk} = \dfrac{1}{dk/dm} = \dfrac{1}{3}$

(viii) Partial differentiation rule

Let us consider, the function

$K = f(m_1, m_2 \ldots m_n)$, where variable m_i, $i = 1$ to n, are independent variables. In this function m_1 variable undergoes a change with other variables remaining fixed. The partial derivative of K with respect to m_1 indicates that all the other variables, i.e. $m_2 \ldots m_n$ are held constant, when taking this particular derivative. The process of taking derivative is called partial differentiation.

Let $k = 5m_1^2 + 2m_1 m_2 + 3m_2^2$

Then, its partial derivative will be

$$\frac{dk}{dm_1} = f_1 = 10m_1 + 2m_2$$

$$\frac{dk}{dm_2} = f_2 = 6m_2 + 2m_1$$

(ix)   Total differentiation rule

Consider a general utility function in the following form.

$U = f(m_1, m_2 \dots m_n)$. The total differential of this function is written as

$$dU = \frac{dU}{dm_1} dm_1 + \frac{dU}{dm_2} dm_2 + \dots + \frac{dU}{dm_n} dm_n \qquad \dots(A\,1.14)$$

$$dU = U_1 dm_1 + U_2 dm_2 + \dots + Undm_n = \sum_{i=1}^{n} = U_i dm_i \qquad \dots(A\,1.15)$$

On the right side of the equation each term denotes the amount of change in 'U' resulting from a very small change in one of the independent variables, say m_1.

For example, the term $U_1\, dm_1$ is the marginal utility of m_1 commodity times the increment in consumption of m_1 commodity. Similar interpretation holds good for other terms. The sum of these terms represents the total change in utility that is du. For example.

$$U = 3m_1^2 + m_1 m_2^2$$
$$f_1 = 6m_1 + m_2^2$$
$$f_2 = 2m_1 m_2$$
$$dk = (6m_1 + m_2^2)\, dm_1 + (2m_1 m_2)\, dm_2$$

Total Derivative

Let the function $K = f(m_1\, t)$ and $m = 2t^2 + 3t + 4$. Then the total derivative

$$\frac{dk}{dt} = K = 3m + 25$$
$$= 3\,(2t^2 + 3t + 4) + 2t$$
$$= 6t^2 + 9t + 12 + 2t$$
$$= 6t^2 + 11t + 12$$

$$\frac{d^2k}{dt^2} = 12t + 11$$

APPENDIX B

MANGO ORCHARD

TABLE B-1
Total Cost of Mango Orchard (10 Acres)

Sl. No.	Particulars	Amount (in Rs)
1.	Cost of land development @ Rs 800 per acre	8,000
2.	Cost of cultivation of mango orchards @ Rs 7,500 per acre	75,000
3.	Cost of three bore wells with 7.5 H.P. submersible pumpsets	1,41,000
		2,24,000
	Total financial outlay	2,24,000
	Margin @ 25%	56,000
	Total bank loan	1,68,000

TABLE B-2

Cost of Development of 1 Acre Mango (in Rs)

Sl. No.	Particulars	I	II	III	IV	V	VI	Total
					Years			
I.	LAND DEVELOPMENT							
1.	Uprooting of stubbles	150	—	—	—	—	—	150
2.	Levelling of land	500	—	—	—	—	—	500
3.	Formation of internal bunds and removal of stones	150	—	—	—	—	—	150
II.	DEVELOPMENT OF ORCHARD							
1.	Preparation of land	240	—	—	—	—	—	240
2.	Digging of 40 pits 3' × 3' × 3'	250	—	—	—	—	—	250
3.	Filling back of pits	100	—	—	—	—	—	100
4.	Cost of mango grafts	800	80	—	—	—	—	880
5.	Planting & staking	80	—	—	—	—	—	80
6.	Irrigation	250	210	210	210	210	210	1300
7.	Manures and fertilizers	260	260	300	360	400	450	2030
8.	Interculture	120	120	120	120	120	120	720
9.	Plant protection	60	120	140	140	160	180	800
10.	Intercrops	600	—	—	—	—	—	600
11.	Fencing	500	—	—	—	—	—	500
	Total	4,060	790	770	830	890	960	8,300

TABLE B-3

Yield and Income From Mango Orchard with Bore-well

Year	No. of fruits per plant	Yield/10 acres (Rs)	Gross income (Rs)	Cost of maintenace (Rs)	Net income (Rs)	Total repayment (Rs)	Net surplus
7th	150	60,000	45,000	9,6000	35,400	25,112	10,288
8th	200	80,000	60,000	9,600	50,400	25,562	24,838
9th	300	1,20,000	90,000	9,600	80,400	26,702	53,698
10th	400	1,60,000	1,20,000	9,600	1,10,400	27,377	83,023
11th	500	2,00,000	1,50,000	9,600	1,40,400	27,587	1,12,813
12th	500	2,00,000	1,50,000	9,600	1,40,400	35,660	1,04,740

Spacing: 33' × 33'
No. of plants per acre: 40
Cost of fruits: Rs. 75/100 fruits

INLAND FISH CULTURE

TABLE B-4

Capital Outlay and Income for One Acre of Fish Pond

Particulars	Amount (in Rs)
(a) Capital cost	
i) Escavation of ponds	14,250
ii) Providing inlets/outlets with shutters	4,000
iii) Contingencies	720
Sub-total	18,970
(b) Operational cost	Rs. 19,880
Total financial outlay 18,970 + 19,880 = Rs. 38,850	
MEANS OF FINANCE	
i) Borrower's contribution	9,750 (25% of total cost)
ii) Bank loan	29,100 (75% of total cost)
Total	38,850
Gross income	Rs 55,880
Net income over recurring expenditure = Rs 36,000	

TABLE B-5

Recurring Expenditure Per Acre

	Particulars	Amount (Rs)
1.	Ploughing of land twice crosswise per acre	100
2.	Cost of lime of 200 kg @ Rs. 1.50/kg	300
3.	Cost of cow-dung of 8000 kg @ Rs 20 per 100 kg	1600
4.	Cost of superphosphate of 150 kg @ Rs 2.50/kg	375
5.	Cost of urea of 200 kg @ Rs 3.10/kg	620
6.	Cost of potassium permanganate	100
7.	Cost of muriate of potash of 50 kg @ 1.70/kg	85
8.	*Cost of feed:*	
	2500 kg of rice bran @ Rs 1.80/kg	4500
	1000 kg of oilcake @ Rs 3.00/kg	3000
9.	Cost of seed 2000 Nos. @ Rs 1.50/ each	3000
10.	Salaries to watch and ward staff	
	one person for 12 months @ Rs 400 per month	4800
11.	Harvesting charges	300
12.	Insurance charges	400
13.	Pump-operation and maintenance	800
	Total recurring expenditure	19,880

TABLE B-6

Repayment Schedule for One Acre Water Spread Area

Year	Loan outstanding (Rs)	Net income (Rs)	Loan repayment			Balance of the loan outstanding at the end of the year (Rs)	Net surplus (Rs)
			Principal (Rs)	Interest (Rs)	Total (Rs)		
1.	29,100	36,000	3,300	4,075	7,375	25,800	28,625
2.	25,800	36,000	3,800	3,610	7,410	22,000	28,590
3.	22,000	36,000	4,400	3,080	7,480	17,600	28,520
4.	17,600	36,000	5,000	2,465	7,465	12,600	28,535
5.	12,600	36,000	5,800	1,765	7,565	6,800	28,435
6.	6,800	36,000	6,800	950	7,750	—	28,250

FINANCING SERICULTURE

TABLE B-7

Economics of Sericulture (Unit: One Acre)

Particulars	Amount (in Rs)
I. CAPITAL EXPENDITURE	
A. Cost of construction of rearding shed of 20' × 15' size (approximate)	
i) Basement and foundation with random rubble mansory in mud mortar	1,000.00
ii) Super structure with bricks or stones in mud mortar	1,500.00
iii) Doors and windows	750.00
iv) Roofing with straw over country wood rafters	1,000.00
v) Flooring, plastering, etc.	750.00
Sub-Total	5,000.00
B. COST OF EQUIPMENT	
i) Rearing stands 4 Nos	500.00
ii) 80 Nos rearing trays at Rs 10/- each	800.00
iii) 40 Nos Chandrikas @ Rs 60/-	2,400.00
iv) One chopping knife	100.00
v) Nylon net	200.00
Sub Total	4,000.00
II. WORKING CAPITAL EXPENDITURE	
a) Preparatory cultivation of land	300.00
b) Irrigation	400.00
c) 10 tonnes of organic manures @ 75/- per tonne	750.00
d) Planting material & planting	300.00
e). Digging and weeding 3 times in 1 year and 5 times from II year onwards	300.00
f) Plant protection	100.00
g) Application charges with fertilizers	800.00
h) Cost of layings	300.00
i) Leaf picking and transport	200.00
Sub-Total	3,500.00
Grand total	12,500.00

TABLE B-8

Returns From Sericulture

Particulars	First Year	Second Year
i) No. of crops	2	4
ii) Poduction of cocoons @ 90 kg/crop	180	360
iii) Value of cocoons at Rs 60 per kg.	10,800	21,600
iv) Less working capital expenditure covered by term loan (Rs)	3,500	3,500
v) Net Income (Rs)	7,300	18,100

TABLE B-9

Cash Flow Statement of 1 Acre Sericulture Unit

(in Rs)

Sl. No.	Details	I Year	II Year	III Year	IV Year
1.	EXPENDITURE				
	Working expenses per year (A)	3,500	3,500	3,500	3,500
2.	INCOME				
	Sale of cocoons (B)	10,800	21,600	21,600	21,600
3.	NET INCOME (B–A) = (C)	7,300	18,100	18,100	18,100
4.	REPAYMENT				
	Principal	2,500	2,500	2,500	2,500
	Interest	1,300	900	600	300
	Total (D)	3,800	3,400	3,100	2,800
5.	NET SURPLUS (C–D) = (E)	3,500	14,700	15,000	15,300

FINANCING DAIRY SCHEME

TABLE B-10

Income Pattern for Two She-Buffaloes

(in Rs)

Year	Lactation days	Sale of milk	Sale of manure	Total
I	420	20,160	300	20,460
II	480	23,040	400	23,440
III	480	23,040	400	23,440
IV	420	20,160	400	20,560
V	450	21,600	400	22,000
VI	390	18,720	300	19,020

TABLE B-11

Cash Flow Statement

(in Rs)

Sl. No.	Particulars	Years						
		0	1	2	3	4	5	6
I.	Gross income	—	20,460	23,440	23,440	20,560	22,000	19,020
II.	Costs:							
	a) Fixed costs (cost on animals)	12,000	—	—	—	—	—	—
	b) Working costs	—	5,270	6,600	6,600	6,285	6,642	4,902
III.	Net income	−12,000	15,190	16,840	16,840	14,275	15,358	14,118

TABLE B-12

Repayment Schedule

(in Rs)

Year	Loan outstanding at the begining of the year	Net income	Repayment			Loan outstanding at the end of year	Net surplus
			Principal	Interest	Total		
1	9,600	15,190	1,920	1,200	3,120	7,680	12,070
2	7,680	16,840	1,920	960	2,880	5,760	13,960
3	5,760	16,840	1,920	720	2,640	3,840	14,200
4	3,840	14,275	1,920	480	2,400	1,920	11,875
5	1,920	15,358	1,920	240	2,160	–	13,438

FINANCING PIPELINE

TABLE B-13

Cropping Pattern

Without project			With project		
Crop	Area	Irrigated/ rainfed	Crop	Area	Irrigated/ rainfed
Paddy	1 acre	Irrigated	Paddy	2 acres	Irrigated
Groundnut	1 acre	Irrigated	Groundnut	2 acres	Irrigated
Sugarcane	0.5 acre	Irrigated	Sugarcane	1 acre	Irrigated
Fallow land	2.5 acre	Rainfed			

APPENDIX B

TABLE B-14

Unit Cost of 200 Metres Underground Pipeline

Particulars	Amount (Rs)
a) Average cost of 200 mts PVC pipe @ Rs 36/metre	7,200
b) Cost of digging 200 mts trench to a depth of one metre @ Rs 4/metre	800
c) Cost of laying pipeline at Rs 2/metre	400
Total	8,400

TABLE B-15

Cost of Cultivation and Gross Returns Per Acre (in Rs)

S.No.	Crop	Cost of cultivation	Yield/ acre	Rate/Qtl/tonne	Value of produce
1.	Paddy	2000	20 qtls	225	4,500
2.	Goundnut	2000	7 qtls	750	5,250
3.	Sugarcane	4000	40 tonnes	350	14,000

TABLE B-16

Benefits of Additional Irrigation

(in Rs.)

Season/Crop	Without project situation				With project situation			
	Area (acres)	Cost of culti- vation	Gross income	Net income	Area	Cost of culti- vation	Gross income	Net income
Kharif								
Paddy	1	2,000	4,500	2,500	2	4,000	9,000	5,000
2. G'nut	1	2,000	5,250	3,250	2	4,000	10,500	6,500
3. Sugar- cane	0.5	2,000	7,000	5,000	1	4,000	14,000	10,000
Rabi								
1. Paddy	1	2,000	4,500	2,500	2	4,000	9,000	5,000
2. G'nut	1	2,000	5,250	3,250	2	4,000	10,500	6,500
Total	4.5	10,000	26,500	16,500	9	20,000	53,000	33,000

Net incremental income: Rs. 33,000 – Rs. 16,500 = Rs. 16,500

TABLE B-17

Cash Flow Statement

(in Rs.)

Particulars	Years					
	0	1	2	3	4	5
a) Incremental income		16,500	16,500	16,500	16,500	16,500
b) Costs:						
i) Cost of pipeline	8,400	—	—	—	—	—
ii) Cost of maintenance of pipeline @ Rs. 500/Year	—	500	500	500	500	500
Total costs	8,400	500	500	500	500	500
c) Net benefits	−8,400	16,000	16,000	16,000	16,000	16,000

TABLE B-18

Repayment Schedule

(in Rs.)

Year	Loan at the beginning of the year	Loan at the end of year	Net income	Repayment			Net surplus
				Principal	Interest	Total	
1.	7,140	5,712	16,000	1,428	893	2,321	13,679
2.	5,712	4,284	16,000	1,428	714	2,142	13,853
3.	4,284	2,856	16,000	1,428	536	1,964	14,036
4.	2,856	1,425	16,000	1,428	357	1,785	14,215
5.	1,428	—	16,000	1,428	179	1,607	14,393

FINANCING SHEEP FARMING

TABLE B-19

Economics of Sheep Unit of Bellary Breed—Meat Type

Year	Parent stock Ewes	Parent stock Rams	80% lambing from parent stock	Preg-nancy	Total lambs born	Sex of lambs Ewes	Sex of lambs Rams	Sale value of ram lambs @ Rs. 250	Sale of heaped manure at Rs.50/ cart load	Total income (Rs.)	Repayment Prin-cipal (Rs.)	Repayment Inte-rest (Rs.)	Insu-rance (Rs.)	Medi-cal expenses (Rs.)	Total expenses (Rs.)	Net surplus (Rs.)
I	20	1	15	—	16	8	8	2,000	400	2,400	900	750	190	110	1,950	450
II	20	1	16	—	16	8	8	2,000	400	2,400	1100	640	190	110	2,040	360
III	20	1	16	6	22	11	11	2,750	450	3,150	1,400	550	190	110	2,250	900
IV	20	1	16	12	28	14	14	3,500	500	4,000	2,000	410	190	110	2,710	1,290
V	20	1	16	18	34	17	17	4,250	500	4,750	2,100	210	190	110	2,610	2,140

Cost of 20 ewes at Rs 410 = Rs 8,200
Cost of ram lamb = Rs 600
Rs 8,800

Bank Finance Rs 7,500
Borrower's margin Rs 1300
Rs 8,800

APPENDIX C

AAP	Annual Action Plan
ACD	Agricultural Credit Department
ADB	Agricultural Development Branch
AFC	Agricultural Finance Corporation
AIGBWO	All India Gramin Bank Workers' Organisation
AIRCRC	All India Rural Credit Review Committee
AIRCSC	All India Rural Credit Survey Committee
AIRDISC	All India Rural Debt and Investment Survey Committee
APCCADB	Andhra Pradesh Central Co-operative Agricultural Development Bank
APCOBARD	Andhra Pradesh Co-operative Bank for Agriculture and Rural Development
ARDC	Agricultural Refinance and Development Corporation
BCR	Benefit-Cost Ratio
BIRD	Bankers Institute for Rural Development
BOP	Balance of Payments
BLBC	Block Level Bankers' Committee
BRIMS	Block Rural Industries Marketing and Servicing Society
CAB	College of Agricultural Banking
CADA	Command Area Development Authority
CALCOB	Committee on Agricultural Loans through Commercial Banks
CAS	Credit Authorisation Scheme
CCA	Capital Consumption Allowance
CIS	Crop Insurance Scheme
CRAFICARD	Committee to Review Arrangements for Institutional Credit for Agriculture and Rural Development
CRR	Cash Reserve Ratio
DBOD	Department of Banking Operations and Development
DCC	District Consultative Committee

DCCB	District Central Co-operative Bank
DCP	District Credit Plan
DICGC	Deposit Insurance and Credit Guarantee Corporation
DIRS	Differential Interest Rate Scheme
DISCOBARD	District Co-operative Bank for Agriculture and Rural Development
DPAP	Drought Prone Area Programme
DRDA	District Rural Development Agency
DTC	District Technical Committee
EC	Encumbrance Certificate
ECGC	Export Credit Guarantee Corporation
FSS	Farmers Service Society
HADP	Hill Area Development Projects
IBRD	International Bank for Reconstruction and Development
IDA	International Development Association
IDADA	Integrated Dryland Agricultural Development Agency
IDBI	Industrial Development Bank of India
IFAD	International Fund for Agricultural Development
IFC	International Finance Corporation
IMBP	Individual Maximum Borrowing Power
IMF	International Monetary Fund
IRDP	Integrated Rural Development Programme
IRR	Internal Rate of Return
LAMPS	Large-Sized Adivasi Multipurpose Co-operative Society
LDB	Land Development Bank
MFALDA	Marginal Farmers and Agricultural Labourers Development Agency
MPCCS	Multipurpose Co-operative Credit Societies
NABARD	National Bank for Agriculture and Rural Development
NCA	National Commission on Agriculture
NCDC	National Co-operative Development Corporation
NIBM	National Institute of Bank Management

NPW	Net Present Worth
NREP	National Rural Employment Programme
PACS	Primary Agricultural Co-operative Credit Societies
PBP	Payback Period
PLDB	Primary Land Development Bank
RBI	Reserve Bank of India
RLEGP	Rural Landless Employment Guarantee Programme
SAA	Service Area Approach
SAO Loans	Seasonal Agricultural Operations Loans
SAP	Service Area Plans
SCB	State Co-operative Bank
SFDA	Small Farmers Development Agency
SLBC	State Level Bankers' Committee
SLR	Statutory Liquidity Ratio
SSI	Small Scale Industries
TADP	Tribal Area Development Programme
TRYSEM	Training of Rural Youth for Self Employment
VAS	Village Adoption Scheme

GLOSSARY

Advances: It is the amount of loan advanced by an institution, during a particular period; year or season.

Agribusiness: The sector of the economy concerned with the production, processing and distribution of agricultural products, including farm supplies (machine labour, human labour, bullock labour, fertilizers, pesticides, etc.) essential for farm production, various agricultural services (processing, storage, etc.), and also the economic agencies (financial institutions, warehouses, marketing agencies etc.) that serve agricultural producers.

Asset: An item of value is called an asset.

Average cost: Cost per unit of output, where the cost of all inputs are included. It is written as

$$ATC = \frac{TC}{Output\ (X)}\ or\ AFC + AVC$$

Average Fixed Cost: It is the fixed cost per unit of output.
It can also be written as

$$AFC = \frac{TFC}{Output\ (X)}$$

Average Physical Product: It is the total product divided by the total quantity of inputs being used in production process.

Bad debt: A debt that is difficult to collect.

Backward Linkage: Refers to the relationship between an industry or firm and the suppliers of its inputs. A change in the output of the industry will get transmitted backwards to the supplier of its inputs by changing in demand for inputs.

Bank Credit: Refers to the lending by the banking system by whatever means; bank advances, discounting bills or purchasing securities.

Bullet Loan: A single repayment loan, having no amortization.

Capital: It is a produced means of production. Karl Marx defined capital as a crystallised form of labour.

Capital Consumption Allowance (Depreciation): The charges reflecting the estimates of wear and tear, obsolescence, destruction and accidental losses of physical capital.

Capital Goods: These are the economic goods which are used in the production of other goods. Farm structures, machinery, trucks, bullocks and tractors can be classified under capital goods. Land and money are not usually considered capital goods. Goods that enter into production of other goods are called intermediate goods, i.e. fertilizers, seeds, chemicals, etc.

CIF (Cost, Insurance and Freight): Term used of goods shipped where the price includes shipping and insurance charges. A CIF quotation implies that the seller must ship the goods, meeting all charges up to 'on board' and paying freight, insurance, etc. The seller must supply the buyer with all the documents required to enable the goods to be imported. The buyer must pay all expenses, customs duties, etc., on arrival of the goods at the port of destination.

Constrained Optimization: The maximisation or minimisation of an objective function, where the selected variables are subject to some constraints.

Correlation: The relationship between two economic variables using cross-section, time series and pooled data is measured by using the statistical technique known as correlation analysis. Higher the magnitude of the correlation coefficient, greater or closer would be the relationship between the two variables. Positive and high value of correlation coefficient (r) indicates that the variables are moving together in the same direction, similarly negative correlation coefficient ($-r$) indicates that the variables are moving in opposite direction. A correctly estimated and significant correlation coefficient is being used for business forecasting.

Cost Minimisation: A given level of output is produced by choosing that input combination which costs the farmer the least.

Creditor: The party to whom a debt is owed. In the case of a loan, the lender is the creditor.

Credit Rationing: It is one of the methods of credit control and regulation of money supply. It is a method by which the Reserve Bank of India (RBI) seeks to limit the ceiling of loans and advances and in certain cases fixes ceiling for specific categories of loans and advances.

If the rationing of credit is done with reference to the total amount, it is a quantitative control, but if it is done with reference to the specific types of credit, then it is qualitative control.

Credit Squeeze: It refers to Government restrictions on the expansion of bank loans and advances as a part of policy to check rising prices in the wake of increased aggregate demand.

Current Assets: The assets that could be quickly converted into cash within a short time, usually a year e.g. agricultural produce, livestock produce, etc.

Current Liabilities: The debts that must be paid in the very near future.

Debenture: It is a bond executed by a company or corporation, showing the debt owed to donor of money. This bond is not generally protected by a specific lien or mortgage on property. These bonds show a specific amount of money, i.e. principal at a specified date or over time period, during which interest is paid to the donor at a specified rate.

Debt Capital: Capital obtained from borrowed funds.

Deed: A deed is a document in writing or printing, which is signed, sealed and delivered by the parties thereto.

Dividend: The share of profits distributed to the share-holder of a company is called dividend. The dividend may be payable at a fixed rate as on preference shares, depending upon the profits that are made.

Down Payment or Margin Money: No financial institution advances the total amount of investment and it generally advances about 75 per cent of the total investment for the project, and the remaining amount is to be borne by the borrower. The amount contributed by the borrower is called margin money or down payment.

Econometrics: It is the branch of economics, which expresses economic theories in mathematical terms in order to verify them by statistical methods. Econometrics seeks to measure the impact of one economic variable on another in order to be able to predict future events or advise the choice for economic policy to produce desired results. Economic theory can supply qualitative information concerning an economic problem, but the study of econometrics provides the quantitative contents for these qualitative statements.

Economies of scale: If the farm expands its size and streamlines its production process of crops and livestock products, its unit cost of production will be reduced considerably. Such reduction in the cost or rise in the level of output is attributed to internal economies. The prospects of increasing returns to farm will also be possible if the farm adopts new technology, new marketing techniques or any other external factors. Such economies of scale are termed as external economies of scale. These are better explained by theory of increasing returns propounded by Adam Smith in his book *The Wealth of Nations.*

Equity Capital: It is the capital obtained from own savings, gifts, etc.

Finance: It is capital in monetary form. It is in the form of funds either borrowed or lent, normally for investment purposes through fiancial institutional agencies.

Financial Intermediaries: All the financial institutions, viz. commercial banks, insurance companies, fianance companies, investment trusts, etc., are included in the term financial intermediaries in a broad sense. But in a narrow sense, it excludes commercial banks.

Firm: In economic sense, any business unit producing goods and services with ultimate objective of earning profits is termed as firm. A farm is said to be a firm, if it acquires and combines necessary resources under entrepreneurial control to produce crops and livestock products on sound business lines aiming at profit maximisation. Managemnt of the firm may take various forms, such as proprietorship, partnership and corporation.

Fixed Asset: An asset that is permanent or that will be used continuously for several years.

Fixed Capital: It consists of investment in land improvements, buildings, irrigation channels, irrigation structures, machinery, livestock, etc.

Fixed Costs: These costs do not vary with the level of output produced by the farm. These are also known as overhead costs. Such costs remain even if no output is produced by the farm hence the name fixed costs. Rental value of land, depreciation of farm machinery, equipment, farm structures, taxes, revenue, cess, interest charges, repairs and maintenance charges, etc. constitute fixed costs. These costs are fixed in the short run, but in the long run there are, in fact, no fixed costs.

Fixed Inputs: These refer to resources or factors which are used by the farm in set amount for producing crops and livestock products. Generally the size of the farm, buildings, machinery, equipment and farm structures at a given point of time whose quality is fixed, are classified as fixed inputs. In the short run these inputs are fixed, but in the long run no input is fixed. All are variable inputs, because the farm can alter its size, its operation and its output.

FOB (Free on Board): Term used for goods shipped where the price does not include shipping or insurance charges. It is opposite to CIF. An FOB quotation implies that the exporter will deliver the goods free at the port named; he pays all expenses up to that point. From then on, the buyer must take responsibility, paying freight, insurance, and all subsequent expenses.

Forward Linkage: Refers to the relationship between an industry or firm and other industries or firms, which employ its output as an input. A change in output or price will get transmitted forward to users of its product.

Gestation Period: It is the period required for the investment in a project to produce a visible return.

Guarantor: Though a bank may be unwilling to grant loan to one person but it may advance loan, if a second person stands as guarantor for him, i.e., he gives an undertaking, that he repays the loan in case the borrower fails to do so.

Hedging: The risk of monetary loss due to price fluctuations is sometimes avoided by a marketing technique known as hedging. This technique is adopted by food grain traders, mostly wholesalers. A food grain dealer buys the product at current market prices (spot prices) and at the same time he sells an equal amount in the future market keeping some normal profit. Thus he guards himself against price decline in the future. This practice is also very common in foreign exchange market.

Heteroscedasticity: An econometric problem in which the variance of the error term in a regression equation does not remain constant between observations. This problem results in the ordinary least squares procedure not producing best linear unbiased estimates.

Hypothecation: In the case of hypothecation, the legal ownership of the borrowed asset, e.g., tractor, remains with lending institution, but the physical possession is with the borrower. The loans for tangible property such as machinery and equipment are generally hypothecated loans.

Income Statement: It is a summary of income, expenses and profit or loss, from farm operations for a given period, usually a year.

Insolvency: It means the state of being unable to pay one's debts. An insolvent person or company may, after various legal processes is declared bankrupt.

Intangibles: Costs or benefits which either cannot be quantified or at least cannot be priced.

Isocost Line: It is a graphic line on X, Y input plane showing various possible combinations of two inputs, X and Y that can be purchased with a fixed amount of money. The slope of the isocost line represents the ratio of prices of two inputs and it is used to determine combination of two inputs to produce a given level of output with minimum cost. This means at the point of tangency of isocost line and isoquant, we get the least cost combination of two inputs to produce a given level of output.

Isoquant: It is a line on the two dimensional graph showing the various possible combinations of two inputs which will yield the same level of output (unit isoquant). The slope of isoquant is negative and indicates the marginal rate of substitution of two inputs at the particular point on the curve. The convex shape of isoquant is due to diminishing marginal rate of substitution. If the two factors are perfect substitutes, the isoquant is a straight line.

Issued Capital: It refers to that part of the authorised capital of a company, which has been subscribed.

Lagrangean Technique: A method for solving constrained optimisation problems in which the constraints written as implicit functions are incorporated along with the objective function to form a new equation called the Lagrangean. If the problem is say, to maximise

$$y = f(x_1, x_2)$$

subject to the constraint $g(x_1, x_2) = 0$

the Lagrangean $L = f(x_1, x_2) + \lambda [g(x_1, x_2)]$

The maximisation of L with respect to x_1, x_2, and will yield the values of x_1 and x_2 which maximise y, while still satisfying the constraint. The term λ is called a 'Lagrangean multiplier'.

Linear Programming: A mathematical technique evolved to select from among alternative courses of action, the one most likely helps to achieve, the objective function, such as producing a product or group of products at the lowest cost possible. It is a management tool, which is employed on a good range of problems such as profit maximisation from the farm as a whole, under resource and technical constraints.

Liquidation: It is the process of selling assets or securities, in order to get a better liquid or cash position. The term also refers to the termination of business for clearing off the obligations and distributing the balance to share holders.

Logit Analysis: A development of the linear probability model (Probit Model) in which the values of the dependent variable are constrained to lie within zero to one probability limits.

Marginal Cost: It is the additional cost of producing an additional unit of output

$$MC = \frac{\Delta C}{\Delta X}$$

Marginal Physical Product: It is the addition to the total output (Y) as a result of using of an additional unit of input (X), keeping other factors fixed.

Marginal Revenue: It is the change in the total revenue resulting from the disposal of an additional unit of output. In a perfectly competitive market, marginal revenue is equal to price, because of infinitely elastic demand curve.

Mortgage: It refers to a legal transfer of ownership of property from a debtor to creditor. The transfer of ownership becomes void as soon as debtor clears off the loan. Land is generally mortgaged for obtaining term loans as a security. Simple mortgage is being followed in financial institutions if the farmer-borrower has ancestral property. Equitable or registered mortgage is followed when the borrower has got self-acquired property.

Net Present Worth: It results when the discounted value of the expected costs of an investment are deducted from the discounted value of the expected returns

$$NPW = \sum_{t=0}^{T} \frac{R_t - C_t}{(1+r)^t}$$

Operations Research: It means the use of certain mathematical techniques in analysing particular activities in order to provide a more or less scientific basis for a choice among alternative means of accomplishing a given objective.

Opportunity Cost: It is also known as alternative cost. It is the value of the enterprise or factor of production in its next best alternative foregone. Assume that the land is put to production of crop or housing units. Then rent that is obtained from housing units would become the opportunity cost for the land, if the land is engaged for production of crops. This cost is a valuable tool for a manager to determine whether or not to invest in additional fixed assets or inventory. An investment is said to be worthwhile, if it promises to earn more than its opportunity cost.

Outstandings: The amounts (Principal + interest) which remain to be recovered on a particular date.

Overdues: The amount which was due to be paid on a particular date, but has not been repaid by the borrowers.

Paid up Capital: It is that part of the issued capital which is subscribed by the shareholders.

Payback Period: It is the time required for an investment activity to produce sufficient incremental returns to offset the initial capital expenditure.

Probit Model: A model in which the dependent variable is a dummy or binary variable, and is expressed as a linear function of one or more independent variables. The model is so called, since its predictions can be interpreted as the probability with which the dependent variable will assume the value of unity. Such models are useful in the analysis of qualitative phenomena.

Production Function: Production function expresses the mathematical relationship between output and various necessary inputs, assuming a given level of technology.

Recovery: The amount of loan which was recovered up to a point of time by the financial institutions.

Repayment: It is the amount of loan, which is scheduled to be recovered from the borrower by the institutional agencies during a specified period of time.

Risk capital: Capital subject to considerable risk. It is also called 'venture capital'.

Returns to scale: The rate at which output changes as the quantities of all inputs are changed. If inputs and output increase by the same multiple, constant returns to scale prevail. If output increases by less than the rate at which inputs increase decreasing returns to scale prevail and when output increases by more than the rate at which inputs increase, increasing returns to scale prevail. The word scale means that all inputs are being varied.

Security Capital: Capital which is subject to a minimum amount of risk.

Social Cost: The sum of money which is just adequate when paid as compensation to restore to their original utility levels of all who loose because of the production of the output. The social cost has been the opportunity cost to society (i.e., to all individuals in society) rather than just to one firm or individual.

Soft Loan: In international trade, a loan that may be repaid in the borrowers' currency, is called soft loan, while, hard loan must be repaid in the lender's currency or in gold. Soft loan is advanced by IDA (International Development Association) to the developing countries. Soft loan does not carry any interest, but a service charge of 0.5 to 1per cent is collected from the borrowing countries.

Solvency: The ability of the business farm to meet its debts or obligations to pay, is referred to as solvency. Actual solvency refers to the ability of the farm to cover all types of liabilities, but technical solvency of the farm enables it to cover its current obligations/debts.

Tangible Assets: The term used for physical assets such as plant and machinery, which are distinguished from intangible assets.

Terms of Trade: The term used for the relationship between the prices of exports and imports. It may be expressed as an index.

$$\text{Index of terms of trade} = \frac{\text{Price index of exports}}{\text{Price index of imports}}$$

The price index of exports measures the change in the aggregate value of a representative selection of exports as compared to the corresponding value in a base year. Similarly, the price index of imports measures the change in the aggregate value of a representative selection of imports as compared with the corresponding value for the same base year. If the prices of imports rise in relation to the prices of exports, then the terms of trade have moved against the exporter.

UNIDO Guidelines: These refer to a technique of appraising projects in developing countries and an alternative to the Little Mirrless Method. It has been essentially a cost-benefit analysis, where the numeraire is present consumption.

Working Capital: It includes such items of capital as seed, feed, fertilizers, pesticides, etc. It is also called as operating or recurring capital.